In this first history of the practice and theoretical underpinnings of colonial psychiatry in Africa, Jock McCulloch describes the clinical approaches of well-known European psychiatrists who worked with indigenous Africans, among them Frantz Fanon, J. C. Carothers and Wulf Sachs. They were a disparate group, operating independently of one another, and mostly in intellectual isolation. But despite their differences, they shared a coherent set of ideas about 'the African mind', premissed on the colonial notion of African inferiority. In exploring the close association between the ideologies of settler societies and psychiatric research this intriguing study is one of the few attempts to explore colonial science as a system of knowledge and power.

Colonial psychiatry and 'the African mind'

Colonial psychiatry and 'the African mind'

Jock McCulloch

Deakin University, Australia

CAMBRIDGE
UNIVERSITY PRESS

Published by the Press Syndicate of the University of Cambridge
The Pitt Building, Trumpington Street, Cambridge CB2 1RP
40 West 20th Street, New York, NY 10011-4211, USA
10 Stamford Road, Oakleigh, Melbourne, 3166, Australia

First published 1995

Printed in Great Britain at the University Press, Cambridge

A catalogue record for this book is available from the British Library

Library of Congress cataloguing in publication data

McCulloch, Jock, 1945–
    Colonial psychiatry and 'the African mind'/ Jock McCulloch.
        p   cm.
    Includes bibliographical references.
    ISBN 0-521-45330-5 (hardback)
        1. Psychiatry–Political aspects–Africa–History.   2. Africa–
    Colonization–Psychological aspects.   3. National characteristics,
    African.   4. Imperialism–Psychological aspects.   I. Title.
        [DNLM: 1. Community Psychiatry–history–Africa.   2. Politics–
    Africa.   3. Knowledge, Attitudes, Practice.   WM 11 HA1 M4c 1995]1
    RC451.A4M35   1995
    616.89'0096–dc20
    DNLM/DLC
    for Library of Congress   94-10754
                                                                         CIP

ISBN 0 521 453305 hardback

To my son Alexander

Contents

Acknowledgements

This book was written because of a chance comment made by a reader whose name I do not know. The comment was wrong. However, finding that out involved an adventure for which I am grateful. There are many people and a number of institutions who have contributed to its research and writing. Funds for travel were provided by the Australian Research Council and by the Schoool of Social Inquiry, Deakin University. Those funds enabled me to work in London, Syracuse, Toronto, Nairobi and Harare and gather the archival materials on which this book is partly based. I must also thank the staff at the National Archives of Zimbabwe and Kenya, The Zimbabwe National Research Council, the Australian National Library, Deakin University Library, the Library of the British Medical Association, the Wellcome Institute Library, London, the British Museum, and the Public Records Office, Kew.

The late Dr Colin Carothers and Mrs Diana Carothers were generous in allowing me to stay at their home in Havant, and provided me with material which proved invaluable. Colin had every reason not to assist me in my research and yet he did so with generosity and a wonderful sense of humour. I also thank Pen Hetherington, the late Geoff Goding, and my friends Jocelyn Dunphy-Blomfield, Puroshottama Bilimoria, Ron Gilbert and Hazel Rowley for many long hours of conversation on the Geelong road. In particular I am grateful to Pavla Miller and Barbara Metzger who both read and commented in detail upon the manuscript. Pavla made me aware of literatures and ideas I did not know existed; she also made certain that my days began with first light. Barbara is a gifted editor with a unique eye for the threads which hold a manuscript together and this book would have been the poorer without her help. I must also thank Jessica Kuper who saw what was not obvious and three anonymous readers whose comments were so useful. The dedication is to a leg-break bowler and half-back flanker who does not (yet) care much about social theory but knows a great deal about having fun.

1 Introduction

In August 1938 a young British psychiatrist named Cobb was dismissed, following a scandal, from his position as senior medical officer in charge of Mathari Mental Hospital, Nairobi. His dismissal had left the colony without a psychiatric specialist and the director of public health had been forced to appoint, temporarily, a physician named J. C. Carothers. As a district medical officer Carothers had had no formal training in psychological medicine, and his appointment was consistent with the low priority given to mental health in the colony. Much to his own surprise Carothers showed such a flair for clinical psychiatry and hospital administration that he was to remain at Mathari for the next twelve years. The research papers he published during that period and after his return to England in 1950 made him the foremost authority on mental illness in the African. From the beginning of the 1960s, however, Carothers's reputation began to wane and by the end of that decade his work, along with that of his fellow ethnopsychiatrists, had been all but forgotten. Despite that demise colonial psychiatry has much to tell us about settler societies in Africa and about the preoccupations that sustained them.

Throughout the colonial period the term ethnopsychiatry was used both by practitioners and their critics to describe the study of the psychology and behaviour of African peoples. It occupied a small and uncomfortable niche between the disciplines of psychiatry and anthropology. In contrast to those two specializations, ethnopsychiatry never achieved the status of a mainstream science. In the mid-1960s it was supplanted by a broader transcultural psychiatry that acknowledged the shift in its clientele from colonial subjects to guest workers and ethnic minorities within Europe itself, and implied a desire on the part of psychiatrists to distance themselves from their discipline's own history. As was the case with social anthropology, it was European colonialism that provided the social setting for ethnopsychiatry and it is impossible to separate the story of the profession from the colonial enterprise. It is to that forgotten past that this book is addressed.

Ethnopsychiatry lasted from about 1900 to 1960, disappearing as the social conditions upon which it rested were destroyed. Clearly demarcated from the adjacent sciences of social anthropology and mainstream psychiatry, ethnopsychiatry had its own subjects, its own plant, and its own areas of expertise. There were hospitals and research. On occasion that research influenced the thinking of other practitioners, perhaps even the decisions of government. In reviewing the history of the science it is important to remember that colonialism in Africa was itself short lived. The great African empires of Britain and France came into being at the end of the nineteenth century, but effective occupation took place only many years later and few peasantries were ever fully incorporated into either wage labour or comprehensive taxation systems. For indigenous populations the most important changes came with the new cities and with the urban culture they brought. It was within an urban context that the most intimate contact between white settlers and Africans took place. It was also from that setting that the majority of African psychiatric patients were recruited. The main science that attended European colonization was tropical medicine, whose role was to make the colonies safe for white settlement. This book traces the history of another science which accompanied the colonial enterprise, one whose history has so far been neglected.

The literature that can be included within the ambit of ethnopsychiatry derives mainly from the clinical work carried out among psychiatric patients by practitioners such as J. C. Carothers, Antoine Porot, B. J. F. Laubscher, Wulf Sachs and Frantz Fanon, who worked directly with indigenous Africans and sought to place them, however imperfectly, within the confines of the human family. As a symbol the primitive was important to successive generations of nineteenth- and early twentieth-century psychologists and social philosophers, among them Freud and the Hungarian-born psychoanalyst Géza Róheim and before them Karl Marx, Max Weber and Emile Durkheim, for whom the history of the non-West was important as a contrast to Europe's own past. Except for a handful of psychiatrists working in colonial areas, most of these academics speculated upon it on the basis of second- and third-hand accounts. Perhaps the best known of those who fashioned careers out of speculating about primitive mentality was the lapsed French philosopher Lucien Levy-Bruhl, a man with no direct experience of the African peoples about whom he wrote. There was indeed little incentive for European psychiatrists to travel to colonial regions. Travel was slow, difficult and hazardous, not least because of infectious diseases. Colonial states expanded slowly and the problems caused by mental illness among indigenes were far outweighed in importance by the need for public health programmes to control diseases such as malaria and cholera. When asylums were established in the first two decades of the twentieth century, they were an adjunct to the penal system. As late as 1944 the annual reports on asylums for British West Africa, for example, appear as a subheading under prisons.

In the 1920s and 1930s few psychiatrists came into contact with Africans, and it was common for a colony as large as Kenya to have only one specialist. Physicians such as Carothers were isolated intellectually and in most cases had no colleagues with whom to share their professional concerns. That so much research was published is testimony to the endurance of these men (there was only one woman in the field) and to the importance that they attached to the pathologies they encountered among their patients. The authors of this literature worked in disparate settings, and the philosophical foundations of their work were heterogeneous. Some were qualified psychiatrists who worked directly with psychiatric patients, others physicians with an interest in psychological medicine but little clinical experience, others were psychologists, and still others gifted amateurs with a passion for a particular school of thought such as psychoanalysis or Adlerian psychology. What they shared was a specific position within settler societies and a desire to explore questions regarding human nature.

With the exceptions of South Africa and Algeria, white settler communities in Africa were small.[1] Faced as they were with armed resistance, drought, disease and fluctuations in world markets for their produce they were also fragile. Where the communities were largest the transition to political independence was most violent: almost one-tenth of Algeria's population of 10,000,000 was killed during the war of national liberation. Settler societies differed in terms of their histories, composition and size but were united by their opposition to majority rule and by their ambivalence towards metropolitan governments and their publics. Perhaps the best portrayals of their character can be found in Albert Camus's Algerian novel *The Outsider* and in Doris Lessing's quintet *The Children of Violence*, which depicts Zambesia (Southern Rhodesia) as the most claustrophobic of societies.

Algeria was first occupied by France in 1830, and by 1891 there were already over five hundred thousand Europeans living in the colony. At the outbreak of the revolution in 1954 about 10 per cent of the population was European. However, only a minority of Europeans or so-called *pieds noirs* were of French origin, and the settler community consisted of various factions including Spaniards and Corsicans. There was also a large Jewish minority. The attitude of the *pieds noirs* towards metropolitan France was resentment. There was no natural community of interests between them and the metropole, and they felt themselves to be misunderstood and ultimately betrayed. After so many generations they considered Africa to be their home. In contrast to South Africa and Southern Rhodesia, Algeria had no official policy of segregation. The whites did, however, hold definite views about the Muslims who were in the majority, judging them lazy, criminal, incompetent and prone to committing rape. These views were strongest among those poor whites who were forced to compete with Muslims for work. In general wages were lower than in France, and for most *pieds noirs* the only significant benefit of colonial life came in the services of cheap Muslim domestic labour.[2]

In comparison with that of Algeria, the white communities of Kenya and Southern Rhodesia were minuscule. At the turn of the century there were perhaps as few as thirty whites living in the Kenyan Highlands and at the outbreak of World War II there were only 21,000 whites in the whole of the colony. At that time there were 63,000 Europeans in Southern Rhodesia. In 1939 blacks outnumbered whites in Southern Rhodesia by twenty-five to one while in Kenya there was one white for each one hundred and seventy-five Africans.[3] Southern Rhodesia had a large South African-born minority, and its proximity to the Union was reflected in its civil service and its legal system, both modelled on South African precedent. In Kenya there was no white artisan class and a disproportionate number of settlers came from upper-middle-class and landed-gentry backgrounds. In the period after World War I many of those who settled there did so because they could not adjust to post-war life in Britain. Restrictive immigration practices generally kept out poor whites, and where that failed deportation was practised. Southern Rhodesia, in contrast, attracted lower-middle- and working-class Europeans like the doomed farming couple of Doris Lessing's *The Grass is Singing*. Despite such differences these settler societies had much in common. Both were driven by a desire for the segregation of the black majority, a desire which was compromised by a dependence upon black labour: in Southern Rhodesia in 1936, when the white population numbered 56,000, there were almost as many registered domestic servants.[4] To control that black majority, both necessary and feared, an elaborate structure of pass laws and masters and servants ordinances was erected. That structure was augmented by a system of petty apartheid which was well developed in both Kenya and Southern Rhodesia. There was, however, no such system in Algeria where the *pieds noirs* were largely indifferent towards the Muslim majority. It is easy to identify any number of other differences among settler societies; even within a single colony white communities were riven by class, politics and temperament. There was, however, one issue about which settlers could and did agree: they alone understood the African and his fundamental inferiority to the white race. It was this conviction that made them so sensitive to any outside criticism.

Colonial racism can be studied in any number of domains. In public policy its influence can be seen in the denial to the black majority of a voice in the affairs of government or the state. In political economy it is apparent in the low wages paid to African men and women and in the exploitation of labour of the kind until so recently practised in South Africa. In the sphere of the law it can be seen in legislation denying civil liberties, which in the cases of South Africa and Southern Rhodesia included prohibitions on sexual contact across racial boundaries. The direct expression of racist sentiments in each of these spheres was often compromised by a face turned towards an audience. Even in the most flagrant cases there was always a self-conscious desire to reconcile liberal ideology with the most illiberal of practices. This, however, tends not to be the case in science, where racism has on occasion found its most strident voice.

In scientific discourse the history of colonial racism has been played out between visions of the body and visions of the mind. The old racism was concerned with measuring the native's body: the literature from the nineteenth and early twentieth centuries is filled with attempts to discover a key to the African's backwardness in the size or structure of his brain. Some of the figures whose work will be examined belong to this tradition, one of the most enduring enterprises in the human sciences. Modern theories about race have tended to concentrate upon the mentality and sociability of colonial peoples, presuming to have found the reason for their backwardness in their personality or culture. While ethnopsychiatry shifted over time from physical to cultural modes of explanation, these approaches were often mixed, and it is not uncommon, within the space of a single work, to find a theorist referring to both. Debates in the ethnopsychiatric literature, however intricate and technical, invariably contain some notion of the imperfectibility of Africans.

Social anthropology and ethnopsychiatry have their antecedents in the same cluster of theories about race and human diversity. Those theories, which were prominent in the second half of the nineteenth century, accompanied Europe's colonization of Africa and the growth of the slave-owning economies of America's southern states. In the first decades of this century such theories, which discriminated between worthwhile and inferior peoples, found their apotheosis in the science of eugenics. Most social anthropologists have opposed this tradition and in so doing have prided themselves upon the liberalism of their science. Social anthropology shares with psychoanalysis a preoccupation with the past. It is no accident that the founder of psychoanalysis should so frequently have compared the lives of European neurotics to the lives of primitives. Yet the relationship between these disciplines has been uncomfortable, and the few specialists, such as Géza Róheim and Georges Devereux, who sought to build a career in the narrow space between them struggled for recognition. For all these reasons it is somewhat surprising that ethnopsychiatry, the science which occupies that same ground, should have had its origins in an anthropological expedition carried out by prominent members of the British Academy.

Modern anthropology emerged after World War I, and it is tempting to take the year 1922 as its base line.[5] There is also good reason to take 1898 as the beginning of the British school. It was between April and October of that year that A. C. Haddon led an expedition to the Torres Strait Islands. Haddon took with him W. H. R. Rivers, C. H. Myers, C. G. Seligman and William McDougall, all of whom were to play an important role in the development of the discipline. While writers such as de Gobineau argued that non-Europeans, and especially primitives, were insensate, nineteenth-century explorers had often remarked upon the powers of visual and auditory perception they displayed. It was this impression that had inspired Haddon to undertake the Torres Straits research.

Rivers, McDougall and Myers lived on Murray Island, the largest of the Torres Straits group, for four months and carried out a range of experiments with a good proportion of its 450 inhabitants. These included studies into sensitivity to light, vision, hearing, sensitivity to pain, memory, mental fatigue and muscular power. In summarizing their results Rivers and Myers concluded that the visual acuity of the savage and the half-civilized was superior to that of the average European but not significantly so and that myopia was much more common in Europe. Native subjects were found to be able to distinguish objects from a great distance, but this was attributed to practice rather than to any innate ability.[6] The expedition's report was restricted to what we know as psychometrics; no attempt was made to reflect upon broad questions regarding mentality or intelligence. Despite its limitations, the expedition was the first attempt to apply the methods of science to an oral tradition about primitives. By legitimizing the study of the psychology of primitives, it could be said to constitute the opening chapter in the history of ethnopsychiatry.

The psychiatrists who worked in Africa had no training in anthropology, while psychiatric theory has never formed a routine part of the education of anthropologists. Although each discipline has often behaved as if the other did not exist, major debates have been conducted across their borders, among them Malinowski's work on the Oedipus complex, Margaret Mead's on adolescence and Ruth Benedict's on personality and culture. Social anthropologists have regarded the ethnopsychiatrists and their research with suspicion, pointing to a lack of methodological precision in ethnopsychiatric studies and a characteristic ethnocentrism. It is true that ethnopsychiatrists eschewed fieldwork and made little effort to appropriate even the rudiments of their patients' exotic cultures. The most serious criticism of all has been that, unlike social anthropologists, the ethnopsychiatrists had no empathy with their subjects.

Ethnopsychiatry was very much a self-enclosed enterprise. What we know of it comes from papers, conference reports, archival holdings in former colonies and departmental correspondence on mental health. There has been little written from outside the discipline evaluating its research or clinical practice. The few full-length reviews by practitioners of the science's past achievements, such as those by Fernando, Littlewood and Lipsedge, are overly generous.[7] Unlike professional anthropologists, most of whom were outsiders, the ethnopsychiatrists tended to be long-term residents of colonial societies. The science they produced reflected all the tensions and peculiarities of the settler class to which they belonged.

Two groups of Africans were represented in the ethnopsychiatric literature: peasants and intellectuals. The literature about the intellectual failings of Africans was often directed specifically against the class of mission-educated men and women living on the fringes of colonial cities. It was from their ranks that the rising nationalist leadership was drawn and the majority of psychiatric patients were recruited. Criticisms of the intellectual and moral failings of urban Africans were therefore, to an extent, criticisms of African nationalism itself. In their relation to the new urban classes, the ethnopsychiatrists stood in a unique position. They were the one group of scientists that worked directly with urban Africans. Their position allowed practitioners to look back to the pre-eminence of their own class, the colonialist bourgeoisie, and forward to the rise of the class that would replace it. There was no other group so positioned, and its strategic location in time and place lent ethnopsychiatry a nostalgia for a colonialist hegemony which, by 1945, had already been lost. The ethnopsychiatrists knew better than their contemporaries the extent of the social changes which were taking place in the colonial towns and cities. They witnessed daily the flood of new migrants, and they saw in the lives of their patients the cost of the social dislocation created by the new economic system. Even though the evidence of approaching change was apparent in many of the texts they produced, with the exception of Frantz Fanon they refused to acknowledge the fragility of the colonial states they served.

In the period after World War I the devaluation of the African past which had accompanied the setting up of the modern colonial empires came under attack for the first time from African nationalists. Many drew upon archaeological evidence which by the 1930s had established the existence in the pre-colonial era of social and political systems equal in complexity to those of Europe. Two other major bodies of ideas flowed into African nationalism: Negritude and the philosophy of the African Personality. Negritude emerged in the West Indies and Francophone Africa in response to European doctrines about African cultural inferiority. The philosophy of the African Personality served much the same purpose in British Africa. While there is no evidence that apart from Fanon any of the members of the nationalist generation were familiar with ethnopsychiatric research, in some respects Negritude is merely the mirror image of ethnopsychiatry, elaborated by the poets of Negritude as they struggled to create a positive value for precisely those traits which the ethnopsychiatrists deplored.

2   Psychiatry and colonial practice

No matter where they practise psychiatrists deal with two main groups of patients: those whose suffering is due to brain dysfunction and a second group who are ill because of a dysfunction of a psychic nature. Although this distinction is frequently blurred it is reflected in distinct medical philosophies, neuropsychiatry and psychoanalysis. Each school tends to minimize the importance of its rival, not least by reducing the apparent incidence of the disorders which constitute the field of its competitor.

British psychiatry, at the beginning of the twentieth century, was dominated by neuropsychiatrists. Freud had found refuge in London at the end of his life, and his presence had given encouragement to the psychoanalytic community, but analysts were few and had little influence on the British mental health system. Until the Mental Treatment Act of 1930, most patients were admitted to hospitals under certificate. The Act was intended to encourage voluntary treatment and to promote psychiatry as a curative rather than a custodial discipline. This change in emphasis was encouraged by the introduction of new technologies such as insulin coma, metrazol and psychosurgery. It was perceived as important by the profession for psychiatrists to be able to compete in terms of philosophies, procedures, and equipment with colleagues in other specialities.[1] The National Health Service Act of 1946 and the Mental Health Act of 1959 enhanced the salaries and status of psychiatrists. In the period since 1945 the Institute of Psychiatry in London has held a near monopoly over the entry of young physicians into this expanding field, with research being centred at the Maudsley Hospital. The dominance of neuropsychiatrists began to decline only in 1971, with the establishment of the Royal College of Psychiatrists.[2]

Psychiatric practice has long been dominated by the disease model: the idea that the recognition of a symptom or disease can be matched with the discovery of an underlying biological abnormality. Unfortunately, while there has been some stability in the classification of the most serious forms of mental illness there are significant variations in diagnosis even between societies as similar as the United States and Britain. In addition, few somatic disorders have a single identifiable cause and in the case of mental illness it is often impossible to locate a biological foundation. Western psychiatrists do distinguish between functional and organic disorders. Organic illnesses are those for which structural abnormalities can be identified and include dementia, delirium and severe mental retardation. In functional disorders no organic cause can be found, and syndromes are formulated descriptively in terms of a loss of function.[3] The hope of neuropsychiatrists has been to reduce the number of functional maladies as greater precision is brought to bear upon the diagnosis and treatment of organic disorders.

Depression is the most common of the affective disorders identified in psychiatric practice and is characterized by an exaggeration of normal mood. It is usually accompanied by somatic disturbances such as a loss of appetite or inability to sleep. Schizophrenia is the most commonly diagnosed form of psychosis and often involves a severe and progressive deterioration of personality. It is usually seen in young people and is frequently irreversible. Since the early 1950s the use of psychotropic drugs has helped to reduce the inmate populations of mental hospitals, especially the numbers of chronic schizophrenic patients. It is debatable, however, whether medication alone has been successful in improving the life opportunities of those individuals.

Within public health systems then, the influence of psychoanalysis has been negligible. Psychoanalysis has, however, influenced a number of theoretical discourses. Freud was confident that a well-preserved facsimile of our own prehistory could be found in the lives of primitives, and he hoped that their study would have relevance to the understanding of his European patients.[4] His *Totem and Taboo* began with the proposition that savages were more sensitive to the practice of incest than Europeans.[5] He cited case material demonstrating the rigidity of the incest taboo from Melanesia, Asia and Africa, and asked why these societies were so consistently severe in the sanctions they imposed. This severity suggested to Freud the strength of the corresponding desire to transgress. In this respect he argued that incest taboos were characterized by the same ambivalence that was found in compulsive neurosis.[6]

Freud used the term 'primitive' in a number of different ways. Most often it designated a particular kind of psychic entity. His 'savages' were men and women in whom the primary process (the force of the id) was much stronger than in the European. Because they lacked a well-developed superego, external sanctions restricting sexual impulses were essential. Without those sanctions primitive societies would have destroyed themselves. According to Freud, the primitive's psychic life was also characterized by a tendency to project feelings onto the outer world.[7]

The primitive's mode of thinking 'is still highly sexualized and ... this accounts for the belief in the omnipotence of thought, the unshaken confidence in the capacity to dominate the world and the inaccessibility to the obvious facts which could enlighten man as to his real place in the world'.[8] Such a mode of thought made objectivity as Freud defined it almost impossible, and lack of objectivity constituted another link between primitives and neurotics. The primitive was imprisoned by myths whose origins were hidden from him and which served no useful purpose. His life, like that of the neurotic, was dominated by the past.

Despite the qualifications Freud made in comparing primitives to neurotics, *Totem and Taboo* is founded on their presumed affinity. At various points Freud spoke of neurotics and primitives as if they were one and the same. He commented, for example, that they shared a psychic process dominated by intellectual narcissism and the omnipotence of thought.[9] According to Freud the primitive lacked the means, the strength and the curiosity to explore the world as it was. Whereas the myths that organized experience for the neurotic were his own, for the primitive they were presented to the individual ready made by his culture.

Totem and Taboo is a rich and complex book, and it would be wrong to reduce Freud's argument to a handful of quotations emphasizing the ethnocentrism he inherited from thinkers such as Comte, Darwin and Frazer. Although his views on the primitive's mode of thinking were shared by most of his contemporaries, parts of *Totem and Taboo* represent a departure from orthodoxy. Freud conceded that the interior life of the primitive, like that of the neurotic, was elaborate, and he stressed the repressive nature of primitive societies. Their world was saturated with fear and their achievement of a culture and a communal life threatened at every point with disintegration. Freud's primitives could not have been further removed from Rousseau's vision of the noble savage or from the unfettered sexuality of Margaret Mead's Samoans.

Freud's views on primitive psychology had their effect on the work of the ethnopsychiatrists. Counterbalancing that influence were the models of normality and pathology, presumed to be universal, inherited from mainstream psychiatry. British psychiatry was founded upon a series of hypotheses about the 'good citizen' and how he should behave. In contrast to social anthropologists, for whom cultural difference stimulated research, the ethnopsychiatrists saw difference as merely an impediment to scientific precision. They suffered greatly from intellectual isolation, and their work rarely reached a non-specialist audience. Like mainstream psychiatrists the ethnopsychiatrists were marginalized within the medical specialities, and their requests for government funding were often ignored. Ethnopsychiatry was practised in urban colonial settings and the subjects for its theorizing were the Africans who had been drawn most completely into the new economies which grew up in the period between the World Wars. There was no social theory about those new classes and there were no flexible models of personality upon which physicians could draw either in their clinical practice or in their research. The ethnopsychiatrists' one advantage was that they were entering new territory: and even that advantage was compromised by the political context in which they worked.

Southern Rhodesia

The history of psychiatry in colonial Africa follows a single pattern. The most elaborate services were established where European populations were largest – in Algeria, Southern Rhodesia and Kenya. Hospitals were also established early in South Africa, and it was common for mentally ill Europeans from neighbouring colonies to be sent to the Union for treatment.

The first asylum in the Gold Coast (Ghana) was opened in February 1888 at Victoriaborg. By 1904 it had 104 inmates, attended by a staff of ten untrained nurses with the assistance of a gatekeeper. The function of the asylum, here as everywhere in this period, was purely custodial, and many of the mentally ill remained within the prison system. In 1906 a new hospital was built at Accra and a visiting doctor, employed at the prison, made rounds of the patients.[10] There were covered yards, an airing court and dormitories, and violent patients were restrained by handcuffs and leg-irons. Overcrowding was chronic, and the only form of treatment offered, apart from farm work for the less disturbed inmates, was arsenicals.[11] With the exception of a brief period in 1929, when a specialist worked for a time at the Accra asylum, there was no psychiatrist in the Gold Coast until 1951. In that year the first African psychiatrist to work south of the Sahara was appointed to Accra. His workload was formidable: in the period from 1947 until 1951, an average of 700 patients a year were processed.[12] In 1960 there was still only one mental hospital in the whole of the country, servicing a population of over six million. The same kinds of conditions, minimizing any chance for therapeutic care, could be found throughout West and Central Africa.

In Senegal the first psychiatric clinic was established in 1956. In the Cameroon a small psychiatric centre with thirty-five beds was opened at Douala in 1957, and a year later a similar centre was set up in the Belgian Congo.[13] In Angola a neuropsychiatric section was established as an annexe to the main hospital in Luanda in 1946. In the Sudan the first mental hospital was opened in 1950, and before that date there were no specialist services. In Ethiopia the first specialist facilities became available in 1940, and by 1958 there was one psychiatrist at the Ammannel Hospital, near Addis Ababa, with 150 beds. At that clinic almost 70 per cent of the cases treated were classified as schizophrenic and another 25 per cent were epileptic.[14] In Mozambique the first asylum for the criminally insane was established near Lourenzo Marques in 1930; mentally ill Europeans were often sent to South Africa or Southern Rhodesia for treatment.[15]

The first mental hospital in Nyasaland, the Zomba Lunatic Asylum, was opened in 1910 as an annexe to the Central Prison. The mission hospitals had consistently refused to admit patients regarded as mad, and reluctantly the colonial administration had assumed some limited responsibility for them. Most of the asylum's inmates were classified as criminally insane, and many were violent. As Megan Vaughan has pointed out, the early establishment of a specialist institution was remarkable, for at that time the total expenditure in Nyasaland on education and health was a little more than £8,000 per annum.[16] Inmates were treated in much the same way as criminals and the asylum remained under the administration of the Department of Prisons until 1951, with the first psychiatrist appointed in 1955.[17] A lack of funds and the absence of an incentive on the part of the administration to segregate the insane from the rest of the community meant that most of the mentally ill remained with their families and continued to be treated by native physicians. European patients were sent to South African asylums or to the Ingutsheni Mental Hospital in Bulawayo.

The history of Zomba suggests that it was not a healthy place to be an inmate.[18] There was an outbreak of pellagra in 1916, and the patients' diet was judged inadequate until the 1930s. A review of the inmates' health carried out in 1936 showed that 26 per cent had malaria, 60 per cent hookworm and 12 per cent pellagra.[19] As late as 1935 the medical superintendent found that thirty of the inmates were suffering from varying degrees of malnutrition. W. H. Watson, medical officer in charge of the asylum and another general practitioner, Horace Shelley, reported to the director of medical services in that year that it housed eighty-four inmates in individual cells: 8 percent were judged psychopathic, 13 per cent epileptic psychotic, 36 per cent schizophrenic and 4 per cent as suffering from an organic brain disease.[20] Shelley and Watson noted marked differences between these figures and comparable returns from Kenya and South Africa and suggested that this might be due to racial factors. They also found that a disproportionate number of the inmates had received some education.[21]

In 1953 a new hospital was built, and its administration was entrusted to the Department of Health. The introduction of psychotropic drugs and electroconvulsive therapy (ECT) in the 1950s changed Zomba as it had changed asylums in Britain and France. By the time of the establishment of the Federation of the Rhodesias and Nyasaland in 1955 the asylum held almost two hundred inmates.[22] In the annual reports for the 1950s a number of causes for this increase were listed, including malnutrition and injuries at birth, but most related to qualities of African culture and to the African mind. Africans' belief in witchcraft was held to create fear and conflict for the individual while the loosening of tribal and familial ties increased emotional insecurity, particularly among the young. In such a climate families were less willing to look after a mentally ill relative, especially where a European hospital was close at hand. The authors of the annual report for 1959 suggested that urban life played some part in the increased incidence of mental illness; 'the emergent African is paying a penalty in neurosis and anxiety states quite unknown in years gone by', with the abuse of alcohol being a contributing factor.[23] Although rates of hospital admissions are unreliable as a guide to the incidence of most forms of mental illness they do suggest a correlation between urbanization and hospital admissions.

During the first decades of European settlement in Southern Rhodesia, when it was administered by the British South Africa Company, the annual budgets for public health were modest, and until 1900 there was no separate allowance for the treatment or custody of lunatics.[24] In 1903 the total budget for the care of such patients was a mere £1,000 or less than 3 per cent of the annual outlay for hospitals and public health.[25] Prior to 1908 there was no asylum, and lunatics were detained in gaols before being transferred to institutions in the Cape Colony, Natal and the Transvaal.[26] On average thirty African and ten European pauper lunatics were receiving treatment in other colonies, at considerable cost to the government, and eventually this expense prompted calls for the establishment of an asylum. In 1907 approval was granted for the building of a hospital at Bulawayo to house all lunatic Africans and Europeans held in local gaols and in South African institutions. Because of the unexpectedly high cost of construction, the final buildings could hold only half of the intended capacity.[27] On completion Ingutsheni Asylum offered beds for twenty African and ten European patients.

Ingutsheni opened in June 1908 and it was located initially on 750 acres of land some one-and-a-half miles from the centre of Bulawayo. Under the Lunacy Ordinance regulations of the same year, a scale of fees was established for European, African, Asiatic and Coloured patients. Ingutsheni accepted African inmates from other territories, and their governments were charged the same fee as for Asiatics. Provision was made also for patients of any race who could not pay. At the end of its first year of operation no reduction had been achieved in the numbers of Southern Rhodesians held in South Africa. Far from reducing the drain on public funds the new facility had almost doubled the cost of caring for lunatics to over £3,500 per annum, not counting the Europeans being cared for in private nursing homes.[28] By 1911 the hospital was judged 'hopelessly overcrowded' and much in need of expansion.[29] Mental illness was, however, of little importance in comparison with the threat posed by malaria, dysentery and typhoid. Making the colony attractive to white settlement meant controlling these diseases rather than providing funds for the care of the mad.

The best-treated patients at Ingutsheni were the Europeans. Few of them paid fees, the majority being supported at public expense. Whereas the diet for Europeans consisted of bread, meat, sugar, vegetables, butter and coffee, the Africans' rations were limited to second-grade meal, coffee, sugar and vegetables.[30] The cost per patient per day at Ingutsheni was by far the lowest of the three major hospitals in the country.[31] The patient-to-staff ratio was high in relation to figures for metropolitan asylums, and costs were further reduced by the inmates working on the hospital farm.[32] It was of necessity a custodial institution; if patients happened to recover, well and good.

Europeans who went mad in the colonies were a strain on their families and often a burden upon the colonial administration. After some years of debate between treasury and the medical director, it was decided to expand Ingutsheni sufficiently to hold all the lunatics then resident in South Africa. The decision required extra facilities and extra staff, and when these were made available in 1917 Ingutsheni could house 196 inmates.[33] The extra room allowed a more conservative policy with regard to the release of patients; where the patients' homes were far from Bulawayo staff members were now loath to discharge them for fear that they would suffer a relapse and have to be readmitted.[34] The hospital farm was expanded to supply fruit, vegetables and milk, with excess produce sold for profit at the Bulawayo market.

During the 1920s the number of inmates increased steadily. The cramped facilities defeated attempts to segregate African and Asiatic male patients. Violent Europeans could not be properly cared for, and it proved necessary to continue to send them to South Africa. In 1924 overcrowding in the African section was eased by the conversion of a storeroom into sleeping-quarters. This, however, did not allow new patients to be housed in single cells; much to the consternation of staff, these patients were placed in wards with long-term inmates. Each of these problems can be traced to the shortage of funds that plagued Ingutsheni throughout its history.[35]

Working conditions for hospital staff grew progressively worse, and in April 1924 the European nurses made a submission to the medical director demanding improvements. They pointed out that they were required to work longer hours for less pay than those employed in other branches of the medical service, and demanded the same rate of pay received by mental hospital employees in South Africa.[36] Their demands were not met, but in August the medical director instructed magistrates not to forward any more patients to the hospital, in order to ease the overcrowding. As a result, an increasing number of psychotic Africans remained in local gaols.

Despite the chaotic conditions on the wards, every effort was made in the official correspondence to present a picture of order and discipline. Correspondence from the auditor general's department indicates that reviews of stores and the condition of the plant were made regularly and careful checks were kept on the use of seclusion and the restraint of violent inmates. Authorization had to be given by the medical superintendent and the procedure justified. However, the recording of the use of restraint and seclusion was restricted to Europeans.[37]

In the five years from 1927 until 1932 there had been a 30 per cent increase in the size of the European population in Southern Rhodesia and this increase, combined with the passage of the British Mental Health Act of 1930, brought about a change in official attitudes towards mental health. Under the Lunacy Ordinance of 1908 no distinction had been made between the mentally defective and the insane, a fact which mirrored the custodial role of asylums in that era. There also had been no provision for treatment. By 1932 the government was committed to appointing a psychiatric specialist to supervise the hospital and to ensure that a curative programme was begun.[38] In that year a psychiatrist, Dr K. M. Rodger, was appointed as the superintendent, and he set about changing the system.

Rodger found that overcrowding made segregation and treatment impossible and urgently requested additional accommodation. He also set about creating an occupational therapy programme with mattress making, woodworking and poultry breeding. Before Rodger's arrival no entertainment was provided for Africans and Asians; Europeans enjoyed the luxury of a ward radio, some old newspapers and magazines, and fortnightly cinema evenings. Within eighteen months Rodger had succeeded in appointing one full-time and one part-time occupational therapist and improving the atmosphere on the European wards with the provision of a weekly cinema and the staging of cricket and football matches on the weekends.

The Mental Disorders Bill of 1936 marked a radical change in mental health care in Southern Rhodesia. Whereas the 1908 Ordinance was in the main concerned with defining the procedures for the committal of the insane and in ensuring the safety of the community the 1936 Ordinance was designed to distinguish between various forms of mental illness, to encourage voluntary committal and to promote the early treatment of curable disorders.[39] Under the 1908 Ordinance a lunatic was defined as an idiot or a person of unsound mind. A person could be committed under the terms of an urgency order initiated by a spouse or relative or at the instigation of a magistrate. The only right retained by the insane was the right to apply to a court for an inquiry into their committal. Courts had the power to appoint a curator to control the estate of a lunatic or even to sell such property. In theory allowance was made for voluntary patients but they were charged double the fee of certified inmates. As was the case in the United Kingdom, the colonial asylum was a place for 'social refuse', and this deepened the stigma already attached to mental illness.[40]

Under the new Act, which came into being largely through the efforts of Dr Rodger, patients were able to gain entry to hospital simply by signing a request for admission. The Act also allowed for the request to be made by a relative on the patient's behalf. In each instance the application had to be endorsed by two physicians, ruling out the need for recourse to a magistrate. Just as important as these changes was the fact that the Bill allowed for the establishment of a hospital administrative board which was empowered to hear patients' complaints about their incarceration or treatment and thereby, to an extent, preserve their civil liberties. The Mental Disorders Act went into effect on 19 August 1936. With it came also no fewer than twenty-seven schedule forms and a complex bureaucratic apparatus which absorbed a considerable part of the mental health budget.

In 1936 there were 379 patients on the hospital's registry. Under Rodger's authority a mattress-making department was established to supply other branches of the government service, giving employment to the inmates and bringing some sorely needed income to the institution. From that same year regular picture evenings were provided for all inmates, a number of concerts were produced by ladies from the Jewish community, and at Christmas a party was held. While all of this must have improved the atmosphere on the wards, the recovery rate, especially among European patients, remained disappointing.[41] A large proportion of the inmates, both African and European, were chronically ill, and over time they simply deteriorated. There was also a sizeable number of mental defectives who were beyond the reach of any known form of treatment. Rodger was sensitive to criticism of Ingutsheni, and in the annual report for 1938 he emphasized the achievements of the hospital. In that year the rate of discharge was 78 per cent for Europeans and 84 per cent for Africans.[42] According to Rodger this showed that Ingutsheni was a place of hope rather than despair.

Like most physicians Rodger was enamoured of new technologies, and in a five-year period cardiazol convulsive therapy, used typically in Europe for depressive psychosis, was administered to 205 patients. Rodger estimated that 31 per cent of patients recovered, while a further 29 per cent showed improvement.[43] While, according to Rodger, the method proved safe with Europeans, this was not the case with Africans. Rodger admitted that although there had been no sudden deaths, in several cases among African patients illness and death had followed treatment. The main danger associated with cardiazol, as with all forms of convulsive therapy, was fractures, and studies carried out in Europe at that time show that complications occurred in as many as 40 per cent of cases.[44] Such events would have been far more difficult to manage in a poorly funded colonial hospital than in metropolitan England, and deaths would have been inevitable.

Surviving records suggest that European patients were far more trouble to the staff than were Africans. Whereas the death of Africans following the use of cardiazol brought no public criticism, the injuries sustained by three young European men following ECT led to an official inquiry into the hospital and its administration. The majority of European inmates were unable to pay any fee and so the cost of their treatment was borne by the hospital. The files of the Department of Internal Affairs are filled with the problems created for their families and the administration by penniless settlers who had become mentally ill.[45] By contrast, African patients remain anonymous; there is no evidence in internal documents of complaining relatives or distressed patients protesting about the violation of their rights.

The typical African inmate had either fallen foul of the law or become violent and unmanageable. A review of district commissioners' records for the period provides the only evidence we have of the circumstances which brought psychotic Africans to the asylum gates. One such case was that of an unnamed woman from the Chipinga district who in early 1942 became violent following the death of her husband. The woman burnt her own grain bin and attempted to set fire to other huts in the village. She was incapable of looking after herself, and spoke gibberish. She would take off her clothes and lie naked in the road inviting cars to run over her. For days on end she would neither speak nor eat and at night she would soil her bedding. In frustration her relatives approached the district commissioner to have her sent to Ingutsheni.[46] During the colonial years this story was repeated innumerable times.

In the early months of 1936, at the instigation of Rodger, a proposal was made for the establishment of a nervous diseases hospital that would treat a limited number of fee-paying Europeans in single-bedded wards with fees sufficiently high to make it self-financing. By allowing for the segregation of respectable white patients from poor white and African lunatics, such a facility would satisfy two of the dominant needs of settler society: to retain a *cordon sanitaire* separating whites and Africans and to discriminate against Europeans whose indigence threatened the prestige of the race. On 15 March 1940 such a hospital was opened at Bulawayo, approximately five miles from Ingutsheni, under the direction of Drs Martin and Rodger. The fees were set high enough to exclude Africans and Asians; inmates were charged 10s per day as against the 5s for European patients in the general ward of Ingutsheni and 1s for African patients who could pay.[47] Originally the hospital was intended to cater for minor mental disorders of a kind never admitted to Ingutsheni, and for alcoholism. The relatives of alcoholics were loath to see them admitted to Ingutsheni, and alcoholics were unwanted on the wards of the Memorial Hospital, where they disturbed other patients. The new hospital was ideal in that it avoided the stigma attached to an asylum.

During World War II Ingutsheni and the Nervous Diseases Hospital suffered from the shortages of equipment, staff and funding that were felt in all parts of the British empire. At the beginning of 1943 the number of inmates at Ingutsheni had grown to 548 and a lack of staff was causing serious problems.[48] Yet the annual report for that year, the last compiled by Rodger, was optimistic, especially about the efficacy of convulsive therapy; in the period from 1938 until the end of 1943 he had administered 30,000 doses of this therapy with, to his knowledge, only three cases of serious injury.[49]

The major innovation introduced after the war was psychosurgery and in 1946 twenty prefrontal leucotomies were performed by two Bulawayo surgeons with what the annual report refers to as 'gratifying results'. The patients, the majority of whom were female Africans, had behavioural problems. The operations were viewed as successful because in the words of the superintendent, 'the nursing difficulties in the native female ward have been greatly reduced by this new operative treatment'.[50] In the following year seventy such operations were performed, but thereafter the number of patients deemed suitable diminished and the procedure was used infrequently.[51] The operation, invented by the American neurologist Walter Freeman, was often used in American hospitals as a means of subduing difficult inmates, and it is hardly surprising it should have been employed for the same reasons in colonial Africa.

During the years of Federation, from 1953 to 1961, the numbers at

Ingutsheni increased dramatically as patients held in Northern Rhodesia were transferred to Bulawayo. By 1960 there were over four hundred Northern Rhodesians in Ingutsheni. There was no specialist facility in Lusaka and the resignation of the psychiatrist at Zomba only served to place more stress on Southern Rhodesia.[52] The number of inmate deaths rose; in 1957 of a total population of 1395 patients there were 85 deaths.[53]

Kenya

From the beginning of European settlement in Kenya the main concern of public health officials was to control the spread of infectious diseases and to cater for the needs of colonial officials and their families, the majority of whom were congregated in the cities of Nairobi and Mombasa. The first African hospital was established at Fort Hall in 1909; at that time lunatics were housed in prisons. In the following year Mathari Mental Hospital, a small facility offering beds for two European and eight African patients, was opened in Nairobi. Until the late 1920s, however, the medical officer in charge of the African and prison hospitals also had the task of supervising Mathari.[54]

From the first days of the Protectorate there was a problem in providing care for mentally ill Europeans. As the white population grew the problem became more pressing. Before 1910 and the establishment of Mathari, all European lunatics were sent to South Africa for treatment and a fee of 5s per day was payable by the British government for each of these patients.[55] This practice continued after 1910, as Mathari was never considered a suitable place to house Europeans. Families that could afford to have their sick relatives repatriated home to England or else sent to institutions in South Africa did so.[56] Where that was not possible the government invariably paid both the cost of transport and hospital fees.

In 1921 there were eighty-eight admissions and twenty-six deaths, and of the one hundred and sixty patients treated two-thirds were male. Most of the patients came from Nairobi itself, and proximity to the hospital was a major factor in the admission of both Europeans and Africans.[57] In the European section the majority of admissions were due to alcohol, and in 1921 the one recorded death on the ward was caused by delirium tremens. All the patients remaining at the end of the year were incurables, and most were kept at Mathari at government expense until the end of their days. The major perceived problem faced by staff was to amuse the white inmates, deemed incapable of entertaining themselves and too few in number to play games such as cricket or football. In the African section fifty-seven patients were admitted during 1921. The majority of these came from settled European areas, and the annual report stated: 'There does not seem to be a great deal of insanity in the Reserves except that of a temporary acute kind, which is responsible for a good many of our criminal lunatics'.[58] Throughout the 1920s Mathari was simply a holding centre for acutely disturbed Africans and chronically ill Europeans.

By 1925 Mathari, especially the African section, was overcrowded, and it was common for patients to be housed in the gaol until beds became available. Many of the Africans were put to work in the hospital's vegetable garden, which produced most of the patients' food. Mathari had no separate facilities for criminal lunatics or for the violent, and the threat of escape was a constant problem. Tennis and indoor games such as draughts and dominoes were used to occupy the European inmates, while the Africans were employed in repair work and gardening. On suitable evenings they were encouraged to play football. It was not until 1929 that the services of a private consultant, Dr H. C. Gordon, were first made available to the European inmates.[59]

In July 1928 construction finally began on a new wing for African women, sick bays and new bathrooms; these additions had taken almost a decade to achieve. Priority was given to segregating the Asians and Africans and to securing the significant number of criminal lunatics. In fact, segregation on the basis of race is a dominant theme in the annual reports during this period. In light of the overcrowding the number of deaths was surprisingly low, for most years of that decade fewer than thirty. In 1927 there were thirty-two deaths, and their causes suggest that many inmates were debilitated and frail.[60]

Despite the constant growth in patient numbers the asylum remained a small part of the health system. For example, in 1930 Mathari had 144 admissions and treated a total of 278 patients. In that year the African hospitals in the colony admitted over 30,000.[61] The prison and asylum populations were to a large extent interchangeable, and the form used to record details of prisoners remanded on a capital charge at Nairobi gaol include various references to the state of the prisoner's mental and physical health.[62] It was hoped that with Gordon's appointment conditions at the asylum would improve; although he had no formal training in psychiatry, he did have a strong interest in psychological medicine. His initial attempts were thwarted, however, by a lack of funds.[63] In 1931 both the prison and Mathari were denied money for extensions.[64]

In his first twelve months at Mathari Gordon succeeded in reducing the number of deaths among inmates from thirty-eight for the previous year to ten, an improvement which was maintained. Admissions were also reduced in order to alleviate the overcrowding; those not admitted were kept in the Nairobi prison.[65] The physical health of the patients was improved, and serious illnesses were restricted to malaria and tuberculosis. Gordon carried out the first survey of the hospital's inmates, initially diagnosing and classifying the male African patients and separating the psychotics from those suffering from physically based disorders such as delirium and stupor. Of immediate concern was the need to segregate the non-violent from the criminal cases. In 1932 Gordon made an appeal for amendments to existing legislation and for the introduction of new legislation to cover cases of mental deficiency. Such changes were to be delayed for many years.

Mathari held African, European and Asiatic patients, a number of whom were native Goanese. Like Kenyan society itself, every aspect of the hospital's life was regulated by race, and each of the above groups was served an individual diet. The hospital's records are filled with complaints about the food and the specific requirements of Europeans and Asiatics. For example, in January 1933 the Portuguese consul general complained on behalf of the three Portuguese citizens detained at Mathari that they should not be served Asian food and he provided the medical superintendent with a detailed menu.[66] One unusual case was that of Father Faustino, a Catholic priest who was an inmate for some months in 1938. As a mestizo he was classified by the hospital staff as Asiatic and placed on an Asian diet. Following an appeal from his superiors, who pointed out that the priest had since his ordination some twenty-two years earlier lived as a European, he was given European food.[67] Apart from the question of cost there is no reference to the food provided for Africans.

One of the original reasons for the establishment of Mathari was to care for unmanageable Europeans whose behaviour threatened their families and scandalized the white community. European men suffering from alcoholic delirium were of particular concern, and in Nairobi they were housed either in the European hospital, the infectious diseases hospital or, much to the horror of their relatives, Mathari. These patients were thoroughly disliked by hospital staff since they were often uncontrollable and required constant attention.[68] Before 1932 there was no policy for dealing with such cases, and alcoholics tended to be shunted between one institution and another. Outside Nairobi, in towns such as Eldoret and Nakuru, Europeans were on occasion placed in African hospitals, a practice which was viewed with concern by the director of medical services. In one such case an alcoholic young man with aristocratic connections had been interned in an African ward.[69] Besides the issue of stigma, the sending of alcoholics to Mathari was, in the view of the chief justice, unlawful, as under the existing Lunacy Ordinance all patients admitted to the asylum had to be certified.[70] This, however, did not stop the practice. The asylum files, particularly during the years of World War II, are filled with stories of European alcoholics who had brought ruin upon themselves and their families. There are no parallel records regarding the lives and families of African inmates.

In 1936 new wards to house sixty patients were opened and in the following year additional accommodation was completed for African men. The persistent decline in the number of deaths, which in the period from 1929 to 1937 had fallen from 10 per cent to just 4 per cent, can be attributed to Gordon's influence.[71] In 1937 Gordon, who had served at Mathari for seven years, was forced to retire because of ill health. There were at that time only a handful of psychiatrists in the whole of Africa, and yet the government succeeded almost immediately in securing the services of a qualified specialist. His name was James Cobb. Dr Cobb had worked previously in mental hospitals in England, and his application was welcomed by the director of medical services. His appointment, however, was to prove a disaster.[72] Cobb came from a good family and was a personal friend of the Prince of Wales. He was also alcoholic, homosexual and thoroughly eccentric, and while his drinking could well have passed unnoticed in Nairobi society his other traits soon caused disquiet. Cobb kept a Great Dane named Obe in the hospital compound and he also obtained two lion cubs. He was constantly drunk and he was given to arriving at the hospital late at night with his drinking companions, entertaining them by showing off the more interesting inmates. Worse still, Cobb made no attempt to hide from the patients or staff the nature of his attachment to the lions. According to Colin Carothers who replaced Cobb as medical superintendent Cobb was actually 'having sex with one of the animals'.[73] It was this that proved too much for the local authorities, who were also unaware that prior to his appointment to Mathari Cobb had been hospitalized in England as the result of a suicide attempt. The Kenya medical board, with John Carman acting as chair, eventually persuaded Cobb to retire on the grounds of ill health. His successor at Mathari was to become the best-known psychiatrist of the colonial era.

During the war years the majority of inmates were of course Kenyans, but there were also residents from the other East African territories of Uganda, Zanzibar and Tanganyika. This diversity encouraged the government to expand the facilities and in 1944 an allocation of over £17,000 for capital works was made. The new buildings were intended to house European and Asian patients from other territories.[74] At that time the charge per day was set at 24s for Europeans and 10s for Asians and Cape Coloureds. Few of the inmates could afford such high fees, and their purpose appears to have been to enable the government to obtain full compensation from other territories for treating non-residents.

At that time it was customary to confine lunatics, under temporary detention orders, in local gaols until such time as they recovered spontaneously or could be transferred to Mathari. Kenya is, however, a large country, and there were often long delays in transferring psychotic patients from outlying districts. Apart from the problem of distance and transport there were delays due to a lack of available beds. The surviving correspondence from the District Commissioner's Office of the Central Province in the period from 1932 until 1956 contains many references to the problems posed by the housing of lunatics at the Fort Hall prison. There were no proper facilities at Fort Hall or at Nairobi Gaol to accommodate such people, and their presence added to the difficulties faced by prison staff. In June 1946 there were twenty-four non-violent and nine criminal lunatics held at Fort Hall, which was already over-crowded. The commissioner of prisons requested, without success, that observation cells be built in order to accommodate these inmates.[75] The gaol had only two small cells and two wards that could be used for lunatics, which meant the majority of patients were housed with the rest of the prison population. In the words of the commissioner, the situation was 'shocking', and in desperation he wrote to the Fort Hall medical officer: 'If you agree, any cases for observation which have no violent tendencies could be more easily confined in the tool store at the detention camp.'[76]

The experience of Central Province was repeated throughout the colony, and in the correspondence from the Prisons Department and the Department of Medical and Sanitary Services there are numerous complaints on this subject. As the district officer at Machakos pointed out in a letter of protest in December 1950, there were no provisions, even under the new Lunacy Act of 1949, for the treatment of these patients. They were dependent upon the goodwill of African warders who were not trained to deal with the mentally ill, and given the same diet and physical care as criminals. In the case of Machakos the district officer's request in December 1950 that adequate rations and a nursing orderly be attached to the Machakos prison was ignored.[77] The situation in other provinces was even worse and in Nyanza in 1950 there were 128 such cases in the four local prisons, with each lunatic spending an average of fifteen days in gaol before certification or discharge.[78]

The official response to this problem indicates the low priority given to mental health by the colonial government and by the Department of Medical and Sanitary Services. As early as July 1939 the Colonial Office had laid down a policy on the detention of lunatics. First, prisons were never to be regarded as suitable for the insane, and their use could be justified only as a temporary measure. Second, even where lunatics had committed a crime they were to be treated as ill rather than as offenders.[79] This did not stop the practice of holding lunatics for prolonged periods in prisons, and it took almost fifteen years before wards in African hospitals were set aside specifically for the temporary accommodation of the insane. By the end of 1952 such wards were operating at Nakuru, Kisumu, Nyeri, Fort Hall, Kitui and Embu, and further extensions were commenced in 1953 at Mathari. Despite these changes, many of the mentally ill continued to be housed in gaols.

In 1948 Mathari treated a total of 750 patients. Of these sixty-eight were Europeans, sixty-two were Asians and the rest were Africans. In that same year the European hospitals in Nairobi treated 1,464 in-patients and a further 2,122 out-patients. The African civil hospitals in the capital treated a total of 21,181 in-patients. In addition a further 2,007 cases were treated at the prisons hospital.[80] Apart from the usual range of ailments dealt with at public hospitals, venereal disease clinics alone in the colony were treating many more patients than was Mathari. For example, in 1948 almost 40,000 cases of syphilis and gonorrhoea were deal with at such clinics. There appear to have been ample resources to limit the spread of venereal diseases and yet Mathari and the provincial hospitals always lacked funds to provide even the most rudimentary care.

Tuberculosis was a constant problem among Mathari's inmates, and the rate of infection was at least four times higher than in hospitals in the UK.[81] Besides mental illness many of the patients carried self-inflicted injuries, and suicide attempts by hanging appear to have been common. Occupational therapy was confined to gardening, painting or minor repairs. On three nights each week football matches were organized for the African inmates, and an annual sports day was held at Christmas on which the visiting British Red Cross Society distributed sweets and cigarettes, and the superintendent's wife presented the prizes. On Sunday mornings regular services in Swahili were held by the Church of Scotland Mission. Patients were allowed newspapers and periodicals, and books were also distributed by members of the Red Cross.

In 1948, under the direction of Carothers, a training programme was begun for African staff. With the use of St John Ambulance Association first aid textbooks in Swahili and a series of lectures delivered by Carothers himself, every effort was made to improve the skills of the nursing staff. After only a few months Carothers was forced to admit, however, that whatever their practical experience many of the staff lacked the qualities necessary for nursing the mentally ill.[82] In contrast to the situation at Ingutsheni, ECT was used sparingly at Mathari, and in 1948 only thirty patients, mostly Europeans and Asians, were given that form of treatment. Carothers was reluctant to use it with Africans because they tended to develop complications, including lung abscesses as the result of ingesting pus from mouth ulcers. In 1948 insulin coma was used for the first time on four African inmates; however, this form of treatment was seldom employed because it demanded the presence of a physician to monitor the patient's progress. Prefrontal leucotomy arrived at Mathari in 1948, when it was used on four occasions. One of the patients died, and two of the surviving three improved sufficiently to be released.[83]

Until 1949 the mental health system operated under legislation drawn up originally in the middle of the previous century. The Indian Lunacy Asylums Act of 1858, which was used extensively in British East Africa, was aimed at protecting the community from the insane. It made few concessions to preserving the rights of patients or ensuring that they received care. Under the Act it was the duty of district police officers to send before magistrates all persons found wandering at large who were deemed insane. The magistrate was to examine such persons with the assistance of a medical officer, and if in agreement they were to sign an order for the person to be sent to an asylum. If a relative or friend so wished, the patient could be sent to a licensed asylum rather than to a public institution, but only if they also agreed to pay all costs, including care and clothing. The Act allowed for a period of detention of ten days to enable a medical officer to determine whether the person was insane. In authorizing the incarceration of mentally retarded individuals the Act was out of step with twentieth-century medical philosophy. Its most serious flaw, however, was that it made no allowance for voluntary patients. Certification, with its attendant stigma, was the only means of gaining admission to Mathari.

In only two respects did the Act provide protection for the insane. The procedures of committal were carefully laid out, and where those procedures had not been followed the detention of any person was considered illegal. Such problems arose frequently at Mathari, and there were many cases in which committal papers had not been correctly signed.[84] The Act also offered some provision for lunatics who were not in proper care or control, or were being treated cruelly; a magistrate had the power to order that any person be gaoled for up to a month for mistreating a lunatic. There is no evidence, however, that either of these provisions was ever acted upon. Once drawn into the committal procedure, the insane were at the mercy of magistrates, physicians and, of course, their own relatives.

After several years of lobbying by Carothers and many months of negotiations, a new Lunacy Ordinance was approved by the attorney general in February 1949. It completely revised the existing Indian Lunacy Asylums Act, which on the sub-continent had been replaced in 1912. It made provision for the custody, care and treatment of the mentally ill and the mentally defective. Like the previous Act it encompassed the management of the estates of the insane and the administration and control of mental hospitals. It also covered reception orders, the admission of members of the armed forces, the discharge and transfer of patients and their removal to other countries. Carothers played a major part in the drafting of the Ordinance, and his influence can be seen in the emphasis placed upon voluntary admissions. For example, any person over the age of sixteen years could be admitted voluntarily and retain the right to leave, without written notice, within the first seventy-two hours. Patients who could express themselves coherently could not be detained against their will for more than forty days. Visiting committees were established as an outside panel of review for inmates' grievances. To change Mathari, however, required more than a new legal framework protecting the rights of patients.

Perhaps the best way of gauging the quality of life for Mathari's inmates is to be found in the annual budget estimates, as these list the hospital's acknowledged deficiencies. The Department of Medicine's estimates for 1951 contain familiar appeals for extra accommodation, for male and female patients, of the kind that had been ignored over the previous ten years. Much to the relief of the superintendent, in March 130 additional beds for Africans became available. The beds were in effect to replace those that had been requisitioned by the army in 1941. In the interim of more than a decade, many inmates had been forced to sleep on the floor. As the superintendent pointed out, it was difficult to refuse the hospital's services to patients who were dangerous, yet giving priority to such individuals meant refusing entry to patients who could benefit from hospitalization. In his estimates submission for 1951 the superintendent, Dr E. L. Margetts, requested urgent funding for African interpreters; over a quarter of the inmates could not express themselves in Swahili.[85] He also requested additional staff and special equipment including a new ECT apparatus. One curious item refers to the need for sterilizing equipment; with the exception of a primitive stove, Mathari had no means of sterilizing instruments or dressings. We know from internal correspondence that self-inflicted injuries among the patients were common, and we also know that a number of inmates had undergone prefrontal leucotomies. One can only guess at the kinds of circumstances in which even simple surgical procedures were being performed. At that time the hospital had no adequate lavatories for African and Asian patients, as the use of pedestal-style facilities was embarrassing for these groups, which formed the majority of the inmates.

Throughout the 1950s, psychiatric services in Kenya were static. There was one specialist who was assisted by a junior medical officer. Most of the supervision at Mathari was carried out by the seven European couples who occupied the senior nursing positions. By 1958 the hospital also had the services of one part-time occupational therapist. Ideally Mathari had space for five hundred beds, but in 1958 it contained over seven hundred patients.[86] Of those more than a hundred had committed serious criminal offences, including murder. In the view of the senior medical officer, the hospital had too many patients and not enough staff.[87] The major forms of treatment used were ECT and phenothiazines. Each month an average of 500 doses of ECT and 22,000 chlorpromazine pills were administered. The bulk of the work at the hospital, including care of patients, cooking, cleaning, interpreting and some of the clerical work, was carried out by untrained African staff. In 1960, of the sixty-one African men employed in nursing, only ten had any formal qualifica- tions.[88] Most attendants were illiterate, and their major role at Mathari, like that of the institution itself, was custodial. The colony had no specialist facilities for old people, the feeble-minded, alcoholics, epilep- tics or the criminally insane. Neither was there a mental hygiene society. Despite severe limitations in terms of funds, staff and plant, much good work was done in caring for incurably ill men and women who would otherwise have died alone. In reviewing its history it is important to recognize the efforts made over a fifty-year period by senior medical officers such as Gordon and Carothers and by the African staff to make Mathari a humane institution.

In the Kenyan National Archive there is an abundance of material documenting the history of Mathari. The files stretch back into the first decade of the asylum's existence, and it is possible to recount that history with some precision. There is little remaining evidence, however, of the lives of the men and women who comprised the majority of its inmates and who in some cases spent years in the asylum. Although eight out of ten of the patients were Africans, their stories have simply disappeared. There are no case-histories, and there is no correspondence from relatives or friends or from government officials inquiring as to their welfare. In contrast, the archive files are filled with the stories of insane Europeans and their relatives who were ruined by the loss of a husband or wife. These files show the fragility of settler families and the intensity of the stigma which, throughout the colonial era, was attached to mental illness. It was the fate of these people which helped to establish Mathari's reputation as a dirty, overcrowded and unpleasant place. This judgement was made, however, from the perspective of the white minority, and there is no documentary evidence as to what Africans thought of Mathari. All that we do know is that African families were willing to place their sick members in the asylum.

3   Some contemporary reviews of colonial mental health systems

Judgements made of past medical practice may enjoy the advantage of historical reflection, but they tend to be misleading. Fortunately, during the colonial period a number of reviews of asylums were commissioned by governments, and these provide us with insight into contemporary judgements of the hospitals. They enable us to identify their recognized failings and also to assess the extent to which the asylums functioned according to the intentions of their creators.

In June 1936 Dr R. Cunynham Brown arrived in Lagos to begin a survey of the care and treatment of lunatics in the West African colonies of Nigeria. His commission from the Colonial Office included a review of the role of African doctors in treating the mad. Cunynham Brown's survey was a pioneering work, and his references to African healers suggest a willingness to take their methods seriously. He visited most of the asylums in the colonies but, as he acknowledged in the preface to his report, Nigeria is a large and diverse country of which he was only able to see a small part. There were major differences between tribal groupings in their treatment of the mad, and he could find no reliable data on the number of the mentally ill.[1] He was certain, however, that the large number of urbanized Africans in asylums was the result not of any 'clash of cultures' but of proximity to the asylums. The major flaw in the existing system was that the majority of the ill remained in their homes without access to European medicine while the asylums were filled with chronic patients who could not be helped.

Cunynham Brown reported that each tribe had particular views as to the causes of insanity, among them witchcraft, the trespass of sacred places, the influence of evil spirits and the working of charms. Similarly, the methods used by witch-doctors in treating the mad varied. African doctors who specialized in mental disorders served a long apprenticeship and Cunynham Brown found that they did much good for the patients in their care. Only a small number of the insane ever came to the attention of the colonial authorities, and for the majority of Nigerians the only form of medical care was that provided by African physicians. In Cunynham

Brown's opinion the work of such doctors was vital to the future of any mental health system.

The majority of the 142 lunatics Cunynham Brown saw in traditional care were in good physical health and even the vagabond lunatics were given sufficient food by strangers to survive, as if 'fed by God'. Eleven per cent of the cases in northern Nigeria and over half of those in the south were under some form of physical restraint. The preferred method was a primitive form of stock which prevented the patient from moving about freely and therefore from harming himself or others. The majority of patients appeared to recover within three months. Under the traditional system, patients would pay for their care by working for the doctor when they recovered. Cunynham Brown found little evidence of physical abuse, although he did discover a number of female lunatics who made a living by combining begging with prostitution.

The government-funded institutions Cunynham Brown visited were all found to be deficient. The Zaria Asylum had ample room for its patients but the buildings were dark and quite unsuitable for long-term care. The Lokoja Prison Asylum held 167 inmates – far in excess of its capacity – and was run down and poorly serviced. The asylum at Kano resembled a fortress rather than a hospital, while the Jos Prison Asylum was nothing more than a prison. The Yaba Asylum in Lagos was antiquated and needed replacing. The Port Harcourt Prison Asylum which at the time held over six hundred inmates had no segregation of patients and simply held them in custody.

Cunynham Brown reserved his strongest criticism for the use of prisons to house the insane. According to him asylums were at best holding centres for a particular class of patient; their very design precluded treatment. The prison asylums were staffed by warders who were untrained to provide anything other than confinement for the inmates. They lacked facilities for work and occupational therapy, and there was an urgent need for out-patient programmes. Cunynham Brown estimated there were as many as forty thousand people in Nigeria who required institutional care and that the vast majority of these remained in the village setting. It was rare for a person having a psychotic episode for the first time to be seen by a Western physician, and only the chronic and incurable cases ever came to the attention of the authorities. Cunynham Brown recommended the use of village asylums as an adjunct to the state system so that patients could remain within a traditional setting while receiving modern medical care.

What is most notable about Cunynham Brown's report is his sympathetic attitude towards traditional medicine at a time when Western physicians were hostile towards it. He commented that the modern asylums in Nigeria did not help the insane and that removing them from their familiar surroundings often increased their suffering. Like the nineteenth-century European asylums the colonial institutions had become dumping-grounds for the incurably ill. Such patients had come to dominate the hospitals, and their presence hindered efforts to provide care for those who were still reachable.

Nearly twenty years later, in November 1955, J. C. Carothers conducted an official review of mental health in Nigeria for the federal government, visiting the main asylums and examining all the problems associated with what he called the 'confused and unsatisfactory treatment of the insane'.[2] He travelled more than six thousand miles and inspected all types of institutions where the insane were kept, including prisons and local facilities. Even so, because of the size of the country, like Cunynham Brown he managed to visit only the major centres.

Carothers reported difficulty in identifying a concept of normality, given Nigeria's cultural diversity, but he did find that insanity everywhere carried a stigma both for sufferers and for their families. The insane were often kept confined to the family hut or chained to a log, and the vast majority of them never found their way to an asylum. The treatment provided by traditional healers was determined by the dominant theory of causation. In the south Carothers found that insanity was believed to arise from the transgression of a taboo or from the casting of a spell, while in the north a djin or spirit was assumed to have gained control over a person who 'had walked in the night'. In both regions there was an attitude of tolerant forbearance and while to Western eyes the treatment of the insane may have seemed harsh, within the context of rural Africa it was, in his opinion, compassionate.[3]

Apart from home care, Carothers identified two types of African mental hospitals. The 'crude' type was found in the townships, where a self-taught doctor would operate a single-roomed hospital consisting of a mud-walled hut with no furniture, no windows, and one small door. The huts were intolerably stuffy and dark, and the patients were usually chained. As many as three lunatics would be kept simultaneously in one of these huts, where they were treated with chants and with fumigation by burnt prayers. The African doctors chose their patients according to their ability to pay. The second kind of facility, the 'developed type', was found in rural areas. The doctor was invariably an old man who had studied general medicine for five years, usually under his father, and had then spent a further three years specializing in psychiatry. Such hospitals resembled traditional villages with a large number of individual huts in which the better-behaved patients stayed, sometimes with relatives who acted as guardians. There was also a refractory ward for the acute cases, who were chained to logs or pinioned by the ankles. Treatment consisted of herbal remedies and the performance of rituals. When they had recovered sufficiently, the inmates were set to work producing food or tending animals, such labour being performed in the place of a fee. Carothers found that relations between doctors and their patients were excellent and concluded that the work of such physicians was necessary, humane and intelligent.

Like Cunynham Brown, Carothers found that only the violent or vagabond mad came to the attention of European authorities. Certification was generally avoided because of the stigma and, more important, the scarcity of places to house the officially mad. Many were kept in prison asylums, where they were often sent on trivial charges.[4] Carothers visited several of the seven prison lunatic asylums, all of them located in the south and administered on behalf of the federal government by the director of prisons. These asylums formed part of the prisons to which they were attached, but their inmates were segregated from the rest of the prison population. Most of the insane were held in single cells, often shackled to an iron ring set in the concrete floor. All of these facilities were over-crowded, with little effort at segregating the violent from the docile inmates. During the day the inmates were kept in small courtyards; in wet weather they remained in their cells. Many had been brought to the asylums from distant regions and had soon lost contact with their families and friends. The staff were overworked, and visits to the prisons were usually but one of the many duties of the attending medical officers. Carothers considered these asylums out of keeping with the requirements of modern psychiatry. They were also unsatisfactory in comparison with institutions he had visited in other undeveloped countries.

In the north there were ten local administration asylums, where inmates were housed in mud or clay cells of various sizes, sometimes in a prison yard. Almost half of the inmates were criminal lunatics. The exercise yards were small, and many inmates spent all day in their cells. However, in contrast to the situation in asylums in the south, little use was made of chains or shackles. At best a local medical officer would visit the asylum once a week, and this gave him little opportunity to treat individual inmates. The rest of the staff were untrained.

It was the four lunatic asylums – Yaba, Calabar, Lantoro and Aro – administered by the federal government which in Carothers's opinion would have to form the nucleus of any refurbished mental health system. Yaba, with 237 inmates, was the largest of these and Aro, with only 98 patients, the smallest.[5] When Cunynham Brown had visited Yaba it was in the countryside outside Lagos; Carothers found it submerged in sprawling suburbs. Its buildings were mostly wooden, gloomy and forbidding, and the conditions Cunynham Brown had found unsuitable nineteen years earlier were now hopelessly inadequate. The Calabar asylum was now also located in a thickly populated suburb, but in contrast to Yaba it offered generally good accommodation. Its location, however, made it inaccessible to most of the region, and it had no psychiatrist. Lantoro was built originally for the Department of Prisons which had then leased the buildings to the Medical Department. It was surrounded by farmland and provided accommodation only for male patients. Lantoro was close to Aro, and Carothers suggested that in the future it could be used as an adjunct to that hospital.

At the time of his visit Aro was still under construction, but an effective programme of out-patient care had already begun. Carothers was so enthusiastic about the achievements of Dr T. Adeoye Lambo and his staff that he suggested that Aro be used as a model for the whole of Nigeria. The modes of treatment employed included ECT, deep or modified insulin therapy, occupational therapy and group psychotherapy. The patients, accompanied by relatives, were housed in villages where they could continue to live an ordinary life while receiving treatment. The programme thus eased their fear of institutions and with it many of the problems of institutionalization. Carothers cautioned, however, that relatives were often the worst people to care for the mentally ill and that suicide and other complications following insulin coma were reason for concern. Two-thirds of the Aro patients were psychotic schizophrenics and the rest were suffering from various forms of psychoneurosis. There was also a separate clinic for epileptics. Prior to the opening of Aro the lesser forms of mental illness had never come to the attention of Western-trained physicians.

Over a quarter of the patients in Nigerian asylums had committed some crime, and to local psychiatrists this suggested an association between insanity and criminality. Rejecting this idea, Carothers observed that in England and Wales the majority of mental patients would eventually commit a crime if left outside institutions and in Nigeria such people were not treated until they had transgressed. It was the process of recruitment of inmates which explained the large number of criminal lunatics rather than the nature of mental illness itself. His was, however, a dissenting voice, and the idea that the African psychotic was atypically violent remained part of ethnopsychiatric orthodoxy until the 1960s. There was a total of 1,171 persons held in asylums at that time, and of those the vast majority were men. Carothers considered this imbalance to be due to the fact that Nigerian women lived in a traditional village setting and were less exposed than men to the stresses of social change. Using comparative figures from England and Wales, he estimated that there should have been at least 30,000 psychotic and severely retarded men and women in the colony. His estimates confirmed the evidence from other sources that few of the mentally ill ever came to the attention of the state. While the other areas of medical care in the country were, in Carothers's opinion, of a high quality, the mental health system was, even by African standards, poor.

Carothers made a number of recommendations for the improvement of the Nigerian mental health service.[6] He observed that most asylum inmates came from regions remote from the places where they were interned, so that besides the burden of illness they felt keenly the loss of the support of friends and relatives, and their chances of recovery were thereby diminished. He suggested that a well-equipped mental hospital be organized in each region and that priority be given to out-patient care along the lines established at Aro. Such hospitals should provide at least three hundred beds to allow for segregation, but the kinds of massive institutions built in Europe should be avoided. Auxiliary units should also be established at general hospitals throughout the country, and these should eventually replace the existing prison lunatic asylums. The programme of change suggested by Carothers involved a devolution of the existing system into smaller, specialized units and the bringing of care within the reach of local communities. He also recommended an overhaul of the training programme for senior medical staff and nurses. Most particularly, he wished to see Nigerians encouraged to train in psychiatry as, in his opinion, psychiatrists could not be effective without understanding (in depth) their patients' cultural backgrounds. Perhaps most striking of all, along with Cunynham Brown he supported the work of African doctors and attached importance to their role in any future mental health system. During his travels in Nigeria he found that the local doctors had no serious rivals in treating minor mental disorders, including non-psychotic depression, and while he considered their methods obscure and sometimes crude he saw their work as important. Western psychiatry, according to Carothers, would be of little use to such patients, and the state should not interfere in the work of local healers (although they should not be officially recognized as physicians).[7]

In the Gold Coast as in Nigeria, psychiatry and mental illness were of little importance to colonial administrators, and a review of the annual reports for the period 1946 to 1954 reveals that in three of those years there was no reference at all to mental health. In 1949, however, the Colonial Social Science Research Council commissioned Dr Geoffrey Tooth to study the mental abnormalities associated with trypanosomiasis (tryps) as part of a broader survey of mental illness (which, however, was never completed). Tryps, or 'sleeping sickness', is endemic to large parts of West and Central Africa and in its final stages can cause gross mental derangement. Tooth estimated that among tryps patients receiving medical care gross lunacy occurred in 10 per cent of cases.

Tooth found the only specialist institution in the country, the Colonial Mental Asylum in Accra, severely overcrowded. Patients were usually isolated from their relatives, and accurate case-histories were seldom obtained. Attitudes towards insanity varied from region to region, and only in the north was no stigma attached to it.[8] He reviewed the cases of 400 inmates and found that for half there were no proper records. In the material available he perceived major discrepancies in psychiatric responses, which led him to question the validity of using the same nosological frameworks for African and European patients. The ratio of male to female patients was two to one, similar to the ratios recorded by Carothers in Nigeria. Tooth concluded that all the varieties of mental illness that afflicted Europeans were found also in Africans, although the same diagnostic criteria seemed not to apply to the two groups. The organic cases were dominated by tryps, epilepsy and cerebral syphilis, but there were relatively few cases of mental deficiency.[9] In addition, there were a number of unclassifiable psychotics.

Although the terms of reference for Tooth's study were narrower than those employed by Cunynham Brown and Carothers, this did not prevent him from commenting on broader issues. Perhaps the most significant aspect of his report was the importance he attached to the unclassified cases he found at the Accra asylum. There were not many such psychotics in Tooth's sample – fewer, in fact, than identified by Carothers or Cunynham Brown in Nigeria – yet, in contrast to his contemporaries, Tooth questioned the applicability to African patients of European-based diagnostic categories.

A contemporary review of a colonial mental health system of a rather different kind is available from Algeria. In 1955 five physicians employed at the Blida asylum near Algiers, writing out of frustration with the conditions endured by patients and staff and in protest at the unwillingness of French authorities to remedy the situation, produced a report structured around the patients' experience of the service. The leading signatory to the Algerian study was a young physician named Frantz Fanon.[10]

In 1955, they reported that there was an estimated deficiency of several thousand beds for psychiatric patients in Algeria; there were not even adequate facilities for urgent cases. Overcrowding was so severe that many Muslim patients were being held indefinitely in metropolitan French hospitals awaiting repatriation. The requirements for an adequate psychiatric service in Algeria had first been raised in 1912, but it was more than twenty years before a system with facilities at Blida, Oran and Constantine was established. As early as 1935 there were problems of overcrowding and despite frequent protests from medical staff these were never resolved. By 1955 Blida, with its capacity of less than a thousand beds, held over two thousand patients, and almost all the refectories and bathrooms were being used as dormitories. Such overcrowding made it impossible to implement any 'proper' programmes of psychiatric care. At that time, in a country of ten million people, there were eight psychiatric specialists and an average of one hospital bed for each four thousand inhabitants.[11] While these figures suggest a far more sophisticated service than was to be found in Nigeria or Kenya, because of the large white population the situation in Algeria was perceived to be unacceptable.

Admissions took place only when there was a vacancy, either through the discharge of a patient or because of a death. In September 1954 there were 850 patients awaiting admission to Blida alone. Many had been waiting months and some as long as a year. Such delays caused all kinds of problems, especially with aggressive or violent cases, and there were occasional scandals involving patients protesting outside the hospital gates for admission. In most wards the patients were simply released into courtyards after breakfast to fill in the days as best they could. Entertainment for the inmates was restricted by the lack of a recreation room which had been promised but not built for each of the past fifteen years.

The admission and discharge of patients was often compromised by the lack of regional facilities, and the problems of readjusting were often greater for Muslim women than for men. Many insane women were immediately abandoned by their husbands, who were permitted to remarry under Muslim law. At Blida it was common for female patients to remain in the asylum for months after their recovery before they could find a place in the community. Contact with families hundreds of kilometres away was difficult, and releasing patients into a strange environment often brought about a relapse. A lack of facilities also meant that discharged patients were left to fend for themselves.

Fanon and his colleagues concluded their study with a plea for new equipment and additional funding to reduce overcrowding, especially at Blida. They also suggested that out-patient clinics be established at general hospitals and that new asylums be built at Oran and Constantine. Their appeals to the Health Department were ignored, and no major renovation of the mental health system was undertaken. The tone of the article was in fact restrained, as one would expect given Fanon's position at the time, and the group authorship of the piece. There was no suggestion that overcrowding and shortage of funds and qualified staff were in any way connected with the colonial status of Algeria or that the bulk of French investment in the colony was being spent prosecuting an unwinnable war. The report made only passing reference to the need to modify Western medical techniques and philosophy when dealing with North African patients, even though a year earlier Fanon had published a long article on that very question.[12]

These four surveys had much in common. The major problems they identified in the services were due to lack of funds and lack of staff – something that could have been said at that time of any mental hospital in Birmingham, Lyon, Melbourne or Toronto. There is a congruity between colonial sites and the metropoles in the low status of psychiatry among medical specializations and the stigma attached by the public at large to mental illness. Although conditions in the so-called native hospitals were poor and the majority of the indigenous population in colonial Africa were unlikely ever to receive Western medical treatment, the mental health systems described by Tooth, Cunynham Brown and even Carothers were surprisingly well developed. The authors of these reports found no evidence that treatment was offered in any of the state-run asylums but neither did they discover widespread infectious disease among inmates or any suggestion of brutal or arbitrary violence against patients. In colonial Africa most psychotic men and women never reached an asylum; those who did received food and shelter.

Whereas these surveys provided overviews of colonial mental health systems, two official inquiries into conditions at particular asylums tell us something about what life was like there for patients and staff.

An official inquiry set up to evaluate the operation of Mathari Mental Hospital in 1931 dealt with the administration of the hospital, the accommodation for African patients, and patient management.[13] The board of inquiry found that, despite the poor facilities, especially for African patients, the hospital was well administered and that Gordon's presence had improved conditions considerably. It did, however, recommend the appointment of a medical officer experienced in mental health and hospital management. Accommodation at Mathari was found to be unsuitable and, with the exception of the male European ward, in need of replacement.[14] Because of overcrowding, a number of female European patients were housed in the male block. Others were kept in a small bungalow close to the African wards. The African wards were found to be not only poorly designed, with little light or ventilation, but practically derelict: 'The general design and layout of the buildings renders them totally unsuitable for a mental hospital. They may be described as being unfit for human habitation as they are a serious menace to the health of the inmates.'[15] There was no special accommodation for the physically ill, and many patients did not even have a bed to themselves.

Despite the poor facilities the board found that the African inmates were well cared for and well fed, and that the European patients were as comfortable as inmates of lower-grade mental hospitals in Britain. It reported itself as 'not aware that any systematic treatment is given'.[16] In the case of African patients the board argued that there was need for basic psychological research before adequate treatment could be provided. The final report pointed to the need for some form of segregation of the criminal and non-violent lunatics, who mixed freely in the courtyards and on the wards, and for games and amusements to fill in the patients' barren days. Most of the board's recommendations were never acted upon.

In response to a number of complaints about conditions at Ingutsheni a commission of inquiry was established in 1942; its three members included a South African psychiatrist brought to Bulawayo especially for the hearings. The commission interviewed a total of forty-one witnesses, including staff, patients, their relatives and a number of individuals who were regular visitors to the asylum, to produce a picture of life at Ingutsheni which is not available from any other source. In his testimony before the commission Dr MacKenzie, who had been appointed in 1938 to assume responsibility for patient care, asserted that the death rate among African inmates was five or six per month and many of the deaths were probably due to the indiscriminate use of ECT. According to MacKenzie, practically all African inmates were given ECT, regardless of their physical or mental condition, and even patients suffering from general paralysis of the insane (GPI) were convulsed in order to sedate them.[17] He had, he said, witnessed the head apparatus (conducting the shock) mistakenly applied over a patient's ears; one such patient had become deaf as the result of perforated ear-drums.

An African named Namisaku, suffering from schizophrenia, was found on 21 June 1941 to show signs of active tuberculosis; on 16 September he was given a series of ECT, and within three months he was dead. The post-mortem showed that he had generalized TB of the liver, intestines and both lungs. It was MacKenzie's opinion that Namisaku should never have been convulsed and that such treatment may well have contributed to his death. A patient named Tozwinini, identified in January and May 1941 as showing signs of chronic lung and cardiac disease, was given ECT on 16 October 1941, and within a few weeks he too was dead. A man named Mukopa who, when examined in November 1941, displayed a masklike expression, had a gross tumour on his tongue, and an abalition of the right reflex and was scorbutic. On 5 January 1942 he was given ECT; within six weeks he died. According to MacKenzie this patient was suffering from GPI, and there was no justification for subjecting him to such treatment. Finally, an unnamed African man suffering from GPI was found to be in poor physical condition in January 1941; on 6 March he was given ECT, and he died three months later. There was no post-mortem, as it was presumed that he would have died in any case. Apart from the details of these cases, it is significant that they all occurred within the space of just seven months. Concluding his account of conditions at Ingutsheni, MacKenzie said: 'There was treatment going on at Ingutsheni that no civilised community would have tolerated at all. For instance there were no facilities for doing clinical work, patients were lying on the floor in their own filth. Very often you saw that a patient was ill and you took his temperature it was one hundred and three degrees, and that was the first you knew about it.'[18]

Three members of the hospital board who appeared before the inquiry spoke of the distressing conditions in which the inmates lived. Mrs Esther Greenshields, who had served on the board for five years and visited Ingutsheni each month during that period, spoke at length about the lack of amenities and of the terrible conditions on the African and coloured wards. She was also critical of the African staff, the kitchen facilities and the lack of segregation. Her testimony was supported by the evidence of fellow board members H. Shannon and Henry Low. Acknowledging that Ingutsheni had changed considerably, Low commented that there were still major problems with the facilities and that in his experience the European patients led a miserable and hopeless existence: 'I have never had a more depressing job than the one I had in connection with this hospital. I always came away from these visits thoroughly depressed about conditions there.'[19] In Low's experience, when in competition for funds with other hospitals Ingutsheni always did poorly. Members of a charitable organization that regularly visited the asylum, the Toc H Committee, made a brief written submission expressing concerns about the filthy appearance of the wards, the dejected and ill-clad patients, the lack of supervision, the inadequate sanitation and the necessity for the European inmates to mix on occasion with African patients.[20] They suggested that a separate institution be built for Europeans. The evidence taken from European patients and from the nursing staff was predictable. The inmates aired various grievances about the food, the staff and other patients, while the staff complained at length about pay and conditions and the inmates. None of the staff corroborated MacKenzie's allegations about the excessive use of ECT.

The most important issue examined by the commission was the use of ECT, and here it found no proof that such treatment had contributed directly to the patients' deaths, although it determined that in one case ECT had been negligently given to an inmate suffering from tuberculosis. The commission concluded that although the inmates at Ingutsheni gave the appearance of neglect there was no evidence of mistreatment. It did, however, recommend the restructuring of the hospital's administration and the use of ECT only with the express approval of the medical director in Salisbury.

On 15 February 1945 an article appeared in the *Bulawayo Chronicle* suggesting that conditions at Ingutsheni had improved. In 1943 a building programme had begun; African and European inmates were to be fully segregated, and new wards for chronic cases and admissions had been established. There was now a workshop and a manager had been appointed to run the asylum farm. According to the *Chronicle*, with the construction of a block for female European patients Ingutsheni would finally be transformed into a modern hospital offering facilities as good as those found in England. A review of the asylum's correspondence during this period shows this optimism to be misplaced. In January 1945, for example, the director of medicine received a complaint from the Coloured Community Services League about conditions at the asylum, where over three hundred and fifty non-European patients were being kept in squalid conditions under a single roof.[21] There are similar complaints in the files regarding the treatment of juvenile patients and mental defectives. Criminals continued to be kept with other inmates, and throughout the colonial era effective segregation except on the basis of race was never achieved. In January 1946 the medical director described the female African block at Ingutsheni as 'appalling and pitiful'. During a tour of this section he had found a woman dying alone in one of the buildings' 'dungeons'; she was lying naked on the floor and the attendants were unaware of her condition.[22] Such correspondence shows that while the inquiry of 1943 may have restricted the use of ECT, in other respects Ingutsheni remained largely unchanged.

The inquiry at Mathari was established in order to improve the existing service and to identify problems of management. The inquiry at Ingutsheni was initiated in response to allegations of medical malpractice, and its purpose was to prevent a scandal. Although these differing contexts determined the focus and outcome of each investigation, the inquiries revealed that both institutions were starved for funds and in need of specialist staff. With the glut of patients, the lack of facilities and the professional isolation, few psychiatrists were attracted to the colonial service. Apart from ECT, no treatment was offered, and inmates, both African and European, did not recover except spontaneously.

The histories of colonial asylum systems have much in common. Mental health services were established on an *ad hoc* basis and took many years to develop. All institutions began with a handful of patients and no specialist staff. In the southern half of the continent, nurses were often recruited from South Africa, and there were significant numbers of such men and women among the staff at Ingutsheni, Zomba and Mathari. As in England, France and the United States, mental health was at that time a backwater of medicine. The asylums had the last call upon public funds, as it was hard to justify spending large sums of money on forms of illness which in themselves had no economic significance. One of the major reasons for the establishment of asylums arose from the problem of what to do with mentally ill Europeans. Such people caused financial and emotional distress to their families and posed a financial problem for the colonial state. It was the reduction of the considerable cost of keeping such patients in South African institutions that was used to justify every major infusion of funds to Ingutsheni. In each asylum the bulk of the inmates were African, and the desire to manage such people was also important in the establishment and expansion of mental health services. Yet until the introduction of ECT in the early 1940s, asylums offered no treatment.

The files of European inmates indicate that they either went into spontaneous remission and were released or deteriorated and spent the rest of their lives in confinement. The attitude of staff appears to have been unsympathetic; in any case, staff who were overworked and under-paid had little opportunity to minister to the psychological needs of their charges. The asylums offered benefit to the families, who were relieved of their mad relatives but that relief was bought at the price of the stigma attached to mental illness; settler communities were small and gossip ridden, and to have an insane relative cannot have been a pleasant experience. The question of stigma did not seem to arise with African patients; this much is obvious from the willingness of their families to leave them at the asylum gates.

In the 1920s and 1930s there were high death rates in these institutions, mainly because of the prevalence of infectious diseases. The physical conditions were primitive, but there was ample food and shelter, and the inmates were not subject to physical abuse. The men and women who ended their days in the asylums would most certainly have perished miserably if left to their own devices. African families, especially those living close to major towns, used the asylums as dumping-grounds for incurably ill relatives, and therefore Mathari and Ingutsheni came to be filled with patients suffering from chronic organic disorders. The same, of course, had happened in Western Europe and North America a century earlier.

For the state the asylums fulfilled one significant function: their existence allowed for some segregation of prison populations. The insane, both non-violent and criminal, were almost impossible to manage within the walls of an ordinary gaol, and it was to the provincial gaols that vagabond or violent lunatics were first sent. The establishment of Ingutsheni and Mathari allowed, in principle, a distinction to be made between criminals and the mad, even if in practice psychotics continued to be kept in prisons. No doubt this was some comfort to prison directors and also to attorneys general determined that the insane be accorded their rightful place within the legal system. If the system did not work properly, it was because of limited funding and not because the distinction between criminals and the mad enshrined in law went unrecognized.

Throughout colonial Africa black patients were recruited from urban areas, and there was a close correlation between urbanization and the size of the asylums. The physicians who worked in these institutions were well positioned to view the social changes that wage labour and land alienation were bringing to indigenous communities. While social anthropologists were intent upon documenting the vanishing world of primitives, the ethnopsychiatrists were watching a world being born. Their patients included the first elements of urban proletariats and landless peasantries who had come to the cities to find work. Unlike other members of settler communities, the ethnopsychiatrists were formally assigned to deal with Africans as persons and at least to understand something of their biographies.

In Africa at the time when asylums were being built, the state was rudimentary and essentially extractive. Colonial state institutions were never as elaborate or extensive as their European counterparts, and in the first thirty years of empire their role was devoted, in the main, to military control, the expropriation of land, the collection of taxes, the extraction of labour and the provision of basic infrastructure. The colonial state was never designed to incorporate or absorb the indigenous population. Indeed, it corresponded more closely to Lenin's notion of the repressive state apparatus than it did to Foucault's smooth, machine-like capitalist republic. In every part of Africa rural populations retained some degree of autonomy from state control.

The history of mental health systems, in Africa as in Europe, is often written as a history of reform. Within the historiography traditional methods are viewed as inadequate both as ethical systems and as science. And yet if those systems are evaluated in terms of the direct benefits to patients and their families, a rather different picture emerges. The asylums in colonial Africa did not offer effective treatment; most patients were unreachable, and there was never sufficient staff to cater for anything more than their physical needs. Their *raison d'être* lay elsewhere.

According to the official history of colonial asylums, what went wrong at Mathari, Zomba and Blida was that there were too many patients and too little money. The inquiries into Ingutsheni and Mathari and the reviews of servicing in Nigeria, the Gold Coast and Algeria accepted without question the asylum model. The physicians who wrote those reports were concerned about the quality of care and suggested ways in which conditions could be improved. Presumably with adequate supplies of trained staff and funds the asylums would have functioned effectively. There was no suggestion that Western medical models were in any sense unsuitable for Africa or that asylums were an extravagance.

In nineteenth-century Europe the reform movements which helped create asylums were motivated by the best of intentions. Reformers angered by the cruelty of the existing system believed that the new institutions could only improve the plight of the mad. They wanted science to replace custody as the means of treating the mentally ill. Their good intentions, however, brought few benefits to patients, and the large institutions of nineteenth-century America and Europe were little better than the system they replaced. In colonial Africa asylums were established for much the same reasons but with one notable difference: when the question of what to do with lunatics was raised, there was already the precedent of European experience. Liberal ideology and the myth of colonialism as a civilizing mission demanded that some form of care be provided for Africans suffering from mental illness. In each colony those disabled by tryps, tertiary syphilis, mental deficiency, epilepsy or brain injury filled the asylums. The surviving documents reveal the gulf between the intentions that helped to establish these institutions and the conditions under which the inmates were kept.

Before 1938 there was virtually no treatment provided in any colonial state, and when treatment did begin it was in the form of convulsive therapy. This therapy was cheap and easy to administer, and it was effective in altering the mood of some patients. It also gave psychiatrists their own technology, thereby confirming their professional independence. At that time ECT was commonly used in European mental hospitals where it was the preferred treatment for depressive illness. This makes its use in colonial Africa somewhat puzzling. As there was no discrete theory about mental illness in the African before the establishment of the asylums, the science itself cannot be used to explain the creation of these institutions. There was a body of theory, namely, European psychiatry, which was believed to be universal, but there was nothing in the theory itself which demanded the setting up of expensive mental hospitals in colonial sites. Therefore the building of asylums such as Mathari and Ingutsheni requires a different kind of explanation.

From the work of contemporary social historians we know that the building of asylums in Europe and North America led to an increase in the numbers of psychiatric patients and that to an extent those numbers were an artefact of the institutions themselves.[23] For example, in England in the period from 1806 to 1844 there was a sixfold increase in the total of certified cases, with the majority of new patients being paupers.[24] The birth of the prison and the asylum in the period from 1780 to 1840 saw a transformation from squalid neglect to hygienic order and until the 1960s that transformation was viewed by historians as beneficial. However, revisionist historians such as Foucault and Scull have argued that such reforms were designed to control and regulate Europe's working classes. According to these theorists, such total institutions were intended to inculcate the middle-class virtues of conformity and obedience. Invariably such intentions were hidden beneath liberal rhetoric which subsequent historians tended to accept without question. Two of the key terms in Foucault's theory of the 'great confinement' are 'power' and 'the individual'. Foucault associates the existence of total forms of power in Western states with the emergence of psychiatry as a profession and argues that it was at the moment when a new science of personality was born that the new technologies of power were implemented.[25]

The problem with this theory is the presumed symmetry between intentions and outcomes. It is one thing for the state or the ruling class or, as in the work of Foucault, some ill-defined social force to establish institutions to regulate and control citizens. It is quite another for those institutions to achieve their purpose; in fact it is more common for social reforms to have unintended consequences. The histories of Mathari, Ingutsheni and Blida are replete with good intentions. In the absence of such intentions it is impossible to explain the willingness of colonial governments to spend so much money on institutions which brought so few benefits.

Foucault writes of a type of society which did not exist in Algeria or Kenya or Southern Rhodesia. Colonial states were never so widely influential or so well developed as their metropolitan counterparts, and they were incapable of providing the kinds of surveillance of which Foucault writes with such imaginative force. In none of the colonial sites was there an attempt at a 'great confinement', and the procedures for identifying and then incarcerating the mad were *ad hoc*. Those procedures always relied upon some dramatic event or the decision by a family that a relative was unmanageable. Even with the new legislation enacted in the 1930s and 1940s, the majority of the African mentally ill never came to the attention of district commissioners or mental health authorities. Within the settler communities of Southern Rhodesia and Kenya there was a fear of leprosy and venereal disease, and those who were infected were subject to quarantine and regulation. In contrast, the insane were considered simply a nuisance.

Asylums in colonial Africa never played the role currently ascribed to parallel institutions in Europe, but they certainly served the interests of the medical profession: although psychiatry was a backwater, the expansion of its domain helped to increase the power of physicians by giving them exclusive competence in treating mental illness. They also served the interests of white settlers by affording them a haven for their mad relatives and by providing a means for disposing of dangerous African employees. Perhaps most important, they were evidence of the civic virtue of settler societies, symbolizing their ability to construct a state which mimicked the grand configurations of the metropoles.

4   Towards a theory of the African mind

To European science the most primitive of all peoples were to be found in Australasia and Africa, and it was the inhabitants of those regions who excited the greatest interest. Theories about the mind of the African were abstract; their inventors had no direct contact with the peoples about whom they wrote. Indeed, the theories preceded by several decades the introduction of Western psychiatry to colonial areas. Through historical accident the first literature about mental illness among people of African descent was published in the United States. It was only much later that a parallel literature, written from within the continent, was produced about the indigenous African.[1]

Once mental health services were established in Africa, a scholarly literature dealing with the African soon began to emerge. Like the asylums themselves the literature was most elaborate where settler populations were largest, and so Kenya and Algeria were fertile sites for ethnopsychiatric research. The most prolific and long the most cited of these ethnopsychiatrists was J. C. Carothers. When Carothers arrived in Kenya in 1929, he was introduced to psychological medicine by H. L. Gordon, one of the most senior physicians in the colony and the author of numerous papers presented to the Kenyan branch of the British Medical Association in Nairobi.

In 1934, in the prestigious *Journal of Mental Science*, Gordon gave an account of European psychiatry as practised in Kenya and offered a number of observations about the mentality and culture of the African.[2] According to Gordon the most serious problem for the physician in dealing with the African was distinguishing between normal and abnormal behaviour. The African had no regard for the sanctity of life, no sense of decency; by European standards he was simply abnormal. As a consequence, African forms of mental illness were singular and at best a poor imitation of European disorders. Schizophrenia was limited to the Europeanized tribes, and in all his years in Kenya he had never seen a case of paranoid insanity or manic-depressive psychosis. The majority of patients at Mathari came from urban areas, and Gordon believed that native Africans often broke down when they came in contact with civilization. Gordon further developed this idea of a 'clash of cultures' in a paper presented in Nairobi in December 1935.[3]

During his period at Mathari Gordon had conducted a study of the inmates, noting the frequency of certain disorders and the dearth of particular illnesses common among Europeans. He had identified a pattern of absence of affective and paranoid psychosis and high incidence of mental illness among adolescents as the key to the African personality. According to Gordon, under ordinary circumstances only those with the weakest frontal brain suffered from mental illness, and yet in colonial Africa a disturbing number of adolescents were becoming ill. Gordon believed the reasons were obvious: 'The evidence today is against our Natives being as well equipped in the frontal brain as the average European. Under a traditional environment their adolescent breakdowns may be few. Under the stresses and strains of the foreign environment we are introducing who will say they may not be many? A specimen of these stresses and strains should be found within what is vaguely called the impact of civilisation.'[4] He was particularly concerned about the effect European schools were having upon the 'undeveloped minds' of the young. From a brief study of nineteen of Mathari's younger inmates, all of them educated, he concluded that exposure to Western education was the reason for their illness. The education system had placed too much strain on these young men who, because of their brain structure, were incapable of assimilating complex forms of knowledge. Gordon was unsure what policy the colonial government should follow, but he was confident that science would eventually provide an answer.

Gordon was convinced that an effective eugenics programme could solve most social problems, including mental inferiority and the perversions of masturbation and homosexuality.[5] In a 1942 paper in the *East African Medical Journal* he praised the German government for its efforts at improving the quality of its racial stock.[6] He was concerned, however, that the war would sift out the most able-bodied citizens, leaving behind a pool of inferior individuals who would then breed freely. He deplored the British government's allowing the least able to reproduce while the lives of the most talented were wasted at war.

Gordon's views on social engineering were not necessarily typical of physicians working in the colonial period, but in other respects he was representative of his generation. Many of his contemporaries, including many socialists, supported eugenics programmes and believed that the imprint of race could be found in the structure of the brain. Gordon gave a number of lectures in Nairobi about the brain of the East African, and over a two-year period he carried out thousands of measurements and physiological tests on Kenyan subjects.[7] He also encouraged F. W. Vint of the Pathological Research Laboratory, Nairobi, in researching cranial capacity and brain weight. Using material obtained from the autopsies of Africans carried out at Nairobi hospitals, Vint conducted a study of 351 brains. At Gordon's invitation, in March 1932 Vint presented his findings to a meeting of the British Medical Association in Nairobi. The acknowledged limitation of the study was that it contained no evidence of ante-mortem mental capacity. Vint was confident, however, that the brains were if anything representative of the best Africans, since most of the subjects had been in the employ of Europeans.[8] He weighed the brains immediately after removal from the skull and found the average weight to be 1,276 grams. This compared unfavourably with the average weight from five major studies of the European brain, which was 1,428 grams.

Research into brain volume or weight had been popular for more than a hundred years but by the turn of the century had begun to fall into disfavour. Vint's research, however, was concerned particularly with evaluating the cortex, which he believed gave a better guide to intellectual capacity than did simple measures of brain weight. He studied the five layers of the cortex of his Nairobi sample and discovered what he believed were significant variations, especially in the pyramidal cell layer. He concluded that in terms of cortical development the brain of the adult African corresponded to that of a European child of seven or eight years of age. He was uncertain, however, whether under different cultural and educational circumstances the African's brain would develop to maturity. In the lively discussion that followed his paper Gordon and another physician commented upon the widespread incidence of mental retardation among the African population. Gordon claimed that almost half the inmates at Mathari were mentally deficient, while the second physician, named Anderson, remarked that in his thirty-two years in Africa he had never met a native who had achieved the intelligence of a normal European.[9] Both were impressed by Vint's research, and both expressed concern that the African was in danger of being forced to live in an environment unsuited to his intellectual capacity.

Two years later Vint published a second paper on the brain of the African, this time in an international journal.[10] Studying 100 (half from Kikuyu subjects), once again obtained from autopsies of apparently normal adults performed at Nairobi hospitals but this time excluding samples originating from either Mathari or the gaol, Vint found that on average the samples were 152 grams, or 10.6 per cent lighter than the average European brain.[11] He suggested that 'from these figures it would appear that the native brain reaches its full weight prior to the age of eighteen years, and that there is evidence of decrease after the age of forty'.[12] He also noted that the African brain had a flattened appearance and that a failure of development was evident in its height. The cortex was undeveloped and weighed on average almost 15 per cent less than that of European subjects. Vint's paper, apparently verifying the opinion most whites held about the African majority, attracted much interest in the settler community. In an editorial on it in the *East African Medical Journal*, Gordon praised the pathologist for having confirmed the results of his own research on African intelligence.[13]

Beyond the surviving studies of Gordon and Vint, few attempts were made to employ the sciences of anatomy or pathology to explain the differences between the ruling colonialists and the subject people.[14] Their work was distinctive in that it focused upon brain structure rather than brain function and disregarded the significance of culture. Those who came after them would adopt rather different approaches.

John Colin Carothers was born in Simonstown in the Cape of Good Hope in 1903.[15] His father was a civil engineer who worked for the Admiralty at various ports throughout the British empire. Carothers was educated in England at Portsmouth Grammar School and in October 1921 he passed the London matriculation examinations in the compulsory five subjects and was admitted to St Thomas' Hospital, University of London. At that time his major interest was in biology, but his mother believed that medicine offered a better career and he followed her advice. At the end of his undergraduate course he held a position for six months in the ear, nose and throat ward at St Thomas'. Carothers toyed with the idea of a career in public health and had indeed begun a diploma in that discipline when, by chance, he saw an advertisement for employment in Kenya offering £600 per year. He applied for the job through the Colonial Office, pleased with the prospect of returning to Africa, which in a sense he saw as his home, and to be going to East Africa, which he believed was safer for his health than the west.

In August 1929 Carothers embarked for Kenya. On his arrival he was posted to a rural station where, like any district medical officer, he was expected to perform all kinds of medical procedures. As a young physician he knew little about practical medicine, but he learnt quickly in a job that was varied and challenging. Keen to see as much of Kenya as possible, in the next ten years he moved from one station to another. He served at Kisumu, which was at that time at the end of the railway; then spent two years at Lake Victoria. It was while working in North Kavirondo that he met his future wife, Diana, having been introduced to her by his superior, a Dr Anderson, with whose family she was staying. Colin and Diana shared a common interest in butterflies and they discussed at length the best means of killing the insects without damaging their wings. Their solution was to place cyanide at the base of a wide-necked jar; the insects would die instantly and they could then be set. Colin and Diana married in 1933, when Colin was thirty.

At that time rural Kenya offered a rich social life, and as a DMO the Carotherses mixed with the 'best people' in the European community. In the smaller towns there was always golf, tennis and parties. Following leave in England in 1937, Carothers returned to his post at Kavirondo, in the north west close to the Ugandan border, where his responsibilities included public works such as clearing swamps to reduce the incidence of malaria. In August 1938 he wrote to a friend at the head office in Nairobi saying that he wanted to remain where he was, and received permission to do so. Then, within a matter of weeks, he received a telegram ordering him to report to Mathari, where he was to serve as acting senior medical officer. Carothers was to replace the only psychiatrist in the colony, Dr Cobb, who had been forced to resign.

Carothers's appointment was temporary, and at first he did not consider himself qualified to supervise a mental hospital. To his surprise he enjoyed the work, and after a month he asked to be kept on until a qualified replacement could be found. A replacement proved impossible to find, and the war intervened before Carothers himself could return to England to complete a diploma in psychiatry. Six one-hour lectures on psychology at St Thomas' constituted his only training in psychological medicine, and apart from Gordon there was no one in the colony from whom he could seek advice. Carothers attempted to educate himself by reading the standard psychiatric texts, but many of the cases at Mathari failed to correspond to the clinical profiles.[16] He felt that his lack of formal training was at fault. When the war began a number of army physicians arrived in Kenya, and this reduced his sense of isolation. He worked with the British army and treated a number of soldiers for mental illness.

In 1946 Carothers spent six months at the Maudsley Hospital, London, completing his diploma. On his return to Kenya he was appointed to the post of specialist psychiatrist and neurologist. Before his studies at the Maudsley, Carothers had published little, feeling unqualified to participate in academic debates. On returning to Mathari he began to publish widely and found that writing helped to clarify his ideas about his clinical practice. In 1948 and 1949 he visited Northern Rhodesia and Uganda and wrote reports for their governments on their existing mental health services.

Carothers took early retirement in May 1951 and accepted a post as a psychiatric specialist at St James's Hospital, Portsmouth.[17] In 1952 he was commissioned by the World Health Organization (WHO) to write a monograph on mental health in Africa which helped to bolster his growing reputation. In 1954 the British government approached him to write a report on the psychology of the Mau Mau rebellion and it was published as a White Paper in the same year. In 1955, as we have seen, he was again commissioned, this time by the government of Nigeria, to review its mental health services. His experience as medical officer in charge of Mathari had placed Carothers in an excellent position to carry out research, and he had done this to such effect that his publications in the period from 1940 until 1960 eventually made him the most frequently quoted psychiatrist of the colonial era. Carothers's influence was such that Frantz Fanon was moved to include an attack upon him in *The Wretched of the Earth*, one of the best-known polemics to come out of the African independence movements. Carothers was an inventive and original thinker and his influence crops up in unlikely places, including Marshall McLuhan's *The Guttenberg Galaxy*.

Carothers's first publication, in the *East African Medical Journal*,[18] was a review of the inmates at Mathari with some reflections on the distinctive features of mental illness in the African. The most striking characteristic of the Mathari community, according to Carothers, was the predominance of men, who outnumbered women two to one (the reverse of the pattern found in mental hospitals in England and Wales). One possible explanation might have been that women were less violent than men and therefore more easily looked after at home, but African women at Mathari were noisy and aggressive and more troublesome than the men.[19] He argued instead that the behaviour of women on the reserves was more stereotyped than that of men and therefore they were able to maintain their places in the community despite severe mental illness. He believed it significant that they were also less exposed than men to an alien European culture. Few mental defectives were brought to Mathari because of their deficiency. As had Gordon before him, Carothers commented on the absence in Kenya of any adequate standards of normality for judging Africans' behaviour.

To his surprise, Carothers found very few cases of manic-depressive psychosis at Mathari, and this led him to reflect upon the reasons for its absence.[20] The melancholic, he reasoned, felt wicked, and manics had an exaggerated sense of superiority. In both instances there was a strong sense of personal responsibility, a quality originating in European culture. In his opinion, then, African culture precluded the kinds of attitude associated with manic-depression.

In 1939 thirty-three cases of schizophrenia were admitted to Mathari, representing almost one-third of new patients. Carothers employed Henderson and Gillespie's prosaic account of the causes of this illness.[21] According to these British authorities, whereas most people confronted the problems and challenges of their lives directly some indulged in day-dreams as a substitute for action, and over time this pattern led to withdrawal and a loss of contact with the real world. Adolescence was the most dangerous period for the development of this pattern. The typical schizophrenic was self-absorbed and morally lazy. Carothers saw the African personality as displaying some notable parallels with that of the schizophrenic. By European standards Africans lived in a world of fantasy. Rather than observing their environment in a detached or scientific way, they projected their own qualities and emotions onto the world about them. For Africans, all matter, both animate and inanimate, had a spirit. When things went wrong the cause was always seen as some external agency, be it gods, enemies or ancestors. The African, Carothers wrote, 'seldom blames himself, but projects his guilt. He sees no sharply defined aspects of reality: wish and truth, possible and impossible, dreams and waking thoughts, phantasy and reality are one to him'.[22]

For the Africans the world was vast, strange and awesome, according to Carothers, and the African family was designed to provide individuals with some sense of security. It furnished them with specific rules for every situation, to the extent that 'initiative, personal responsibility, self–reliance are foreign to [the] system, and are even suspect'.[23] In situations in which no rule was prescribed they felt lost, for they had no experience of accepting responsibility for their own actions. The common element linking schizophrenia and the African personality was this denial of responsibility. According to Carothers, 'the normal African is not schizophrenic, but the step from the primitive attitude to schizophrenia is but a short and easy one'.[24] He believed that in traditional society few Africans would have gone mad; those who became psychotic under European rule had done so as a result of their contact with the more advanced European culture.

Carothers's linking of insanity in the African with European contact was conventional. What was distinctive about his work was his development of a theory about African culture and mentality: that culture made Africans vulnerable to mental disorders, such as schizophrenia, whenever they were confronted with new or unforeseen situations. The most debilitating of all circumstances appeared to be those in which they were forced to choose between alternative modes of action or accept responsibility for their behaviour. It was these failings that made Africans such poor employees. Unlike previous researchers, Carothers was careful to attribute these qualities to their culture rather than to their race, but he did characterize Africans as, in effect, delinquent children.

The relationship between culture and mental illness was further explored by Carothers in his first article in an international journal,

published in 1948, in *Psychiatry*.[25] The article was a review of his first
seven years at Mathari and his work with the inmates of Nairobi prison,
and a discussion of the impact upon mental health of Africans' transition
from traditional rural to urban life. Many of the subjects of his study were
members of Kenya's nascent proletariat. Carothers limited his study to
the 558 patients admitted to Mathari and Nairobi prison in the period
from January 1939 until December 1943.[26] This number was, he pointed
out, no indication of the actual incidence of serious mental illness in the
colony. African communities rarely expelled a member; the sick were
cared for within the family and problems arose only when they wandered
into a European settlement or township where their odd behaviour was
conspicuous. On average, new arrivals to Mathari had been cared for at
home for a period of six months before admission. Although nine in ten
Africans lived on the reserves, only half of Mathari's patients came from
that source. Africans remaining on the reserves were unlikely to be
certified. Once they joined the migrant labour force attracted to the towns
and cities, however, they became prone to serious mental illness. Detribalization was a complex process drawing the individual into contact with
the Christian churches, secular education, government officials and white
employers, and with the dangers of alcohol, drugs and venereal disease.
The Kenya census for 1943 revealed that there were over 300,000
Africans, mostly men aged between fifteen and forty-five years, employed
away from home and that a further 165,000 worked as resident labourers
on white farms. Most of the patients at Mathari came from these two
groups.[27]

Although Carothers characterized the problems experienced by
migrant workers as a conflict between modern and primitive modes of
thinking, he made no attempt to analyse the process of detribalization.
Most important, he ignored the impact of urbanization upon a migrant
labour force. Migration was a stressful experience, and migrant workers
were likely to fall victim to a range of pathologies, including mental
illness. If anything those stresses were even greater during the colonial
period when the segregation policies common throughout British Africa
forcibly separated male Africans from their wives and families. Whereas
Carothers elsewhere referred to the influence of social structure on mental
disorders, he ignored its influence on mentality. In his view the suscepti-
bility of migrant workers to mental illness was attributable to one source
alone: their rigid and unstable personality structure.

According to Carothers, the Africans' attitude towards life was con-
ditioned by three factors: their inherent mode of thought, their relations
to the natural world and their relations to a social environment. He had
little to say about the natural environment other than to note that

Africans' strong religious sense came from living close to nature. He had much to say, however, about their natural mode of thought and their social world. Their inherent mode of thought was dominated by fantastic thinking such as day-dreams and myths. It was an immature mode characteristic of children and primitive peoples. Fantastic thinking was directed by fleeting emotions rather than by conscious effort. It was automatic and spontaneous. Observation was often superficial, and Africans did not progress from observation to establishing causal relations. Similarly Africans' imagination was immature and egocentric; they had little capacity for self-criticism and no inclination to accept blame or responsibility. They also had little ability to discriminate between fact and fantasy: 'The ability of the African to lie convincingly is notorious, and one is entertained to believe at times that the story-teller has also temporarily convinced himself'.[28]

Africans' social world was arranged, according to Carothers, in such a way as to produce security for the individual and the group. Social activity was regulated by meticulous rules. The individual would as a young adult have acquired a grasp of the group's entire culture, in which status depended upon age rather than achievement or intellect. In all African communities there were strong forces for equality and conformity. There was no room for original thought, for innovation, or for transgression. Following Freud, Carothers suggested that there was a strong obsessive–compulsive element in primitive society.[29] In contrast to the Africans, Europeans would behave according to a set of general rules and feel responsible for their degree of conformity to those rules. In the European the strength of personality derived from the individual alone.

Among these patients mania was common but depressive illness rare.[30] Carothers argued that the absence of repressive or inhibiting factors in African culture could well encourage mania while excluding depression. Among the patients exhibiting mania at Mathari Carothers found that almost half had held positions of responsibility under European employers prior to becoming ill. He was convinced that in attempting to develop self-reliance and initiative Africans were likely to become deranged.

At Mathari there was a constant stream of patients who simply did not fit the established nosologies. For instance, a disorder that he called 'frenzied anxiety' was like running amok and in Carothers's opinion was probably one of the original reasons for the establishment of the asylum. Patients suffering from this disorder, invariably men, had committed senseless violent acts such as arson or murder. They seemed possessed by the desire to kill someone, anyone, and their victims were often strangers or bystanders. The behaviour seemed to have arisen from a sudden psychotic episode, but because of the great distances involved, the patient had often recovered by the time he arrived at the asylum. Carothers had often had difficulty in convincing a court that such a man had been insane at the time of his crime.

'Frenzied anxiety' was the one disorder in his work that could be termed culturally specific. In such cases a high level of anxiety was diffused throughout the mind, and the individual felt impelled to act. Because of his poorly developed powers of self-criticism, the African would look outside himself for the cause of his distress. The most common result was a senseless murder or act of arson.[31] 'It seems likely therefore that the condition we have labelled frenzied anxiety tends to replace in Africans many of the types of anxiety neurosis, and perhaps some of the depressions, that are seen in Europeans.'[32] Where the European would commit suicide, the African turned instead to murder. Carothers's essay carried a clear warning to the white community, as the Africans who were most likely to commit such crimes were those who lived in urban locations and were in the employ of settlers.

Although Carothers attributed the differences in mental illness between Europeans and Africans to the influence of culture, he was of course familiar with the work of Gordon and Vint, and his post-war training at the Maudsley had also concentrated on the brain and its structure rather than on the influence of cultural variables upon behaviour. It is not surprising, therefore, that in his next publication, 'Frontal Lobe Function and the African', Carothers should have turned to physiology.[33] Most immediately, this study arose from a request by the Kenyan director of laboratory services for a 'test of character' which would permit the selection of reliable Africans for laboratory work. He approached this task by reflecting upon the forms of mental derangement, which he related to personality structure in Africans. He also solicited the comments of three Europeans on their experiences with African employees. Surprisingly, he did not list the qualities required in an efficient employee – indeed, one can best identify such qualities by their absence in his African subjects. Pointing once again to the rigidity of African culture, the absence of generalized rules and the suppression of individual initiative, he also remarked that Africans had no conception of universal truth or justice; that they were prone to rapid mood changes and often responded without consideration for the consequences; that they possessed no genuine social sense and would laugh at the misfortune of others; and that while living on a reserve they conformed passively to community expectations but in all other respects resembled European psychopaths. In fact, he concluded, the pattern of psychopathology in Africans revealed the inability of their culture to produce a responsible citizenry.

The failings of African servants were a staple topic of conversation among white settlers, and Carothers cited thirty-three examples of those failings that seemed to him to reveal an inability to see an event within a context – a tendency to follow routine procedures blindly, and lack of interest in any activity unless it happened to appeal in a direct or personal way. A number of cases can, however, be seen as examples of passive resistance by powerless employees while others can in fact be interpreted to the servant's advantage. A house-boy was instructed never to place black shoes on top of white shoes and never to place heavy shoes on top of light shoes; he followed these instructions for several days and then reverted to his old habits, which damaged the shoes and infuriated his employer. House-boys would dust certain items in a room but fail to keep the rest of the room clean or tidy; they could not be taught to put furniture back against the wall or to hang pictures correctly. Carothers may have been correct that such anecdotes demonstrated a literalism on the part of the servant. They may also have betrayed cultural arrogance and a lack of clear instruction on the part of the employer. Alternatively, the servants may well have been conserving their energy or expressing their hostility. Along with most members of the expatriate community, Carothers assumed that anyone who made a poor servant must be mentally impoverished.

A second theme in Carothers's case-studies was Africans' lack of long-term goals and their inability to pursue the kind of self-interest that was so much a part of middle-class European culture. In exploring these issues Carothers discussed at length the case of an African mental attendant with fifteen years' service who had informed him that he had to go home because a distant relative was ill. This was not allowed, and he was told that if he insisted he would be discharged and would sacrifice his high pay and a gratuity which was due to him. He insisted on leaving but said he would return and begin again at the lowest rank, which is in fact what he did. Carothers commented: 'This is an example of the precedence accorded to primitive custom even when it may ruin the subjects' prospects within the European system, and the latter is treated as quite unimportant and irrelevant when it conflicts with the African.'[34] Another way of interpreting this story would, of course, recognize the merit of the attendant's choice to place the needs of a relative above his own immediate interest. Such a view would also take note of the unfairness of the hospital's work practices.

According to Carothers, Africans' education was focused upon particular, concrete situations; they never came to understand or to apply general rules. As servants they would absorb explicit instructions but fail to comprehend an abstract idea such as tidiness or cleanliness. They had no respect for the truth, and their understanding of what was true would vary from one moment to the next.[35] Carothers concluded that the differences between Europeans and Africans were so great that the African was hardly in fact an individual in our sense of the word, but a series of reactions.

How, then, were these differences to be explained and what were the prospects for training Africans? In answering these questions Carothers turned once again to psychopathology. As a student at the Maudsley in 1948 he would no doubt have learned of the technique that its originator Egas Moniz called prefrontal leucotomy, a procedure that involved destroying part of the patient's brain. The procedure was introduced into the United States by Walter Freeman, who during a career spanning three decades carried out hundreds of these operations, and for a time per-formed them at his New York office using electroconvulsive therapy for an anaesthetic and an ice-pick for an instrument.[36] Few such operations were performed on the inmates of Mathari, and Carothers had access to the patients before and after surgery. He also had read at least some of the literature on the subject. In general patients who had undergone Free-man's operation were assessed to have suffered no intellectual impairment but displayed an emotional shallowness, a loss of creative activity and a tendency to live in the present. Freeman found that his charges had a diminished ability to deal with spatial relationships. They exhibited cheerful self-satisfaction and had little desire to learn anything new. Where there was any personality change it consisted in an inability to see an event as an element in a total situation – to perceive not just details but concepts.

This portrait struck Carothers as familiar, and he commented that except for the ability to verbalize and conjure up fantasies the resemb-lance between Africans and leucotomized Europeans was complete. Carothers goes on to explain: 'It seems not without significance that at least one of the few Europeans leucotomised in Kenya has, since his operation, consorted much more happily with Africans than with Euro-peans, in marked distinction from his previous behaviour, and to the great embarrassment of his relations'.[37] The function of the frontal lobes is to integrate stimuli, and according to Carothers Africans (and leucotomized Europeans) made little use of this region of the brain.

The conclusions he drew from all of this were somewhat ambiguous. Whereas he agreed with Vint that the African brain was smaller and less well developed than the brain of the European and felt that this explained their relative positions on the scale of human achievement, he argued that Africans' peculiarities were due to their culture and that there was no reason to assume that they suffered from any constitutional deficiency. He then commented that all peoples get the culture they deserve.[38] These references to culture were intended to suggest choice and malleability, but they were the only assertions in 'Frontal Lobe Function and the African' which allowed for such variation. The weight of Carothers's argument was upon the gulf separating Africans from civilization: a people incapable of mastering the simple rules required of domestic servants was unlikely to be able to govern its own affairs.

Carothers's essay was cited frequently in the clinical literature in the next decade. For example, in an article published in 1956, C. G. Smartt agreed with Carothers that Africans were unreliable and irresponsible and had little ability to tolerate mental or physical stress. Like leucotomized patients they lacked initiative: 'There is no doubt [that Carothers's] summary of the changes which may follow leucotomy presents a graphic picture of the East African native; one with which most people whom have had experience with Africans would agree'.[39] Within the space of six years Carothers had become the most prominent psychiatrist in the field. His work was widely read and well received, and there were no protests from his colleagues about the parallels he drew between brain-damaged Europeans and normal Africans. His publications were carefully written, and he had little difficulty in gaining access to the best academic journals. In contrast, Frantz Fanon was publishing the results of his own clinical research in Algeria at the same time as Carothers, but he had to content himself with obscure forums such as *Conscience maghrebine* and *Maroc medicale*. It is not possible, therefore, to dismiss Carothers's work as an aberration. In the immediate post-war era it represented the mainstream of ethnopsychiatric science.[40] Significantly, the same period saw the rise of African nationalism.

In 1952 Carothers was commissioned by the World Health Organization to write a monograph on mental health and disease in Africans. That he was appointed over a number of prominent competitors, including Melville Herskovits, was evidence of his standing. In the nine months he spent researching the monograph he travelled widely in Africa, Europe and the United States, and had access to numerous eminent practitioners, including two of the leading physicians from Francophone Africa, H. Aubin and P. Gallais. While writing up the report he spent some time attending WHO conferences in Geneva, where he met such prominent intellectuals as Konrad Lorenz and Margaret Mead. His monograph, *The African Mind in Health and Disease*, published in 1953, provided a survey of the problems of mental health on the African continent. While conceding (for the first time) that there were important variations in setting and environment and endorsing the need for detailed ethnographic studies, Carothers's analysis again centred upon an abstraction. He quoted at length from the work of a number of his colleagues and contemporaries, and in many ways the monograph was more a review of the literature than a breaking of new ground. What was novel in it was the bringing together of these disparate sources.

The framework for the study was provided by an exposition of the impact of physical illness upon mental health and a review of the concept of race. The study dealt at length with the literature on physical anthropology, focusing upon physiology as the key to both culture and personality. Carothers began the study by asking to what extent the distinctive mental attributes of the African were due to genetic factors (that is, to race) and to what extent they could be attributed to environment. The question of race, then, was once again central to Carothers's project but for the first time explicitly acknowledged. The study also contained a long section on environment in which Carothers refers at length to infectious disease and diet. He stressed the fact that throughout Africa disease was a major cause of mental illness.[41]

One of the key questions addressed in *The African Mind* was whether the African's mentality was fundamentally different from the European's and, if so, how the difference could be explained. Here he linked the research of Gordon and Vint with American studies showing the brain of the Negro to be inferior to that of the Caucasian.[42] Acknowledging that brain weight is relative to body size, he emphasized the part of Vint's research that dealt with brain height and shape. He also reviewed the research carried out in 1949 and 1951 by a number of Francophone physicians who had pioneered the use of electroencephalographs (EEGs). One of these projects had compared the EEGs of 100 apparently normal African soldiers with a cohort of 3,000 Europeans. The rate of abnormality among the European subjects was about 14 per cent while well over half of the African subjects (58 per cent) returned abnormal readings. The results were consistent with those of an earlier study which had purportedly revealed evidence of neurone immaturity in Africans, a finding that appeared to verify Vint's research.[43] Carothers was delighted at this correspondence, which he believed established the importance of neurological factors in African temperament and culture. For better or worse, however, the findings of Vint and the French researchers were never duplicated.[44]

Not content with confining his research to physiology, Carothers devoted part of a chapter to the influence of child-rearing practices upon intellectual and emotional development. He quoted at length from the Freudian J. F. Ritchie's *The African as Suckling and as Adult*, which attributed African temperament to family structure and an absence of sexual repression. Carothers agreed with Ritchie that African child training stunted curiosity and prevented the development of mature individuals. In the sexual domain, men's preference was for restless philandering, which confined emotions to the superficial and ephemeral.[45] In turning to Ritchie when there was already ample explanation for the differences between the African and the European in the literature he cited on the brain, Carothers made no attempt to order these levels of causation. He did, however, draw a distinction between culture and race, the first presumed to be dynamic and, at least to some extent, open to change, while the second set immutable limits to human achievement. Paradoxically, his treatment of culture precluded the idea of plasticity which is axiomatic to the concept as it was used by anthropologists such as Franz Boas.

In a section titled 'Psychology in Relation to Environment', Carothers explored the intellectual development of the African child in relation to cultural influences. The section on infancy was once more drawn largely from Ritchie, although Carothers disputed Ritchie's emphasis upon infant experience in the shaping of adult behaviour.[46] He also relied upon the work of Jean Piaget, especially *The Child's Conception of Physical Causality*.[47] Carothers applied Piaget's schema not just to the African child but to the adult, in whom he believed the powers of cognition were deficient. According to Carothers, until the age of seven or eight years the African developed in the same way as the European, but then the process of development suddenly comes to a halt. 'Piaget's descriptions of the second developmental stage', he explained, 'accord closely with the thought patterns of even adult rural Africans, and not one of the developments observed in his third stage is characteristically seen in them.'[48] This argument gave the sanction of scientific truth to what so many white settlers in Kenya and Southern Rhodesia already believed: that the adult African was simply a child.

In his account of childhood, Carothers emphasized the inconsistencies in the attitudes of parents and the intellectual and social impoverishment which he considered characteristic of African culture. He claimed that there was no secure foundation for mental development and that 'the child's life was governed by interlacing networks of rules and taboos, whose origins are prehistoric'.[49] Those rules served to integrate members into the community, but also stunted individual development. Integration was social rather than cerebral, and the individual was integrated into the society but not into himself. Presumably this pattern formed a corollary to the lack of integration which Vint had discovered in the structure of the cortex. Carothers agreed with Piaget that full intellectual development required certain forms of infantile and childhood experience and added that those forms were not available to Africans.

During adolescence the same pattern was maintained and the child's experience was if anything more limited. Carothers rejected the idea that sexuality was to blame for the intellectual dullness of African adolescents. According to him, 'the trouble is much more deep seated: and the whole-hearted concentration on sex which characterises the African adolescent is, in the present writers' view, merely one symptom of a general condition.[50] The individual, he argued, had no proper means to distinguish between object and subject, and no balance was achieved between love and hate. While acknowledging that malnutrition and disease probably played some part, Carothers concluded that the emotional life of Africans was distorted and that the psychology of the adult might be described as 'monodeic'.

Carothers acknowledged that Africans did have some strengths, such as loyalty, self-confidence, sociability and forgiveness, and that their culture fostered an aptitude for dance and music. However, in summarizing the African temperament Carothers lost sight of those frail virtues:

The African accordingly has been described as conventional; highly dependent upon physical and emotional stimulation; lacking in spontaneity, foresight, tenacity, judgment and humility; inapt for sound abstraction and for logic; given to phantasy and fabrication; and in general unstable, impulsive, unreliable, irresponsible and living in the present without reflection or ambition or regard for the rights of people outside his own circle.[51]

The portrait could not have been more damning.

The African Mind represented the distillation of more than ten years' research and over twenty years of clinical practice, and in it Carothers made the most succinct presentation of the theory of African inferiority. The key to that theory was his reliance upon the work of both Vint and Ritchie and his references to both environment and race. At first glance it seems curious that Carothers should have made reference to modes of explanation that are usually seen as exclusive. It was not, however, sufficient for him to restate the deeply held belief of white settlers that Africans were intellectually and culturally inferior. Because for him science had to be comprehensive, he expanded his explanation of the Africans' deficiency to include culture, race, brain morphology, morality and intellectual endowment. It was as if the theory had to colonize the whole of African society, past, present and future. Seen in this way, *The African Mind* was not a study of mental health but a politics of possibilities – a theory of citizenship, economic behaviour and moral failing.

The book went through two impressions in three months. It was the first study of its kind and it differed from other WHO publications in that it was presented as the work of a single, acknowledged author. Given the originality of the project and the fact that much of the material fell into territory controlled by social anthropologists, it was bound to arouse some controversy. It was subtitled *A Study in Ethnopsychiatry*, and its readership included physicians as well as a range of social scientists. It was the only ethnopsychiatric publication ever to reach a wide audience, and for the first time it exposed the research of Carothers and his colleagues to the judgement of a broad intellectual community. One would expect Carothers's use of the concept of race to have provoked the ire of any anthropologist who read the study carefully, but the monograph was well received, and only one reviewer, Jules Henry, took exception to its argument. One of the most positive reviews came from Margaret Mead.

Mead's review, in *Psychiatry*, recognized the importance to Carothers's argument of 'frontal lobe idleness' and noted a number of weaknesses in his approach, in particular the lack of reference to modern studies dealing with social organization.[52] Mead predicted that his conclusions would arouse dissent among religious groups which emphasized the importance of religious belief and among anthropologists who insisted upon the maintenance of traditional values. She questioned whether the WHO should in future employ such original researchers as Carothers, with his heterodox approach to the African literature, suggesting that this heterodoxy could well encourage criticism of the kind frequently directed at non-specialists. Yet she found this approach fresh and interesting. Mead argued that Carothers had addressed important questions about the relationship between cultural forms and mentality, questions that had been ignored by social anthropologists, and in this way had opened up new theoretical ground. He had also, in her opinion, made a striking contribution in identifying the importance of auditory imagery to African belief systems.[53] She judged the monograph as a whole 'a brave adventure into new and untried fields, a tremendous undertaking in a few months by a physician who has spent his life working among the peoples of Africa'.[54]

Mead's failure to recognize the status of many of Carothers's arguments, especially those regarding race, culture and psychological type, is difficult to excuse, but in this she was not alone. Other reviewers, although less sympathetic to Carothers's achievements, also failed to object to his opinions about African inferiority.[55] The one critic to take exception to the monograph, Jules Henry, was as much perturbed by Mead's review as by Carothers's theory: 'Indeed the reader scarcely gets an idea of the really deeply prejudiced character of Carothers' point of view. In Mead's discussion Carothers becomes almost a hero, jousting with the windmills of conservatism conjured up by Mead.'[56] Henry was also outraged by the way in which Carothers used the terms 'race and culture', calling him 'a racial determinist in spite of his repeated insistence on the importance of cultural factors.'[57]

In his defence, Carothers claimed that Henry and others had misread his argument. He explained that his use of the terms 'intelligence and mentality' assumed that both were dependent upon environmental factors, with intelligence also containing a genetic component. He vehemently denied that he was racially prejudiced.[58]

Historically, the terms 'race' and 'culture' represent alternative modes of thinking about human communities. The term 'race' involves attributes that are immutable, and the association of particular features (most commonly failings) with racial identity implies that the power relations between different human groups can and should never change. This was the way de Gobineau used the term, and it is exactly the way it has been used by minority regimes in Southern Rhodesia and South Africa. In contrast, the term 'culture' suggests choice. Cultures are not static and they can be changed and adapted to differing circumstances. Furthermore, people can modify their cultural affiliations. In *The African Mind* 'culture' denoted a type of personality rather than an ensemble of customs, institutions or forms of behaviour. The burden of the argument was that environment and its correlative culture were fixed. The Africans' inferior culture was the product of a particular physical setting and genetic disposition, neither of which was susceptible of immediate transformation. Cultures might change and could be enhanced, but by implication at a rate as slow as the rate of natural selection. It therefore mattered little which term Carothers favoured: the result was the same.[59]

Because of their interest in cultural variation, anthropologists were better equipped than specialists in other sciences to situate Carothers's work in its theoretical and historical context. In *The African Mind* Carothers favourably reviewed the research of his contemporaries and quoted from their work, sometimes at length. Consequently, the judgements of Mead and Herskovits were not just of Carothers but to a large extent of his discipline as a whole. Yet neither reviewer showed any apprehension about how that literature perceived the Africans' intellectual, cultural or social world, and the only critical comments they made related directly to their own areas of technical expertise. Perhaps, in the light of Carothers's professional standing, these reviewers were unwilling to judge a science about which they knew little or nothing. Again, the monograph's focus upon pathology was somewhat removed from anthropologists' concern with normal patterns of sociability. Whatever the reason, it is surprising that social anthropologists, who prided themselves upon their custodial role in regard to primitive peoples, should have raised so few objections to the theory of African inferiority.[60]

5   Theory into practice: Carothers and the politics of Mau Mau

J. C. Carothers's appointment in 1954 as a one-man commission of inquiry into the Mau Mau rebellion immersed him directly in the world of political strife. On 21 October 1952, a state of emergency had been declared in Kenya. In the next six years a total of thirty-two European settlers were killed, along with sixty-three members of the security forces. British soldiers and Kenyan police in turn killed over eleven-and-a-half thousand purported members of the Mau Mau. In addition, several hundred Africans were hanged.[1] British troops detained over ninety thousand Mau Mau suspects, and torture was widely used. The emergency jolted the British government and helped to bring forward independence for the colony, finally achieved in 1963.

The historiography of the Mau Mau has changed several times since the 1950s, and there have been a number of dramatic shifts in the ways in which the movement has been understood. The Mau Mau was confined largely to a single tribe, the Kikuyu, and it gained its impetus from that tribe's claims to the area of Kenya then known as the White Highlands. The Kikuyu first laid claim to this land, which they believed had been illegally appropriated by white settlers, in 1913, and in 1920, under the leadership of Harry Thuku, the Kikuyu Association was formed with the intention of forcing the issue of its return. The colonial government was slow to respond to these demands, and it was only in 1932 that the Kenya Land Commission was appointed to investigate all aspects of landholdings in the colony. While there was some increase in land grants, in its 1933 report the commission ruled against the Kikuyu. Kikuyu resistance was then contained for almost a decade, but the Great Depression and the drafting of large numbers of Africans into the British army during World War II set the stage for a more militant struggle over land in the post-war years. In 1944 the Kenya African Union (KAU) was formed and it was this organization that eventually gave birth to the Mau Mau. Land became an intense political issue from late 1946 with the return to the colony of the Kikuyu leader Jomo Kenyatta. According to the official British government history the Mau Mau began to be politically active around 1947, and within the space of five years it had brought economic activity in the colony to a virtual standstill.

Contemporary histories of the Mau Mau give a very different account to that rendered by post-independence historians. The first of these, published in 1954, comes from John Wilkinson, a physician working in the South Nyeri District of Kenya. According to Wilkinson the aims of the Mau Mau were to unify all black Kenyans under its leadership and to end immigration to the colony. The basic features of the movement were its secrecy, its use of terror, and its anti-Christian and anti-white ideology. The Mau Mau was inspired by a hatred of Europeans, and it sought to impose a form of totalitarian control over the whole country. Wilkinson was outraged by the Mau Mau's oaths which in various ways parodied the Christian sacrament. He also emphasized the violence used against enemies and in particular the use of the panga (a large bush knife). Wilkinson made no reference to Kikuyu demands for land rights or to any coherent political programme. He tended to view the movement as pathological and, along with the British government, believed that negotiating with the KAU or the Mau Mau was useless.[2]

In 1957 Michael Kirby, who like Wilkinson was a European physician, published his own interpretation of the Mau Mau.[3] Dividing the Kikuyu's life into three phases Kirby examined in some detail the stresses confronting the new generation of young men. (He had nothing to say about the young women who also joined the movement.) As a child, the typical Kikuyu was torn between an educated father who lived, at least in part, in contact with the European world and a mother who was conservative and still believed in magic. Torn between these conflicting realities, his conscience became 'ragged and uneven'. As a result 'each parent dominates the child separately through the day, with the result that he is doomed to lifelong misery and drifts into a state of guilt and neurosis'.[4] As an adolescent he was exposed simultaneously to traditional practices such as circumcision rituals and to the influence of the Christian churches. It was the conflict of these realities that would later encourage him to take the Mau Mau oath. The Kikuyu were menacing but servile, aggressive but frightened. They were also, according to Kirby, inherently cowardly.[5] Once again, there was no reference to the land issue.

The leading European authority on the Kikuyu at the time was the Kenyan-born anthropologist L. S. B. Leakey. Leakey's parents had been missionaries, and he had spent his childhood among the Kikuyu and, unlike other commentators, was fluent in the Kikuyu language. He was greatly disturbed by the movement, which he considered destructive, and wrote two books on the subject. In contrast to Wilkinson and Kirby, he commented at length upon the contemporary history of the Kikuyu, addressing the strength of their claim to the White Highlands and evaluating the disruption caused by the growth of settler society. Traditional Kikuyu education was, according to Leakey, both practical and theoretical and it perfectly served the needs and interests of the individual and the community: 'As such, it was fundamental education which made good citizens, honest men and women, and wise parents and leaders of the community, in which a sense of responsibility to those in the lower grades and of the tribe as a whole, was very strongly developed.'[6] Despite his sympathy for Kikuyu culture, Leakey considered the Kikuyu claim to the Highlands unfounded. He did, however, comment upon the injustices of colonial society, which saw an African worker receive only one-quarter the rate of pay given to a white man, and he argued that many government policies were self-defeating and dangerous.[7]

Contemporary accounts of the Mau Mau, including those by Leakey, were based on the idea of a clash of cultures between the Kikuyu and the European settlers. No distinctions were made between different segments of the African population, nor was there any reference to the varied impact over time of a cash economy, wage labour, urbanization or the segregationist policies of the colonial government. The Kikuyu were particularly affected by those changes, since they were drawn into the new economy not just as producers but as wage labourers. Over time demographic pressures and evictions had created a landless class; by 1953 over half of the Kikuyu on the reserves were without land.[8] In his study of the origins of the Mau Mau Frank Furedi traced the process whereby the Kikuyu had come under pressure to supply labour rather than to work as tenants. Prior to 1945, squatters were obliged to provide labour rent for ninety days. In return they were allowed to work five or six acres of land held by white farmers and to run twenty-five to thirty sheep and goats. By 1946 labour rent had grown to 240 days a year and squatters were restricted to half an acre of land and five sheep. Because the monthly wage of eight to ten shillings was not raised, within a few years squatters suffered a decline in income of over 40 per cent in real terms.[9] The squatters were also disadvantaged in the selling of their produce, as the maize marketing board paid them far less than it did European farmers. As a result, many squatters left for the towns, where they eked out a precarious existence.[10] The growth of the Mau Mau was connected to squatter resistance, and it was at least in part a protest against evictions. In contrast, the leadership of the Mau Mau was drawn from the class of traders, artisans and teachers which had emerged out of the market economy established by the settlers. Subsequent histories have interpreted the movement as part of the nationalist struggle against British rule, pointing to obvious parallels between the Mau Mau and movements that emerged during the same period in Tanganyika, Nyasaland, and the Gold Coast.[11]

Mass oath-taking in Nairobi began in 1950. The Mau Mau found support among the urban unemployed and destitute whose ranks included many of the dispossessed squatters from the Highlands. According to David Throup, squatter discontent alone was insufficient to produce a rebellion. The rebellion was made almost inevitable, however, by social changes which created simultaneously a class of Western-educated intellectuals and an urban and rural proletariat. Since this process was most advanced among the Kikuyu, it was they who were most involved in the Mau Mau.

Given these circumstances, it is significant that when the British government sought to explain the rebellion it turned not to an anthropologist or historian but to a psychiatrist. In late November 1953 Carothers, by then resident in Portsmouth, received a letter from S. R. Mortimer, Member for Health, Lands and Local Government in Nairobi, explaining that while the rebellion was being suppressed, the government of Kenya was concerned about its long-term consequences: 'The eradication of the deep-rooted and widespread suspicion and bitterness is a much more difficult problem, the solution of which will require all the skilled advice and assistance we [the government] can obtain.'[12] Mortimer asked Carothers to accept a commission to write a report on the Mau Mau and its causes, and he ended the letter with a request for discretion about the appointment: '[We] are endeavouring to avoid any publicity for your visit and I hope that you will be able to avoid it in the United Kingdom.'[13] It was Carothers's special knowledge of the African mentality that the Kenyan government sought in its efforts to retain the support of the loyal members of the Kikuyu, Meru and Embu tribes. His advice was also considered valuable in helping to rehabilitate Mau Mau adherents. With the consent of his employer, the British National Health Service, Carothers was to spend two months in Kenya researching the rebellion.

The Psychology of Mau Mau, the only study of its kind commissioned by a colonial government to be written by a psychiatrist, represented a landmark in the history of ethnopsychiatry.[14] It also represented something of a landmark in the history of the Mau Mau rebellion. The report was twenty-eight pages in length and provided what was intended to be a comprehensive analysis of the troubled psychology of the Kikuyu. The first two chapters were devoted to the psychology of the native African and the problems of transition between traditional and modern cultures. The last two chapters were addressed to the psychology of the Mau Mau and included recommendations in treating the problem over the long term. Much of this material had direct relevance to the demands of native

Kenyans for political independence. In his report on the Mau Mau, Carothers wandered a considerable distance from the cloistered world of clinical psychiatry.

Carothers began by conceding that no biological distinctions between the African and the European had been proven but maintaining nevertheless that there were important differences. Despite the European presence in Kenya, traditional African culture, with its emphasis upon magical and animistic modes of explanation, remained strong. This culture shaped a mentality in the African which in ways resembled that of the European child. According to Carothers, all traditional belief systems, but especially animism, stifled curiosity to such an extent 'that the individual remains relatively unintegrated – an assemblage of memorised and disparate rules. Reflection, foresight and responsibility are rather components of this culture than of himself: misfortunes are never wholly his own fault'.[15] In his view traditional culture was by its very nature oppressive. Carothers also observed that in African culture outsiders had no rights. If they were powerful they would be feared, but if weak they would be treated in the most vile way. In situations where there were no specific rules to govern behaviour, Africans' conduct would be dictated by spontaneous emotion. They lacked the strength to tolerate anxiety, and where anxiety could not be allayed by ritual it would often lead to violence. Because of the nature of African society and because of the lack of asylums to segregate the insane, it was difficult to establish a boundary between the normal and the pathological.

Addressing the problems caused by the clash of African and European societies, Carothers focused on culture and personality type, with no reference to land or nationalism. In his view African societies had never been entirely static, but their rate of change had, in the past, been very slow. Consequently, the European presence had had a dramatic effect upon every facet of African culture which, because of its rigidity, had been unable to adapt or change. Africans' sense of security derived from their attachment to some external power, usually embodied in the gods. The arrival of the Europeans had sounded the death knell of that culture by rendering the gods impotent. More than anything else, it was the Europeans' material success that made Africans feel weak and caused them to lose faith in the benevolence of the supernatural and hence in their own culture.

According to Carothers the Kikuyu were individualistic, scheming and litigious. They were also hardworking and better able than other tribes to delay gratification. Of all the tribes of Kenya they were in his opinion most likely to achieve success within a European culture, and he saw the future of the colony as depending largely upon their co-operation with government. Historically, the Kikuyu had lived on the edge of a forest and at risk of attack by other tribes. The forest had been seen as protective and supportive but had also helped to encourage secretiveness, suspicion and scheming. A 'forest mentality' had remained important in Kikuyu culture and contributed to the Mau Mau rebellion. Even before the arrival of the British, the Kikuyu had had little sense of personal security. Authority had been maintained by fear rather than respect or love; the severity of Kikuyu initiation rituals was a sign of the culture's weakness.

Child-rearing practices had remained static, but traditional beliefs held no conviction and so Kikuyu were left without a sense of direction or purpose. Living in a world they felt to be malevolent, they blamed that malevolence upon Europeans. They had no home in a traditional society and in the new one had been unable to find the material success they craved. Carothers noted the striking inequalities in Kikuyu society between men and women, inequalities which were reinforced by the practice of female circumcision. Women were rarely allowed to attend European schools, and were forced to accept the role of wife and mother. Trapped in a traditional world which the men were trying to escape, Kikuyu women were confused and resentful.

Having established a model of the Kikuyu personality, Carothers turned to the history of the Mau Mau. Written almost as an appendage to the section on personality, that history represented the events of the emergency as pathological. Like many other European commentators, Carothers was appalled by the oaths, which blended Christian symbolism with various sexual practices.[16] He suggested that in form and content they were similar to those used by witches in Europe during the Middle Ages, and he was convinced that Jomo Kenyatta, the Mau Mau's purported leader, must have studied European witchcraft. Carothers even analysed a number of oaths, dividing them into various grades and noting that the oaths initially employed to induct new members were very different to the obscene rituals used later. Many of the oaths involved the deliberate violation of certain traditional Kikuyu rituals, intended to fill the oath taker with terror. The fourth or platoon oath, in particular, was aimed at destroying the oath taker's attachment to customary law.

A major problem confronting the Kenyan government was whether oath takers were redeemable, and it was one of Carothers's tasks to assist the government in framing policy for the treatment of Mau Mau detainees. In addressing this question he turned not to the history of the Kikuyu under British rule but to the literature on psychopathology. According to Carothers, Africans had a facility for dissociation which enabled them to live incompatible lives simultaneously and to reconcile contradictions in behaviour which for Europeans would be inconceivable. This facility was characteristic of the Mau Mau; many of the rebels could, he said, be classified as psychopathic criminals. For this reason Carothers feared that even if screened carefully many of the Kikuyu rebels could never again be trusted and that the seeds of evil might lie dormant within the tribe for many years. He was also concerned that other tribes might have been infected by the events of the emergency, making stable government impossible.

Carothers commented at length on the disloyalty of the Kikuyu towards the British government and often towards their employers: 'Indeed the behaviour of the Kikuyu men in recent years has closely simulated the attitude of a jilted lover, whose love of learning had been scorned and had been turned to hate of all the latter stood for. The attempt to reinstate the old ways was mainly based on this, and when this Emergency is over, it will be seen for the artificial thing it really was.'[17] The Kikuyu had expected too much of the British, and their neurotic behaviour was artificial in the sense that the Mau Mau's demands could never be resolved within the domain of politics. Armed with this insight, Carothers made a number of recommendations for the Kenyan government in dealing with the Kikuyu's special needs. He assumed that above all else the Kikuyu wanted security, and once this was given the Mau Mau would hold little appeal. He suggested the introduction of a 'villiagization programme' resembling that used in Malaya during the insurgency and later employed by the Americans in Vietnam and the Smith regime in colonial Zimbabwe. The villages so created could become the foundation for a new society; the establishment of light industries could provide employment and halt the drift of young men to the cities where few could find work. Keeping the young men at home would also strengthen the family and help to bridge the gulf separating men from women, a gulf Carothers believed had contributed to the rise of the rebellion.

Another suggestion Carothers offered was the re-establishment of a home hygiene programme so that the domestic skills essential for managing a family could be taught to African women. Such a programme had been introduced into Kenya in 1924 by the Jeanes' Movement, the aim of which was to institute Western family practice into African villages.[18] For various reasons, including the emphasis placed upon individual achievement, the movement had had little appeal, and by the outbreak of World War II it was in decline. Carothers was concerned that African adults were handicapped in the context of a modern culture and hoped that measures such as these would help foster curiosity and initiative among children so that a new type of personality could be developed. He also recommended the establishment of a moral education programme aimed at instilling notions of truthfulness and accountability in the young so as to produce a generation of Africans with a sense of social duty.[19] Above all the Kikuyu needed to be taught that to earn the right to political power they would have to demonstrate a sense of responsibility. To reach that goal they needed to be given firm and clear direction by the European community.

These recommendations for social improvement were founded upon the idea of Christian stewardship, and he applied the same principles in evaluating the attitudes and behaviour of the European settlers toward Africans. He was obviously disappointed with many of the settlers he met during his brief return to the colony, and he suggested that in future there should be a strict screening of white immigrants. More than twenty years earlier H. L. Gordon had made a similar suggestion, noting the significant number of mad young European men sent to Kenya in order to save their families embarrassment.[20] Carothers was no doubt aware that many of the Kikuyu who opposed the Mau Mau were Christians, and his criticism of the white community for its failing to live according to the Gospel carried a certain self-conscious irony.[21]

A villiagization programme based on the Malayan model was in fact instituted in Kenya, and Carothers's monograph was influential in shaping the official history of the emergency. Yet Carothers's report contained many silences. As psychology, its focus was upon the individual rather than the group. Carothers ignored the Kikuyu's claim to the White Highlands and had little to say about their history under colonial rule. Instead he concentrated upon their transition from a traditional to a modern culture and the stresses this transition placed upon the individual. He had nothing to say about the circumstances under which this process was experienced by the Kikuyu as peasants, as wage labourers and as a sub-proletariat. As a psychologist, he framed the problem solely in terms of childhood experience, child-rearing practices and personality development. His concern was with the emergence of a healthy, mature individual of the kind produced by middle-class British families. He stressed the importance of adhering to rules through internal constraints rather than through coercion. If Europeans behaved well it was because they adhered voluntarily to principles of duty and responsibility; if Africans behaved well it was because they feared the consequences of transgression. These mental structures, according to Carothers, were very different, and it was only by embracing the one and abandoning the other that Africans would be able to enter the modern world.

With Carothers's monograph the science of ethnopsychiatry formally entered the domain of political action. *The Psychology of Mau Mau* showed how well suited ethnopsychiatry was to the shaping and rationalization of conventional settler beliefs about Africans. It was the one science that was capable of providing a strictly hierarchical definition of human nature, and in that sense it was the one science whose shibboleths corresponded perfectly with the structures of colonial societies. Ethnopsychiatry lacked the tensions of social anthropology, which even in the form of structural functionalism had to struggle with problems associated with the ethics of fieldwork. For a psychiatrist such as Carothers, equipped with unambiguous definitions of normality and pathology, the task of understanding Africans was far easier.

By 1957 the Mau Mau rebellion had been quelled, and the British government decided it was time to commission an official account of its causes. It chose a career colonial official named F. D. Corfield, who was at that time resident in Kenya. Over a period of almost forty years Corfield had enjoyed a successful career in the Sudan and Palestine, and Evans-Pritchard, in his foreword to *The Nuer*, thanked him for his generous assistance. Corfield's task was to study the origins and growth of the Mau Mau and to explain the reasons it had developed so rapidly. He was also to report on any deficiencies in the government's handling of the emergency. Although the terms of reference were very different to those provided for Carothers, the conclusions Corfield reached were in various respects identical to those in *The Psychology of Mau Mau*.

According to Corfield, the history of the emergency could not be divorced from contemporary events in other parts of Africa. He insisted that the Mau Mau was a wholly evil manifestation of nationalism.[22] Tracing the history of the uprising from its distant origins in the late 1920s, he placed it firmly within the context of the Cold War. He argued that Kenyatta had exploited the principles of democratic freedom by adapting techniques of revolution learnt in Russia to the perverse mentality of the Kikuyu. Under his guidance the Mau Mau became a tribal religion which closely resembled the witchcraft and black magic practised in medieval Europe; it exploited and abused the liberalism of the British government through a campaign of hate, lies and intimidation.

Corfield identified three distinctive features of the Mau Mau: its origins in a single tribe, its reversion to primitive superstition and its explicit anti-Christianity. He believed the colonial government had shown astonishing sanity in its handling of the emergency. In his key explanatory chapter, Corfield applied Carothers's clash of cultures thesis to the Kikuyu's violent protest.[23] To him it was the Kikuyu's schizoid quality of mind that allowed once-loyal servants to turn violently against their employers. Another source of the disturbances was identified in the 'forest culture' of the Kikuyu and the severity of the impact of Western culture on their traditional way of life. Predictably Corfield accepted the legitimacy of the European settlers' claim to the White Highlands and argued that the Kikuyu's attachment to land was such that they could not be rational on the subject.[24]

In contrast to Carothers, Corfield examined the rebellion as a social movement and critically evaluated the response to it by the colonial government. Yet when he came to consider the character and reasons for the Mau Mau he uncritically adopted Carothers's arguments. For both writers the eruption of the Mau Mau could not be attributed to any failure by the colonial government or white settlers in dealing with the Kikuyu's claims for land or equality. The movement was not political but psychopathological.

The stresses placed upon Kikuyu society could have been conceptualized in a variety of other ways. Apart from the chimera of a 'forest mentality' the Kikuyu needed to come to terms with increasing demographic pressure on a limited supply of land, the extension of wage labour, rapid urbanization, increasing unemployment and the impact of external economic forces upon ceremonial life. In a wider context, the stresses upon the indigenous Kenyans included the influence of the nationalist impulse which had already seen the beginning of the struggle for independence in a number of British colonies. Carothers contributed to the history of the Mau Mau not only by producing a key study of the movement but by influencing the official account of why it occurred.

Carothers wrote about 'the African' rather than the East African or the Kikuyu or the Luo. In this he was following a convention established by earlier scientists such as de Gobineau, Galton and Levy-Bruhl. Surprisingly, such terms were favoured by the African independence movements themselves. Pre- and post-war nationalists, the poets of Negritude and the proponents of the African Personality all used such categories. The contrast Carothers drew between the European and the African was founded upon an idealized portrait of European man, presented as a heroic figure of the kind Karl Jaspers eulogized in his study of Leonardo, Descartes and Max Weber.[25] Occidental man was resourceful, inventive and persistent in the face of adversity. He was imaginative and reliant upon his own efforts. He was guided by a spirit of scientific curiosity, and he accepted responsibility for his actions. He was the kind of rational adult Weber celebrated in his essay 'Politics as a Vocation', 'the mature personality' of Erik Erikson's *Childhood and Society*. This figure was always male; there was as little place for women in Carothers's universe as there is in the theories of Weber or Erikson.

In Africa the first colonial model of social improvement was provided by the Christian missions, which promoted the idea that redemption was to be achieved by the individual alone. This framework, which ran against the grain of traditional societies, fitted well with liberal ideology and with the imperatives of labour markets. It was also less challenging politically than were ideals involving civil liberties or collective rights. It was the material and ideal interests associated with the operation of the colonial economy which provided the setting in which colonial psychiatry was practised. Then as now, European clinical psychiatry possessed no adequate theory of social action or of social change, and psychiatric explanations were frequently offered about individuals abstracted from any recognizable context. To the Kenyan administration the recruitment of Carothers to explain away the claims of a proto-nationalist movement and to justify the continued colonial presence therefore had a certain appeal.

For Carothers, as for Weber, Freud, Jaspers and Erikson, the ideal individual was the scientist, the man committed to objective knowledge. The figure of the scientist was in various ways a perfect vehicle for colonial ideology. Far removed from the world of political strife, the scientist was characterized by his lack of material interests, his intellectual sophistication and his ethical neutrality. He was a middle-class male who seemed to represent the best of a meritocratic society, for in science success and prominence can be achieved only through one's own efforts. In reality this figure was the antithesis of the kinds of men who dominated the settler societies of colonial Africa; it was a device for judging the African majority rather than the leaders of white society. Carothers believed in the authority of science, and he also believed strongly in a society that rewarded talent and hard work. He hoped that the clear light of science would replace myth and superstition and that by example the European could help free the African from the pull of tradition and custom. These were noble ideals which were often expressed by those who chose the colonial vocation. They were ideals that the nationalist leadership which came to power in the 1960s also endorsed. Ironically, it was the nature of ethnopsychiatric inquiry that made it difficult for Carothers to see that the realization of such ideals would spell the end of the settler societies.

It is easy with hindsight to dismiss Carothers's work as bad science or to accuse him of bad faith. Such an explanation would be adequate, however, only if Carothers's views were heterodox. His theory of the African personality was in fact validated again and again in the research of his contemporaries and therefore his work should be accorded the seriousness it was given in the last decades of the colonial era. It is also important to understand the reasons why a Christian physician who was avowedly anti-racist could have written so disparagingly of African civilization.

The portrait of the African presented by Carothers was original in the sense that there was no reference to the African in the psychiatric texts of the day. Even so, those texts contained parallels to Carothers's portrait and help to explain its origins. In Henderson and Gillespie's *Text-book of Psychiatry*, the standard British manual with which Carothers was familiar, there was a clinical profile of psychopathic states and of a psychopathic type which in various ways resembled Carothers's African.[26] Psychopathic individuals were described as being from early childhood habitually abnormal. Their psychological immaturity prevented them from adapting to reality or profiting from experience. They lacked judgement, foresight and prudence, and often behaved like dangerous children (or women). The category employed by Henderson and Gillespie dated back to 1835, when a Bristol physician named J. C. Pritchard had coined the terms 'moral insanity' and 'moral imbecile'. The disorder had no specific cause but was attributed to a combination of hereditary and environmental influences. Along with many of their contemporaries, Henderson and Gillespie believed that poverty, family breakdown and illegitimacy were major contributing factors. Those factors were of course important elements signifying the boundary between middle- and working-class Britain. It was not coincidental that the particularities of working-class culture in many respects corresponded to the definition of the psychopathic. In the colonial setting the divergence between the cultural practices of Africans and white settlers was even greater and so the concept of the psychopath could readily be applied to the subjects of Britain's African empire. The concept of normality favoured by British psychiatry at that time was rigid and left no space for acknowledging cultural difference without turning that difference into pathology. It was, in part, for that reason that Carothers often referred to the African as a psychopathic type.

Many of the flaws in Carothers's *Psychology of Mau Mau* are due specifically to the limitations inherent in the use of any psychological theory. Carothers was commissioned to explain a social movement with coherent and clearly stated goals, including a demand for independence and the reallocation of land. There was nothing in his method that enabled him to address such issues directly, since the theories he was using included no self-conscious concepts of social class, power or group interests. In the psychiatric theory in which he was trained there was also no formal concept of culture. Henderson and Gillespie's work was of course culturally bound to British middle-class conceptions of normality, gender and maturation. Their anthropology, which Carothers made his own, was that of a single class and gender whose interests were antithetical to social democracy and racial equality.

Outside the boundaries of psychiatric theory there was another source of authority to which Carothers could have turned, and that was the settler community itself. It was a minority to which he had belonged for almost thirty years, and it had shaped his political imagination. Even though he was ambivalent about the white settlers of Kenya and intensely disliked their racism, his response to the dilemma of political choice was to become in effect their standard bearer.

6   African intelligence, sexuality and psyche

Clinical psychologists have long been especially interested in what Francis Galton called the 'serviceable citizen'.[1] In other words they have sought to identify the limits of human nature. These limits have often been pursued negatively: in research conducted in the first half of this century the absence of particular qualities, a certain modality of conscience, a facility for deferred gratification, a particular ability to plan, or a set of attitudes towards the body in women, criminals or 'primitives' was taken as proof of their lack of humanity.

There was little reason for clinical psychologists to take an interest in the intelligence of African peoples, and indeed during the colonial era little research was conducted. What white employers required of blacks was physical drudgery; segregationist policies ensured that skilled work was reserved for Europeans. Stanley Porteus did work briefly among the Bantus of Southern Africa, but his African research was peripheral to his research on the Australian aborigines and the ethnic minorities of Hawaii.[2] By 1940 South Africa had its own intelligence-testing industry, and a number of specialists were working on the subject of African mentality. The best known of the South African researchers was a psychologist named Simon Biesheuvel who during World War II was officer in charge of the aptitude-test section of the South African Air Force. Biesheuvel was also a founder and director of the National Institute for Personal Research, which was part of the Department of Defence, and aimed at improving industrial efficiency. Under Biesheuvel's guidance it developed a range of psychological testing procedures for the screening of black miners.[3] Biesheuvel employed the Porteus Maze Test along with a number of other procedures in assessing the intelligence of black workers, and in 1942 he became involved in a debate about the educability of the African. In *The Education of the South African Native* L. Flick, a psychologist then employed by the Bureau for Educational and Social Research, had claimed that black South Africans could not benefit from education and therefore there was no point in providing schools for African children. In assessing learning ability Flick had used a number of tests including the Porteus Maze and the Goddard Form Boards, and he had concluded that at around puberty the mental age of the African was between four and five years below that of the European adolescent.[4] There is an obvious parallel to be drawn between Flick's claims and those made by Jensen and Eysenck about black Americans some thirty years later.

Flick's book encouraged Biesheuvel to write a monograph of his own which was published in 1943 under the title *African Intelligence*. As a comprehensive review of research on the subject, it was an important addition to the ethnopsychiatric canon. Biesheuvel began by surveying the most popular definitions of intelligence and went on to analyse the methods used for its measurement, the problems of accurate sampling and the influence of culture on test results. He then devoted a chapter to the suitability of existing tests for measuring Africans' performance. In contrast to ethnopsychiatrists, Biesheuvel acknowledged that the context for the debate about African intelligence was provided by the economic and material environment, in this case by the structure of the South African economy. As he noted: 'What the European requires of the African is hard manual labour, a commodity which he does not himself produce, and this at a low wage.'[5] This observation seems an advance over the ahistorical landscape occupied by African subjects in the writings of Carothers and Vint.

Biesheuvel noted that although the cultural settings in which Africans lived were diverse, they invariably disadvantaged African children, who in many cases had never attended school. Most group tests relied heavily upon language skills. Biesheuvel argued that for African children, working in a second language, such tests were discriminatory, and therefore the results had to be treated with caution. Besides the unfamiliarity of the test formats and contents, the emphasis placed upon speed in most tests further disadvantaged African subjects. The skills required by the Form Boards and Maze tests, for example, were culturally specific and unsuitable for testing these children.[6] They excluded most of the auditory skills displayed by Africans and instead emphasized spatial relationships, at which they were less adept. Biesheuvel was concerned that, in the absence of suitable instruments, attempts to measure African intelligence would be unreliable.

The most obvious weakness in intelligence tests, according to Biesheuvel, was their neglect of the social and cultural context of intelligence or even to any definition of intelligence other than as an artefact of the testing procedure itself. He sought to avoid these pitfalls by calling attention to the African home environment and its importance in assessing individual capacity. As he put it: 'African tribal family life develops intelligence in directions entirely different from those of the European home. The goodness or badness of its attributes can only be judged in terms of its effectiveness in achieving its own purposes.'[7] He went on to explain that there was no uniform home setting for the black child, the worlds of urban and rural Africans were entirely different. For example, because of pressure from employers, infants in the towns were not breast-fed for as long as infants in the countryside. In both urban and rural contexts infants were indulged, but it was an indulgence of a negative kind. There was no stimulation in the home to draw out the child's latent talents because mothers did not have the time to spend with their children. Much to the child's detriment, with the arrival of a new baby the mother's indulgence abruptly ended. Biesheuvel explained: 'Hence for the second or third year onward, the African child grows up in an environment which is not only unstimulating on various accounts, but which also lacks that active sympathy between adult and child which is a *sine qua non* of optimum intellectual and emotional development.'[8] The parents' attitude towards the child was now severe, and no respect was shown for the child's feelings. In urban communities, in which traditional forms of sociability had been eroded, Biesheuvel discerned a sterility which greatly affected the child's development. There were no binding constraints on parents' behaviour. The rural African world might be limited but at least it was orderly; the urban setting could not provide a worse environment for the young. According to Biesheuvel, 'it is no exaggeration to say that the average urban African home-environment is bound to stunt very markedly the growth of intelligence of the children reared in it, not only by failing to provide those stimuli which alone enable the most to be made of innate potentialities, but also by creating situations which have an adverse effect on such growth as might spontaneously occur'.[9]

As well as the influence of culture, Biesheuvel considered the material circumstances in which blacks lived. In South Africa those circumstances had not changed greatly in the past twenty years, and neither had the level of political repression. Biesheuvel suggests that the poorest European child probably received a better education than the average African, and this affected the performance of African children in intelligence tests.[10] Biesheuvel also pointed to the poor diet of black workers, rich in carbohydrates but lacking in protein. Up to this point Biesheuvel's argument contained two independent elements; his account of the detrimental effects upon childhood development of African culture and his analysis of the effects of poverty and malnutrition on intelligence. Furthermore, he was critical of the approach used by researchers such as Flick which ignored the culturally specific nature of testing procedures. He even went so far as to acknowledge that existing means for measuring intelligence systematically discriminated against non-European subjects. Each of these elements suggested that Biesheuvel was seeking to break down conventional views about African inferiority. The direction of his argument changed abruptly, however, when he came to consider the influence of temperament upon intelligence.

The concept of temperament was common to theories about race and human type. In works such as Porteus's *Temperament and Race*, 'temperament' was simply a synonym for 'human nature' or for the racially specific elements that define the self.[11] Biesheuvel brought greater precision to the term by identifying three factors which shaped temperament: secondary functioning, activity and emotionality.[12] When a person was conscious of some mental event, the event could be said to be exercising a primary function. Subsequently that event may be absorbed into the individual's chosen pattern of behaviour, in which case it was operating as a secondary function. In some individuals this process was weak; in others it was well developed.[13] Primary-functioning individuals tended to be impulsive, restless and inconsistent in mood. By contrast, secondary-functioning subjects were calmer and displayed better developed patterns of attention. Biesheuvel acknowledged the absence of any systematic research into the African temperament, but then, abandoning the circumspection that characterized the first half of his monograph, went on to speculate on the deficiencies of the African temperament and its influence upon intellectual development. According to Biesheuvel, there was much evidence to suggest that primary functioning was dominant in the African. For instance, because Africans could switch rapidly from primary to secondary modes, they seemed never to brood over their poverty. They were also less inhibited emotionally than Europeans, a fact which corresponded to the primary mode. When rural Africans arrived in the cities, they tended to idle away their time and waste whatever money they might earn. Biesheuvel admitted that this tendency toward idleness might be more apparent than real and that it might be due in part to the hostility of the African towards an urban culture. He also acknowledged that little was known about how cultures, presumably both indigenous and imported, affected Africans' character and motivation. This did not prevent him, however, from concluding that 'if there should be any temperamental difference between the African and the European races, it is most likely to be a difference in perseverance, in drive, in the desire to be active'.[14]

In contrast to Flick, Biesheuvel devoted considerable attention to the influence of the family in shaping adult personality. With Ritchie, Biesheuvel believed that it was within the family that the reasons for Africans' intellectual feebleness were to be found. The family was far more damaging as an influence on intelligence than external factors such as poverty or disease. Africans were intellectually inferior to Europeans because of their temperament, and that temperament was a product of family ethos and child-rearing conventions. Biesheuvel's analysis suggested that the provision of schools or any attempt to reduce poverty would be useless unless the African family were itself refashioned. Increased wages would only be wasted, and improved health would not produce a more efficient labour force. The culture of poverty was the culture to which Africans were best suited and in which they felt most comfortable. Because it would be extremely difficult to change the African family, government would be unwise to expect much of Africans either as labour or as citizens. In most of these conclusions, Biesheuvel's work reflected contemporary English-language progressive literature on the problems of poverty and education failure. That literature was, however, addressed to the pathologies of a particular class; the British working class: Biesheuvel's work was about a particular race.

Ostensibly a refutation of Flick's monograph, Biesheuvel's study should have concluded that no such judgement as Flick's could be made. Yet Biesheuvel ended by restating Flick's findings regarding African inferiority, albeit with one difference: he shifted the ground from the domain of intelligence (about which he admitted little was known) to the domain of temperament, a matter on which every white South African was an authority. In examining African mentality he adopted the perspective of the employer, the same one used by Carothers in his paper on frontal-lobe function. Indeed, despite the progressive texture of his work, Biesheuvel's critique read in places as if it were founded upon disappointment that Flick had failed to provide adequate proof of Africans' intellectual inferiority.

In South Africa in 1943, even more so than in Kenya, Algeria or Southern Rhodesia, the myth of African inferiority was an important foundation for the authority of a white minority regime. Biesheuvel was opposed to that authority, and that was one reason for his setting out to write a critique of Flick's work. Because clinical psychology provided him with no tools to assemble that critique, his monograph is confused between his liberal politics and conservative science. As did his contemporaries, he used the term 'the African', thereby obliterating the variety of social, economic and cultural circumstances under which African men and women in South Africa lived. And yet he also freely acknowledged the importance of the differences between urban and rural environments. Either all African peoples were the same or they were different; Biesheuvel suggested that they were both. Consequently, *African Intelligence* ended as a demonstration that even for a liberal the myth of African inferiority was irresistible.

Although the clinical literature from Algeria, Kenya, South Africa and

Southern Rhodesia repressed the sexual politics of colonialism, making little reference to sexuality, the sexual threat posed by African men to white women was a preoccupation of settler societies.[15] The immorality laws of South Africa and Southern Rhodesia were but part of an elaborate cultural and legislative apparatus designed to prevent miscegenation and to ensure that racial boundaries remained inviolate – inviolate that is in the case of liaisons between black men and white women – a different set of conventions operated in regard to white men and African women, whose sexual encounters produced the sizeable coloured minorities which are conspicuous throughout Southern Africa. One exception to the rule of silence was the work of a South African psychiatrist, B. J. F. Laubscher. For many years the physician in charge of the native wards at the Queenstown asylum, Laubscher took a keen interest in Freudian psychology and, in contrast to his contemporaries, readily acknowledged the role of sexuality in the formation of character and in the production of mental illness. Also in contrast to other practitioners, he was knowledgeable about indigenous culture, being something of an authority on the Tembu of the South Eastern Cape.[16] Laubscher wanted to understand how social practices, beliefs and customs influenced mental illness. He was particularly interested in schizophrenia, which he believed was the most common form of psychosis in the African. It was this interest that led him to an analysis of what he termed 'pagan culture'. In exploring that question he not only studied the inmates at Queenstown but also undertook fieldwork in Tembuland. In this way his work came closest of any ethnopsychiatrist to the methods and preoccupations of social anthropology.

In contrast to academic anthropologists, however, Laubscher interpreted Tembu rituals according to psychoanalytic theory, linking their belief in 'river people', who were the guardians of morality, with the Oedipal drama and the wish for incest. In spite of unorthodox methodology Laubscher's research led him to a conclusion remarkably similar to that of his ethnopsychiatric colleagues: that there was a strong affinity between the European psychotic and the normal African. He also found that patterns of mental illness, especially its less severe forms, varied between the races. 'In view of the superficiality of repression' in the African, for example, 'psychoneurosis, as understood by us, must be rare.'[17] As did Carothers, Laubscher believed that compulsive neurosis and anxiety states were probably unknown in Africans and that the Tembu's culture, especially their mythology, prevented the kinds of refinements found in the European neurotic. When Africans became mentally ill they were more likely to suffer from hypochondria than to display the elaborate symptoms typical of Europeans. Laubscher was much interested in sexuality and described at length what he termed Tembu sexual customs.[18] He did acknowledge, however, that his informants were male and that without access to first-hand information from women or girls the veracity of his material was compromised.

Circumcision of male adolescents was an important ritual for the Tembu and Laubscher, noting the disproportionate number of uncircumcised Tembu men among the inmates at Queenstown asylum, offered a psychoanalytic interpretation of the ceremony. He commented that most male imbeciles, epileptics and schizophrenics at Queenstown were uncircumcised. The first two groups would have been excluded from the ceremony because of their infirmity, and this in turn could only have further lowered their status within the tribe. The schizophrenics in contrast probably had a pathological attachment to their mothers which would have discouraged them from undergoing the ritual (which in Laubscher's opinion offered a resolution to the Oedipus complex). Without circumcision they were impeded from having sexual contact with women, and their decline into mental illness was inevitable. Laubscher also described the initiation ceremonies that marked the passage into womanhood and he noted that as with the men this ritual offered a resolution to the Oedipal attachment.

For Laubscher the culture of the pagan African corresponded closely to European civilization of the distant historical past. Like the European child, the adult African behaved as if words and actions were the same, and ascribed a magical power to language. His universe of thought presented him with limitless possibilities, and when he day-dreamed he slipped back immediately into the world of the child. It was this structure of mind that generated the belief in spirits which played such an important part in African life. According to Laubscher: 'The native in his setting reacts to his unconscious images and fears as does the child to his dreams, and these unconscious impulses, where they fall within the category of forbidden impulses, are transformed into living objects and are viewed as mythical beings.'[19] The African who had received a Western education might on the surface conduct himself according to European conventions, but his perception of objective reality would be based upon archaic emotional needs.

Rejecting Levy-Bruhl's idea that the African's thinking was pre-logical or irrational, Laubscher found it perfectly consistent, although based upon patterns of thought that had their analogy in the behaviour of compulsive neurotics. In fact, as had Levy-Bruhl and others, Laubscher wrote of 'the African' and 'the European' as if they represented polarities. The African's psyche was dominated by the mechanism of projection and his view of the world shaped by mythology, while the world of the

European had science as its foundation.[20] Laubscher had obviously read Freud's *Totem and Taboo*, and he paraphrased that work freely in explaining the modality of African thought. There was, however, little that was novel in his formulation. His one major divergence from Freud amounted to an idealization of Western culture. Freud was never so confident that 'Western man' had transcended the primitive impulses which Laubscher found so conspicuous in the African. Indeed, towards the end of his life, Freud wrote repeatedly that civilization was only a façade.[21] In contrast, for Laubscher the veneer of Western culture which overlay an otherwise primitive emotional life was a distinctive feature of the African.[22]

In an attempt at a theory of mental illness in the African, Laubscher provided a brief account of the Tembu's classification of mental disorders, noting that the mentally ill were always treated by traditional healers before they were admitted to European hospitals. As did Carothers, Laubscher found that in village life the demands of normality were so easily met that many of the apparently insane could live comfortably for years without coming to the notice of European authorities. However, the main reason many psychotics could remain in the villages was to be found in the nature of African culture and the modality of the African personality. The European schizophrenic would display thought patterns, actions and beliefs foreign to his culture, and it was that foreignness which distinguished the psychotic from the neurotic. Because of the myth-ridden nature of their culture, such a distinction was absent among Africans. As Laubscher explained: 'The pagan schizophrenic patient in his regression keeps on the whole within the fold of his cultural belief, expressed as ideas, because the archaic and magical forms of thought are as much part of his normal state as they are of his psychotic state. Hence the great difficulty for the normal pagan native to discriminate between the rational and the irrational.'[23] Like his contemporaries, Laubscher was convinced that Europeans had a greater distance to travel in regressing into psychosis than did primitives, whose culture contained many psychotic elements.

Laubscher's interest in sexual behaviour had been inspired, he reported, by a number of sadistic attacks committed by Africans upon European women. He assumed that this type of sexual crime was restricted to black men. Such attacks, or 'Black Peril' cases were in fact rare, but they inspired a plethora of legislation in the Cape, Natal and the Transvaal, and in Southern Rhodesia, where in 1903 the Legislative Council passed what was perhaps the first legislation in the English-speaking world prescribing the death penalty for attempted rape.[24] That penalty was on a number of occasions carried out, and as late as 1935 an

African man named Ndachana was executed at Salisbury gaol for the attempted rape of a white missionary.

The responses to questionnaires which Laubscher sent to nineteen district magistrates, covering a range of sexual offences likely to be committed by males, including homosexuality, transvestism, indecent exposure, rape and sodomy, indicated that sodomy and voyeurism were rare (although Laubscher believed that bestiality was probably widespread among adolescent boys tending herds in the veld). Sexual offences against children were reportedly confined to sub-normal men who were unable to obtain female sexual partners, the true paedophile apparently being absent. According to Laubscher men who committed rape were invariably uncircumcised or defective, and consequently had been unsuccessful in finding sexual partners. In support of this claim he cited data on a number of men committed to Queenstown who had been charged with that crime.[25] However, he provided no evidence to support his broader claim that normal African men did not commit rape.[26] Few cases of indecent exposure were reported and it was suggested that the practice was confined to old men who had become disturbed. Laubscher, however, mentioned a number of cases from his own experience involving Africans' exposing themselves to European women in the cities.

According to the magistrates, in rural areas homosexuality was rare, and its occurrence seemed to be confined to segregated communities or to the mentally ill. Laubscher commented that homosexuality was almost universal among Africans in prisons and in mental hospitals. In asylums it took the form of mutual masturbation among female patients, while among men pederasty was practised by at least 80 per cent of patients. Upon entering an institution, a male patient or prisoner would take a 'wife' who would gradually become feminized.[27] Laubscher explained this behaviour in terms of the segregation of men from women and 'the primitive organization' of the sexual instinct in the native African. Laubscher argued that the African's sexuality had a compulsive quality, men in particular believing that they had to engage almost daily in sexual intercourse. He tended to equate normal sexuality in the African with sexual pathology in the European. This conclusion was at odds both with the Freudian perspective he employed and with his view that all forms of sexual pathology in the African had a somatic basis or at least some such correlative, Africans under normal circumstances being free of sexual illness. In terms of psychoanalytic theory alone the evidence he presented should have led him to a positive judgement about African sexuality and by implication about child-rearing conventions. His disregard of his own evidence is significant.

Because for Africans it was imperative to engage in sexual intercourse,

Laubscher argued, in the absence of normal outlets they would commit sodomy or rape. His model of sexuality was hydraulic, drawing upon Freud's notion that neurosis was in essence deflected sexual activity. If, as Laubscher suggested, Africans did not suffer from neurosis, then deprived of normal heterosexual outlets they would be compelled to seek alternatives. It was this notion of hypersexuality that was distilled in the 'Black Peril' scares and inflated by Laubscher into a theory. While Africans did not commit rape on the reserves, in the cities where they were deprived of female companions they did, he argued, present a sexual threat. *Sex, Custom and Psychopathology* epitomized the dilemma faced by white settlers in colonial Africa: they needed blacks close by to provide labour and the comforts of domestic service, and yet they greatly feared them. Laubscher's response to that dilemma was to depict the African as a person whose sexuality was at once both normal and aberrant. In the context of the sexual politics of Southern Africa, for him to have reached any other conclusion would have been remarkable.

Freudian leanings were unusual for a psychiatrist working at a public hospital, especially a South African hospital for African patients. One of Laubscher's contemporaries was, however, an admitted Freudian. Wulf Sachs was born in St Petersburg in 1896 and studied neurology and clinical psychology under Pavlov. In the 1920s he emigrated to South Africa, where he soon established himself as a prominent member of the medical community. Like Laubscher, Sachs worked in South African public hospitals treating mentally ill Africans. Unlike Laubscher, he had himself undergone a form of psychoanalysis. Sachs was also, at least for a time, a member of the Communist Party of South Africa. Psychoanalysis presented Sachs with a unique medium through which to approach the pre-apartheid South Africa of the 1930s.

With hindsight it is easy to identify a set of key questions which should have motivated ethnopsychiatric research or at least troubled practitioners. Were there variations in the incidence of the major forms of psychosis or in the kinds of symptoms displayed? Was mental illness identical in form and content in Europeans and Africans, and if not what could account for the differences? These questions were addressed in various ways by Carothers and Gordon, but neither considered them important. Sachs, however, was aware of the consequences of resolving these issues both for practitioners and for patients, and in 1933 he published a study on insanity among black South Africans that addressed them in detail.[28] The study was based upon a review of 100 schizophrenic patients admitted to the Pretoria Mental Hospital in the period from January 1928 until December 1932. Sachs noted that although diagnosing mental illness in the African was more difficult than in the European, schizophrenia appeared to take the same form. Using a model of schizophrenia taken from Freud, he emphasized the loss of object love, the withdrawal of libido and the dominance of autoeroticism, with the patient regressing to an infantile sexual mode. Schizophrenics were usually of high moral character and subject to sexual conflicts which they could not resolve. The most distinctive feature of the illness was a turning away from reality – emotional dullness and a lack of interest in the world. Sachs found each of these features in the African patients at Pretoria. The inmates would, like their European counterparts, sit motionless for hours. Their delusions and hallucinations were also similar, with delusions of grandeur, mania persecution and religious obsessions being predominant. Many of the African patients believed themselves to be King George or his son the Prince of Wales. Significantly, Sachs found that the delusion of being a white man was common.

Sachs concluded his study by speculating upon the normal operation of the mind in the native and the European: 'If the mind of the native in his abnormal state operates on the same principles and finds the same modes of expression as in the case of the European, the working principles of the mind in the normal state must also be identical in both cases.'[29] Like most reviews of mental illness in Africans, Sachs's study was based upon a relatively small sample. However, in contrast to his colleagues he sought to emphasize the similarities rather than the differences between Africans and Europeans. He anticipated that his findings would be viewed with scepticism and was aware of their implications for race relations. In South Africa in 1933 the idea that the African had an emotional life identical to that of the European was original. This innovative article was, however, overshadowed by the work that was to follow. Four years later, in 1937, Sachs published the first psychoanalytic portrait of a native African.[30]

Black Anger was based on a psychoanalysis of John Chavafambira, a native of Southern Rhodesia. Chavafambira was a medicine man and herbalist who was introduced to Sachs by an anthropologist then working in a Johannesburg slum. Sachs's study took place over a period of two-and-a-half years, with individual sessions lasting an hour; Chavafambira would lie on a couch, in classic psychoanalytic fashion, with Sachs sitting behind him, unseen, taking notes. He worked as a kitchen hand in a hotel for £1 per month and felt lonely and depressed in his new life. Sachs chose not to pay his subject, to avoid compromising their relationship. As he explained: 'For the final success of my studies, it was essential that John should become so attached to me that he would be willing to give me information, not to sell it.'[31] The two subsequently travelled together to Chavafambira's home, visiting many of the places and meeting most of the people he referred to in his narrative. Sachs was aware of his own role

in the analysis and admitted that in his relationship with John Chavafambira he was for the first time treating a black man as an equal. That
equality was, however, not without its ambiguities.

As in any psychoanalysis, Sachs focused upon his subject's childhood
and in particular his relations with his parents. Like all African children,
Sachs reported, Chavafambira was breast-fed for several years and spent
that period in perpetual physical contact with his mother. Then, suddenly, the breast was withdrawn, and he was sent away to live in another
hut. At that moment his father, symbolically, took his place. Thus for
John the Oedipal drama was more severe than for the average European
child. The severity of the experience bred hostility toward his father, who
in Chavafambira's imagination became a figure possessing great power.
The impact of that event stayed with him into adult life. As Sachs
explained: 'This dramatic childhood experience had a retarding effect on
John, and on every African child in his fight for independence.'[32]
Nevertheless, in Sachs's opinion this experience in childhood was less
important to Chavafambira's development than were the poverty, economic exploitation, and racism to which he was subjected.

John's marriage was unsuccessful from the beginning, and the arrival
of a child only increased the tension between the couple. Marriage also
increased his awareness of the poverty in which he lived compared with
the obvious wealth enjoyed by white South Africans. He was bewildered
by the lives of the whites, whom he mistrusted and feared: 'The white
people only wish us to suffer. Why has God created such people?'[33] He
mistrusted Sachs as well, believing that like all white men he simply
wanted to use him. He was excited by the story of the American singer
Paul Robeson, and he day-dreamed of the United States as a place where
he could live happily. In contrast, the reality of his life in Johannesburg
was filled with danger, hard work and misery. After a long internal
struggle he began to practise medicine; he had a talent for throwing bones
and settling disputes, for herbal curing of a wide range of maladies, and
his practice soon began to flourish. That brief period of prosperity ended
when he was gaoled for a minor offence. On his release he lapsed into
despair and lethargy.

Despite having acknowledged the political realities of Chavafambira's
life, Sachs assessed this change in the following way:

His tragedy was that of so many Africans. Neither their kraal life nor their early
training, nor their later education, services to strengthen their will power or
imbues them with the perseverance necessary for achievement. Renunciation and
flight were John's choice in any situation requiring strength of will and endurance
of pain... He had not reached that stage of personality or development that belongs

to the healthy human being who is not afraid of being obstinate or amiable, assertive or submissive, active or passive, as the occasion demands.[34]

Sachs's assessment of John Chavafambira's character is probably best summarized in the title given to the British edition of the book, *Black Hamlet*. According to Sachs, most of John's problems were due to his unwarranted optimism and his inability to act: he was the author of his own misfortunes. At the same time, however, Sachs admitted that Chavafambira's misery arose from circumstances over which he had no control.[35] It was as if his psychoanalytic training was furnishing him with one opinion about the reasons for John's fate and his knowledge of the reality of South African society with another. Sachs showed considerable courage in his dealings with Chavafambira, and during their journey to Southern Rhodesia they did become friends. That friendship could not, however, survive the social and racial gulf that separated their lives in Johannesburg. It is significant that Sachs did not reflect upon the reasons why this was so. He was the only colonial psychiatrist to psychoanalyse an African subject, and although that analysis was conducted for the benefit of the physician rather than the patient it remains a significant achievement. The importance placed upon Chavafambira's shortcomings went against the grain of his otherwise progressive politics and of the aesthetic that informed his work. However, in the contexts of South Africa and the history of ethnopsychiatric theory, the very idea that a man such as John Chavafambira might possess a complex inner self was more than sufficient to establish Sachs's radicalism.

John's story was the story of a man moving, under very special circumstances, from life within a rural subsistence economy to life as a proletarian. It involved his adaption to the unique form of subordination endured by migrant labourers in South African cities. This story had been told many times, but it is doubtful that before Sachs it had ever been written in terms of personality. The changes that wage labour brought to Chavafambira's life redefined his vocation, reshaped his social world and determined the nature and circumstances of his marriage. In recording each of these changes Sachs suggested that to succeed in Johannesburg he would have had to change his character or temperament.

Chavafambira's analysis involved a meeting between men standing on different sides of a complicated social, economic, cultural and political process. Sachs presented the record of that analysis in terms of a contrast between traditional and modern forms of mentality. Despite their differences, the two men had much in common. Both were emigres; both were members of political minorities; both were physicians; and they conversed in an adopted second language. Sachs, however, was a member of a dominant culture whose ascendancy was constantly increasing, while Chavafambira found himself more vulnerable and oppressed in Johannesburg than he had been in Southern Rhodesia. Although able to talk to him as no other European psychiatrist had spoken to an African, Sachs was unable to acknowledge the weight of the necessities that shaped Chavafambira's life. He assumed that with greater will John could change the conditions of his life, just as he himself had changed his own life in leaving Russia. Ignoring the importance of Chavafambira's identity as a black migrant labourer, he sought instead to discover within him a potential self which could be liberated. Sachs believed fervently in the authority of such a self and in its powers of transcendence.

As a Marxist Sachs was familiar with a variety of concepts unknown to other psychiatrists, such as the concepts of class, modes of production, and ideology which he could have used in constructing Chavafambira's biography. He chose instead to do so in terms of the idealized categories of traditional and modern, the very classifications that have been used in South Africa to justify first segregation and then apartheid. However, he transmuted those categories by discerning in John a type of inner self from which he supposed it might be possible to construct a rational citizen. Here he violated one of ethnopsychiatry's most cherished truths: that no African possessed a rich inner life. Octave Mannoni, for example, argued that in the African there was no distance between the persona and the inner self and therefore no space in which an analyst could operate. The persona was, in effect, a mask behind which there was nothing. The notion of an inner self for John Chavafambira suggested a private realm of freedom and a set of potentialities which confounded the character of race relations in South Africa. It also suggested the possibility of the kind of equality or equivalence between peoples who, in every other way, were perceived as being fundamentally different. In his analysis of John Chavafambira Sachs accorded his patient the only kind of liberty then available to a black man in South Africa, a liberty which in the absence of civil rights was barren.

7 The African family and the colonial personality

Ethnopsychiatric theory offered various reasons for African inferiority. Vint believed the structure of the cortex to be at fault, while Carothers vacillated between brain morphology and environment. There was no clear progression from physiology to non-material factors, and even within a single work both types of explanation were employed. Even so, over time the analysis of culture became more important. Theorists who were interested in culture were drawn inevitably towards the study of the family.

Laubscher, Biesheuvel and Sachs all made reference to the role of the African family in shaping the child's world, but none of these writers presented an explicit theory of the family or commented at any length upon the relationship between the infant and its mother. In light of the importance attached by psychologists and indeed by colonial practice to familial relations, this silence is surprising. In Britain from the 1880s to the 1930s, many social reformers saw effective mothering as the key to the vitality of the white race, and created various programmes aimed at improving the skills of British mothers. By the end of that period similar programmes, although on a modest scale, were introduced into British colonies. As we have seen the Jeanes' Movement, which was active in four colonies during the 1930s, was dedicated to improving the life and culture of colonial Africans by enhancing the mothercraft and domestic skills of African women.

Nineteenth-century scientists such as Francis Galton sought to discover ways to improve the quality of citizens through various means, including selective breeding. In the twentieth century psychologists have pursued analogous goals through concentrating their efforts upon family life. Like Galton they supposed that by applying scientific principles to child care it was possible to produce better citizens – indeed, a better white race – and to reduce social pathologies such as criminality, poverty, illegitimacy and delinquency. Throughout the present century the ideology of the nuclear family has emphasized the importance of the relations between biological parents and their children in the shaping of character.

In this way the family has been identified with personal life, sexuality and the most distinctive features of individuality. The family has also of course been the major site for the oppression of women, although social theorists have until recently been oblivious to this fact. In most psychological theories the family is, to a degree, a synonym for the mother: everything written about the pathologies of family life can to some extent be dissolved into a pathology of motherhood.[1]

Under the influence of feminist politics and scholarship, the study of the family has, in the past twenty years, gained an important place in both social history and political theory. Research on the history of European family forms called attention to the patriarchal structure of families and familial ideologies. Changes in demography, longevity and modes of subsistence have, in a variety of cultural and historical contexts, been shown to mould familial patterns.[2] In different ways, both historians and sociologists have debunked the idea that, because of its biological function, the family is independent of the economic, demographic, social and political contexts in which it is embedded. Contemporary scholarship has confirmed that there is no necessity for any particular form of domestic arrangements; family forms are constructed rather than ordained.[3] Indeed, such scholarship has thrown into question the very idea of a single transcultural or transhistorical definition of 'the family'. Despite these dramatic changes, the idea of the natural family remains a potent ideology.

In the first half of this century one of the most successful proponents of scientific mothercraft was the New Zealand physician Truby King. King began his career as superintendent of the Seacliff Mental Asylum on the South Island of New Zealand.[4] In 1907, motivated by genuine fears about the mental health and character of the white race, he and his wife, Mary, under the pseudonym 'Hygenia', began writing a newspaper column titled 'Our Baby'. The column, in which they offered guidance to mothers, became immensely popular and by 1913 was syndicated in more than fifty newspapers throughout the British empire. In 1908 King published his best-known book, *The Feeding and Care of Baby*. For over twenty years the book sold in excess of ten thousand copies annually, and King became one of the most influential authorities on the care of infants.[5]

King believed that infants should be subjected to rigorous and unrelenting discipline. The role of the mother was to establish uniformity in every aspect of her baby's existence: feeding, sleeping, bathing and especially bowel movements had to be regulated by the clock. Toilet training was to commence at the age of six weeks and to continue until the child was thoroughly trained. The child was not to be held except during the specified 'holding hour' and at all other times was to be left to cry by itself. The purpose of this regimen was to instil obedience and to establish respect for authority. King believed that spoilt children (by which he meant children who were comforted by their mothers when upset and fed when hungry) would become unproductive and self-indulgent adults. For such children delinquency, criminality and descent into poverty were inevitable. Mothers who played with their infants were, according to King, jeopardizing their children's future. Constipation if left unmanaged would lead to sexual precocity and possibly to masturbation. Sensuality in any form, especially sexual desire, was dangerous both to the mental health of the individual and to the health of the nation. Children were to be trained to control their bodies and subordinate immediate pleasure to some future goal. The views of King and kindred specialists were most influential during the heyday of ethnopsychiatry, and it is not surprising, therefore, that a similar vision of the family, and especially of the mother's relationship with her infant, is found in the ethnopsychiatric literature.

The Rhodes–Livingstone Institute was the first social science research centre of its kind in British Africa. The establishment of such an institute was suggested originally by Sir Hubert Winthrop Young, who became governor of Northern Rhodesia in 1934.[6] Young wanted a memorial to David Livingstone which would serve as a centre for anthropological research. Young had some difficulty convincing the Colonial Office that an institute would be of any value, but eventually, by emphasizing that a centre could assist in the formulation of economic and administrative policy, he gained official backing. Funding for the Rhodes–Livingstone Institute, which was established in 1937, came from the colonial governments of Tanganyika, Kenya, Uganda and Southern Rhodesia. Funds were also contributed by mining companies and by private sponsors. The directors of the Institute included Godfrey Baldwin Wilson and Max Gluckman, who became director in 1942.

In June 1943 a research paper was presented at the Institute by J. F. Ritchie, who for twenty-one years had served with the Northern Rhodesian Education Department. Gluckman was taken with Ritchie's work and encouraged him to write an expanded version of the paper for publication.[7] He wrote a glowing foreword to the monograph in which he praised the author's application of Freudian theory to the study of the African. Twenty-five years later the monograph was reprinted by Manchester University Press.

Ritchie had no formal training in psychiatry, and it is not known whether he had himself undergone psychoanalysis. He was, however, committed to psychoanalytic theory. He was also much influenced by Melanie Klein's work on the development of the infant and child. He had taught for many years at the Barotse National School at Mongu, where most of his pupils were children and adolescents of the Malozi tribe. He had had in addition some experience with other African peoples and he was certain that the patterns of child rearing that he found among the Malozi were typical of the sub-Saharan region. Ritchie believed that while there were no essential differences between the mind of the African and the mind of the European, the two races had very different intellectual and emotional strengths. For example, the African was far more temperamental and given to acute ambivalence.

Ritchie's argument was similar to that offered by Truby King and Melanie Klein in its emphasis upon early childhood and infant experience in shaping character and personality. According to Ritchie, every child brought into the world with him strong feelings of omnipotence. Those feelings were shattered at birth, and the child's first experience of the world made it seem a hostile and painful place. During the process of weaning the infant learned to sublimate its anger and hatred and through that pivotal experience to adjust to the constraints of the external world. The child's major task was to learn the rudiments of a realistic view of objects and events, to balance its emotions and to control its ambivalence. In the process of maturation the tender emotions would triumph as the individual learned to sublimate his hostile impulses. The child traversing this tortuous path required firm guidance from its parents, especially its mother. If a child was indulged it would never learn to distinguish between its wishes and reality. With Melanie Klein, Ritchie believed in the innate destructiveness of infants, and considered envy far stronger than gratitude.[8] This force of destructiveness in the child made the responsibility of the parent all the greater.

During his many years of teaching at Barotse, Ritchie observed the patterns of infant care and child rearing among the Malozi. Much to his distaste he found no regularity in the feeding of infants, who were given the breast on demand. The African mother would carry the child on her back, and at night the infant would sleep in its mother's arms or by her side. While breast-feeding continued, the parents would abstain from sexual intercourse. Frequently this pattern would continue until as late as the age of three. Comparing this pattern with that favoured by European mothers, Ritchie commented: 'In contrast with the normally nurtured child, then, he does not gain early experience of real life, with its many and frequent contrasts.'[9]

The African infant's life was one of unremitting pleasure which ended suddenly with the withdrawal of the breast. The abruptness of weaning, according to Ritchie, was an experience from which the child never fully recovered. The experience was made all the more unbearable by the resumption of sexual relations between the parents. The male child felt betrayed by its mother and grew to resent and hate its father. According to Ritchie this hatred survived into adult life, where 'it lives on in the unconscious, and in later life it colours the whole African attitude to women'.[10] Misogyny was not the only consequence of weaning, for it also provided the foundation for the adult's attitude towards authority. The father became the object of the child's murderous rage and, according to Ritchie, 'this repressed conception of the father as a thief and bully is, I believe, one of the deepest reasons for the typical African distrust of authority, authority being a father-surrogate'.[11] In his imagination the child believed he was hated by his father and felt towards him the same embarrassed uneasiness he would as an adult feel toward all figures of authority.

To compound his problems, while the normally fed child quickly developed a sense of time, the African lived almost entirely within the moment. He could not plan for the future and was often absent minded. His moods would swing between naive optimism and the darkest depression; the optimism came from the prolonged period of breast-feeding, while the pessimism was a reaction to the withdrawal of the breast. Ritchie went on to argue that hardly any African was well balanced and that typically Africans were slaves to their emotions, lacking initiative and utterly dependent upon authority. The child's intellectual development was likewise stunted. According to Ritchie, most (male) members of Western cultures were capable of clear and objective thought and able to change their minds on the basis of rational argument. In contrast, Africans were seldom capable of unbiased thinking, and their thoughts and feelings were poorly differentiated. The typical African had no thoughts of his own; he simply followed the views laid down by authority. In any stressful situation the African adult regressed to an infantile state in which he was incapable of looking critically either at himself or the world around him. He was disinclined to make any effort to improve his situation and he lacked an imagination which could give him a vision of a better life.

The African child projected his own sense of badness onto the symbolic figure of his father and tended to introject or internalize all positive qualities from without believing finally that they originated from within himself. The resulting type of personality displayed a close similarity to paranoid insanity. On this subject Ritchie commented: 'Indeed, we may reasonably say that the typical African is neurotic, but this is not noticeable within his own almost wholly neurotic culture.'[12] This neurosis was seen clearly in Africans' response to education. Although they had no thirst for knowledge and little curiosity, they had an almost morbid obsession with Western schooling. In his many years of teaching Ritchie found that African boys had a passion for mathematics and yet without exception had little ability to master its principles. What these children hoped for was to acquire some philosophy or system which would enable them to create order within their own confused and chaotic minds.[13] They could not assimilate abstract patterns of thinking because there was nothing orderly within themselves. Their lack of initiative and dread of the teacher's authority were further barriers to learning, and within a few years they lagged well behind European students of the same age.

As a Freudian, Ritchie placed much emphasis upon sexuality and the ways in which sexual knowledge and experience shaped personality. He explained that African children would inevitably hear their parents engaging in sexual intercourse and at an early age would themselves imitate adult sexual behaviour. Parents would pretend to disapprove and even threaten their children with punishment, but in effect they connived with this sexual precocity. African children made a rapid transition from anal to genital eroticism, a transition which only stunted intellectual growth. In Freudian terms there was no latency period in their sexual development, the period which according to psychoanalytic theory was so important for the achievement of intellectual and emotional maturity. They might never experience voluntary sexual abstinence, and the codes of conduct among adults reflected the casual way in which sex was treated in childhood. Early sexual gratification led to instability in marriage by loosening the physical bond between parents. In Ritchie's experience, women would use the threat of adultery to punish or cajole their husbands, while men would pursue other sexual partners without thought for their wives. In every respect the sexual behaviour of Africans was irresponsible and chaotic.

Ritchie was certain that the European presence had exerted little effect upon Africans and that the dread of accepting responsibility had always been a prominent feature of the African personality.[14] He was also convinced that, while members of advanced cultures tended to distinguish between rights and privileges, Africans viewed every advantage received as their due. They were generally greedy and acquisitive and lacked completely the objective feeling that Ritchie claimed lay at the heart of gratitude. To be grateful involved a complex process of introjection and projection. Significantly, Ritchie chose to ignore the fact that it also involved an understanding of the independence of both parties and a recognition of their equality.

The African that Ritchie described was almost a parody of human shortcomings: impulsive, self-absorbed, misogynist, angry, ungrateful, sexually promiscuous, passive, ruthless, lacking in intellectual curiosity, emotionally unstable and irresponsible. African culture embodied each of these vices and was as unappealing and neurotic as the individuals it produced. This portrait was close to the model of the narcissistic personality which, during the 1970s, became so fashionable among British and American psychiatrists. In the case of the African, however, the collective traits identified by Ritchie were more infantile and there was a heightened propensity for rage.[15] This picture explained why the colonial relationship should be so difficult for Europeans to sustain; the African lacked every quality that made social relations easy or enjoyable. He was the worst kind of person to engage as an employee and the worst kind of person to have as a fellow citizen. The ideal man in Ritchie's work was emotionally balanced, reliable and realistic in his expectations, able to compromise and to control his anger (which, in any case, was not marked), and capable of empathy with the suffering of others. His life was ruled by rational choice, and he accepted responsibility for his own actions. He was the kind of person who could distinguish between his own wishes and his right to impress his will upon others. In other words, he was the ideal citizen – the most flattering of self-portraits of the males who controlled the settler communities of British colonial Africa.

Torn between the radicalism of Freud's views on sexuality and the conservative opinions of settler society, Ritchie allowed settler opinion to prevail. His commitment to Freudian theory could have encouraged him to find some merit in traditional practices; after all, along with Laubscher, he had found no sexual neurosis among the Africans of Northern Rhodesia. Instead, however, his description of the mother's suckling of her infant – in Freudian theory the archetypal sexual relationship – conjured up an image of depraved sensuality: 'Nursing was one long debauch.'[16] Ritchie claimed that the African infant drank from the breast with such gusto that it invariably swallowed much air along with the milk. The breast was not given when the infant was hungry but offered whenever it cried; this of course produced colic. Consequently the child's stomach wall expanded, acquiring an unusual elasticity, and its need for milk would increase; thus greed became ingrained in its physiology. Far from being joyous or free, African sexuality, beginning with the mother's suckling of her infant, was compulsive and pathological. Significantly, it was that sexuality which threatened the physical safety of every white woman in colonial Africa. Ritchie's argument was, in an oblique way, a restatement of the myth of hypersexuality that Laubscher used to explain the 'Black Peril'; he was the first, however, to offer a scientific justification for it.

References to Ritchie's work can be found throughout the 1950s and 1960s; his research became part of the ruling orthodoxy about African inferiority. At the First Pan-African Psychiatric Conference held at

Abeokuta in 1961, the psychiatrist T. A. Lambo presented a paper titled 'Growth of African Children: Psychological Aspects', which relied heavily upon Ritchie's *The African*.[17] For example Lambo wrote that the African adult 'has no sense of planning. He cannot master his weakness and he cannot express his aggressiveness on account of the shock experience at the termination of the weaning period. He shows neither sympathy with those who suffer, nor with himself'.[18] Breast-feeding on demand, according to Lambo, robbed the child of a sense of time, thereby creating various problems in later life; the unbridled optimism and lack of inhibition, which were dominant traits of the Nigerian personality, probably had their origins in the oral eroticism of infancy.

Ritchie's analysis of sexuality was the most original aspect of his work. It was a subject on which all settlers held strong views but one about which there was little scientific debate. Psychoanalysis did not assuage Ritchie's distaste for the sexuality of Africans, but it did allow him to discuss openly questions that had been repressed in the work of Carothers. The theory of hypersexuality, which Ritchie transformed into a doctrine about child care and cultural preference, was a defining element of settler culture. It had been of particular importance in the histories of Southern Rhodesia and South Africa, where it had been prominent in encouraging and justifying segregationist policies. For that reason alone, Ritchie's observations about breast-feeding regimes fitted smoothly into the theory of African inferiority. It would be a mistake, however, to read his essay as simply a study of the immorality of colonial subjects. *The African* was also an essay about virtue; the virtue of the English men and women who had chosen the colonial vocation.

Although Ritchie's essay was written too early to include serious discussion of nationalism, it did contain clear prescriptions on how settlers should respond to social change. Above all else it contained a dire warning. The essay suggested that the state should behave towards the African with paternalism, fear and mistrust. Those sentiments were already well ingrained within settler culture and there is little doubt that Ritchie's supporters would have seen in his essay ample explanation for the Mau Mau rebellion, which erupted less than a decade later in another British colony.

The psychology of colonization

None of the ethnopsychiatrists with whom we have dealt so far makes reference to colonialism or to the colonial relationship. This silence is striking in that there was a thread in the clinical literature reaching back into the 1930s which presumed that the clash of cultures was likely to provoke mental disturbance among colonial subjects. The sole work that deals directly with this question was written by a Frenchman named Octave Mannoni. Along with Ritchie, Mannoni was also the only ethnopsychiatrist to examine African childhood experience.

Octave Mannoni had lived in Madagascar from 1925 until 1947, working as an ethnologist and at one time serving as director general of the government information service. He had an abiding interest in psychoanalysis, and in November 1947 had entered analysis in Paris under Jacques Lacan.[19] Mannoni later claimed that during his years in Madagascar he had cured himself of an obsessional neurosis. 'I understood, moreover, why Rimbaud had cured himself in the desert. Dislocation can do the job of analysis. Being a white man among blacks is like being an analyst among the whites.'[20] In his 1949 book *Psychologie de colonisation*, released in English under the title *Prospero and Caliban* in 1950, Mannoni sought to explain the factors that had precipitated the riots that swept Madagascar in March 1947 and to analyse the relationship between the native Malagasy and the French colonialists. Although at various points in his study he called his method psychoanalytic, in fact he relied upon the theory of Alfred Adler, who had broken with Freud as early as 1911.

Mannoni considered the colonial situation best characterized not as a relationship between two kinds of civilizations but as the meeting of two different kinds of personality. As the result of that meeting one became colonized and the other a colonial. The European's unconscious reaction to the native prevented him from understanding the colonial situation: 'A colonial situation is created, so to speak, the very instant a white man, even if he is alone, appears in the midst of a tribe, even if it is independent, so long as he is thought to be rich or powerful or merely immune to the local forces of magic, and so long as he derives from his position, even though only in his most secret self, a feeling of his own superiority.'[21] Because of the gulf separating these two worlds, colonized peoples were able to accept only fragments and never the whole of European civilization.

The key concepts in Mannoni's descriptions of the colonized were inferiority and dependence. These terms, extracted from the work of Adler, were taken to represent alternative types of personality and to characterize different types of values. The potentiality for each type was to be found in every individual, and while one was ascendant the other would be repressed. In the Malagasy dependence was dominant, while in the European inferiority held sway. The Malagasy would only feel inferiority when the bonds of dependence binding him to an authority were threatened, a characteristic Mannoni suggested was common to all primitives. Personality structure was the key to the psychology of backward peoples and, according to Mannoni, explained the stagnation of their cultures and their belief in magic. Within the history of social theory this mental structure has a correlative in Marx's concept of the Asiatic mode of production and in Weber's 'garden of magic', by which both men typified the orient.

Prospero and Caliban opened with a fictionalized account of the original contact between the Malagasy and the European, a form of contact presumably reproduced in every successive generation. At some point a Malagasy received a favour from a European. He showed no gratitude but instead came to feel he had some claim on this man who was his protector. He asked for further gifts as reassurance, and if his requests were refused he felt betrayed. The dominant element in the Malagasy's psychology was the desire to avoid the experience of abandonment. From early childhood he learned that final authority rested with his ancestors. Their authority was unassailable, and therefore the child was deprived of believing that one day he might become an authority unto himself. According to Mannoni the dead occupied the place in the Malagasy psyche that in the European was taken by conscience, reason, or belief in God. Unlike the European, who was forced to choose his beliefs, the Malagasy was dominated by the omniscient authority of his father, who interpreted the will of the dead. The European (male) child knew that eventually he would take his father's place and inherit his authority; the Malagasy child accepted, without question, that this would never happen.

The mental structure of dependency was, according to Mannoni, universal among the Malagasy and pervaded their personality. When the need for dependence was unassuaged the individual would suffer a crisis, typically expressed in outbursts of hostility or violence. The Malagasy's childhood, in which he never came into competition with his parents, helped him to avoid the troubled conscience which for the European was the price of progress. If left to themselves, the best the Malagasy could achieve was a feudal type of society dominated by patron–client relationships, for they lacked the courage to fashion a genuine independence. When forced to take the initiative, the Malagasy 'lost their heads'. There was nothing, of course, to prevent a Malagasy from acquiring the same kind of personality structure as Europeans if, for example, he were brought up from infancy in a European environment. Under colonial conditions, however, it was common for them to achieve only the veneer of a European personality. Driven to seek the company of Europeans who never accepted them as equals, these assimilated natives were 'then rather in the position of a repressed homosexual among overt heterosexuals, a situation which, as is well known, is liable to give rise to hatred, either conscious or otherwise'.[22] Malagasy who retained their dependency complex intact were generally not hostile to Europeans. Hostility arose among those in whom dependence had been disrupted. The ferocity of the 1947 riots was due not to a desire for sadistic revenge but to overwhelming feelings of guilt. In the figure of the European the Malagasy saw their master, their protector and a scapegoat for their own failings. Consequently, 'the European is always a source of ill-defined anxiety for the Malagasy: he can do what he likes and is unpredictable: he has no standards, and his attitudes are extraordinary'.[23] The European demanded perfection but rarely met the natives' craving for security.

Mannoni explained that colonization had always required a need for dependence in the colonized and that the craving for such a relationship had prefigured the arrival of the first Europeans. Accordingly, 'not all peoples can be colonised: only those who experience this need'.[24] Armed force alone would never have been sufficient to allow for the conquest of Madagascar (or any colony) if the arrival of the European had not been aided by the unconscious compliance of the native. The strength of the European settlers lay in the weakness of the Malagasy personality, and the white man came to occupy the position in the native psyche hitherto reserved for the dead. When the riots broke out in March 1947, the behaviour of both the Europeans and the Malagasy was determined by the psychology of their relationship. In order to frighten the Malagasy during the riots, Mannoni said, the Europeans resorted to a 'theatrical kind of violence'.

The 'theatrical violence' to which he referred cost as many as eighty thousand lives and was followed by a cruel repression in which torture was widely used.[25] That repression, which saw a large number of rebels imprisoned in France, lasted until the eve of independence in 1960. As with the Mau Mau rebellion, the violence in Madagascar was confined largely to the indigenous community; in the whole of the island only twenty-eight white settlers were killed. In the period from 1945 until the fall of Algeria in 1960 the French resorted routinely to violence throughout their crumbling colonial empire and there is good reason to argue that France, even more than Portugal, was the most brutal of the retreating colonial powers. For example, at Setif on VE Day in 1945, French troops massacred some thirty thousand North Africans; the Algerian war of independence cost over one million lives.

The most innovative element in Mannoni's work was his psychology of the colonizer, especially the connection he made between misanthropy and the colonial vocation. The original colonizers, he argued, were strong and independent adventurers, and it was only later that the colonial type appeared. In portraying this type, he relied heavily upon the fictional characters of Prospero and Robinson Crusoe. He explained that the appeal of these and kindred characters (Odysseus, Sinbad, Gulliver) lay in the desire for a world without men – the wish to denigrate the whole of mankind. The same impulse was present in those who chose the colonial vocation: 'The colonial life is simply a substitute to those who are still obscurely drawn to a world without men – to those, that is, who have failed to make the effort necessary to adapt infantile images to adult reality.'[26] According to Mannoni, Prospero's mistreatment of the slave Caliban was motivated by the ambivalence that played such an important part in colonial racism. Just as Prospero projected his sexual guilt onto the figure of Caliban, so the colonialist projected his own evil intentions onto the African, thereby cleansing his conscience. Using Mannoni's argument, 'Black Peril' scares could be given a very different interpretation to the one favoured by settlers; their source would be the projection by white men of their own sexual fantasies onto the figure of the black.[27] This convincing, if limited, interpretation of 'Black Peril' exonerated the black man, but the absolution did not extend to African women. In discussing sexuality Mannoni's major concern was with the demoralization of those European men who took black women as sexual partners. He described such women as inferior and docile, noting that they sapped the will and intelligence of any white man who came into contact with them. Black women were far more dangerous to the ethos of settler communities than black men. Such views were common in the colonial era, but Mannoni was the only psychiatrist to repeat them.[28]

'What the colonial in common with Prospero lacks', said Mannoni, 'is awareness of the world of Others, a world in which Others have to be respected. This is the world from which the colonial has fled because he cannot accept men as they are.'[29] The behaviour of the colonizer, like that of the colonial subject, was dominated by perverse and infantile needs. The one wanted reassurance from the fears he believed would overwhelm him, while the other was desperately seeking for a world in which he no longer had to treat others as equals. If the colonial subject was pitiful, the colonialist was ignoble. By temperament he was well suited to playing the bully, and it was hardly surprising that colonial officials were prone to displays of petty malice and self-aggrandizement. By its very nature the colonial situation was unstable: it could never adequately meet the psychological needs of its actors.

None of Mannoni's colleagues addressed the colonial relationship and, apart from a few eccentric asides from Gordon, none of the ethnopsychiatrists offered criticism of the European communities they served. The nationalist generation, including Albert Memmi, Frantz Fanon and Aimé Césaire, nevertheless attacked Mannoni with ferocity. Mannoni believed that, at least within the French empire, racism was an aberration: 'France is unquestionably one of the least racialist-minded countries in the world: also colonial policy is officially anti-racist.'[30] This of course was not the experience of *évolués* such as Memmi and Fanon, who were also unconvinced by the distinction Mannoni drew between the heroic Europeans who first settled the colonies and the career colonialists who followed them. Mannoni believed that the Africans' opinion of European culture would often come from the behaviour of some mediocre official who expressed attitudes that were merely personal. He was adamant that 'European civilisation and its best representatives are not, for instance, responsible for colonial racism: that is the work of petty officials, small traders and colonials who have toiled much without great success'.[31] Fanon was sympathetic to the idea that racism had its origins in the recesses of the human personality; he also believed, however, that racism served specific economic and political ends and that to deny the existence of those ends was to legitimize such oppression.

Another reason that *Prospero and Caliban* angered the nationalists was Mannoni's approach to political independence. Ignoring the substance of Malagasy demands for political rights, he treated independence as a psychological problem. The Malagasy, he said, were well aware that they would gain nothing of value from independence and that a nationalist government would only bring more corruption, more taxes and more forced labour. What they were seeking was not political rights but relief from fear of abandonment. They wanted to project their own shortcomings onto Europeans and so they behaved like impossible children who wanted one thing but demanded another. If they were granted self-government at the wrong time, they would simply regress. The average native did not make decisions for himself and was incapable of assuming responsibility for his own affairs. The transition to independence would have to be gradual, and the revival of the traditional village councils, called *fokon'olona*, might help to provide security and continuity.

In 1947 the French empire was under threat on several fronts. France was recovering from the humiliation of the German occupation and was already engaged in an unwinnable war to reconquer Indo-China. Mannoni saw clearly that colonialism had no future; the 'colonialist position was too unrealistic, too emotional – one might even say too neurotic – to last very long'.[32] Yet *Prospero and Caliban* was denounced by both nationalists and communists as an *apologia* for a dying colonialism. Mannoni's critics argued that in treating colonialism as a psychological relationship and by emphasizing its irrationality, he had ignored the economic motives that made colonies so attractive to imperial powers. Neither Fanon nor Césaire in fact had much to say on political economy, preferring instead to document the personal misery which in Africa (and the Caribbean) accompanied colonial rule. Mannoni angered them principally because they recognized only one kind of subjectivity, that of the *évolué* class to which they belonged and about which Mannoni was so scathing. In their writings it was that subjectivity against which the experience of all other classes was judged. Mannoni's critics were adamant that because he could not speak on behalf of colonial subjects he must therefore be speaking for someone else. About that they were correct – but for the wrong reasons.

In *Prospero and Caliban* Mannoni described the settler class (or petty bourgeoisie) as including small traders, officials, shopkeepers, school-teachers and administrators. With the exception of farmers and artisans, these were the men and women who formed the fabric of white communities throughout colonial Africa. It was a class that Mannoni suggested was a miserable failure: greedy, violent and racist, mean spirited and self-interested, incapable of sustaining a metropolitan culture in a colonial setting. In contrast to the metropolitan bourgeoisie, the colonists were a class without vision, and their vices were the vices of those who were not fit to govern. It was this attack upon the settlers and their culture that distinguished Mannoni's work. He did what no other psychiatrist of the colonial era would have imagined doing: he denigrated the class of which he was a privileged member. He claimed to be speaking not for a particular class but for science; in *Prospero and Caliban* the disembodied voice of science was the male voice of the metropolitan ruling class.

The interests of white settlers and those of the metropolitan bourgeoisie were not the same, and in making his choice Mannoni turned his back on the class that had nurtured ethnopsychiatry from its beginning. He did so because in his years in Madagascar he perceived all too clearly the end of France's African empire. In *Prospero and Caliban* ethnopsychiatry arrived at the destination towards which it had been travelling for thirty years: the abandonment of the class the science was designed to serve, a class which like the science itself was doomed.

The literature of ethnopsychiatry was written over a sixty-year period by a diverse group of amateurs and specialists. Carothers, Sachs and Laubscher were qualified psychiatrists, Biesheuvel a clinical psychologist, Ritchie a schoolteacher with a passion for psychoanalysis. Mannoni was an ethnologist. Of this group Carothers was the best travelled and the only one to have contact with other specialists, but even he conducted his research in intellectual isolation.[1] Given the lack of contact between individual psychiatrists, the smallness of the professional group and the absence of specialist journals, their agreement about African inferiority cannot be explained simply by the influence of one upon the other. On the contrary, the science's orthodoxy was spontaneous.

There was agreement from a variety of colonial sites about the major forms of mental illness found among patients admitted to asylums. In Africa as in Europe mental defectives were well represented among the inmates of mental hospitals. In 1950 such patients constituted almost 9 per cent of inmates in South African institutions, while in Kenya in the period from 1939 to 1943 the figure was a little over 10 per cent for first admissions. Carothers found that many of the mentally ill who fell foul of the law were intellectually deficient and that of the psychiatric homicides admitted to Mathari in 1949 almost a quarter were feeble-minded.[2] In all African colonies organic disorders were prominent, and in Nyasaland Shelley and Watson found that 17 per cent of inmates suffered from an organically based mental illness. Epilepsy was also common; in many communities it was greatly feared, and the social ostracism suffered by epileptics encouraged anti-social forms of behaviour. In the 1940s at Zomba Asylum 13 per cent of inmates were found to be epileptic.[3]

Among the major forms of mental illness, affective disorders were the most variable in distribution. In Nyasaland, Shelley and Watson classified almost one-third of patients under this title while Tooth's study of the Gold Coast showed an incidence of around 20 per cent. The figures from South Africa, however, revealed that affective disorders accounted for less than 7 per cent of first admissions. Laubscher, who worked exclusively in South Africa, considered manic-depressive psychosis rare. The most difficult inmates in European and African asylums were those classified as psychopathic. In the colonial period psychopaths accounted for only a small number of asylum admissions, and during his years at Mathari Carothers found that less than 3 per cent of inmates warranted this diagnosis.

The most common disorder in African asylums was schizophrenia, and in the literature it appears as the typical form of psychosis. However, the profile of the disorder and the patient's prognosis in Africa differed from that found in Europe. In the European, according to the texts, schizophrenia was characterized by a slow but steady deterioration of the personality, which most often began in adolescence. The illness was believed to develop in individuals who were shy or reclusive and who early in life displayed a tendency to ruminate upon their problems or to engage in autoerotic behaviour.[4] The typical schizophrenic showed a blunting of emotion and a disharmony between mood and thought. In advanced cases a loss of care for personal appearance was common. For a time there was a belief that schizophrenia was rare in primitives, but with the growth of literature documenting its frequency among African patients that idea was abandoned.[5] However, in the African schizophrenia was poorly defined and was often an intense illness of brief duration. In 1950 the outcome for these patients was probably better in Africa than in Europe where schizophrenia was the most common form of chronic psychosis.[6] Various explanations have been offered for this pattern, most of which ignore the possibility that the reason could be independent of the illness. In Western culture mental illness tends to adhere to the person, and can readily lead to a 'career' as a psychiatric patient. In contrast, Carothers for one believed that traditional societies were undemanding and therefore the mentally ill, along with the sub-normal, could more easily pass muster. It is also possible to view the role of the patient as an artefact of a mental health system: like any form of behaviour, being mentally ill is shaped by social expectations.[7] In Africa, the absence of follow-up procedures and sophisticated means of referral meant that the opportunities for a career as a mental patient were so limited as to explain schizophrenics' enhanced prognosis.

The mentally ill were more likely to find their way into Blida or Mathari if they had committed a murder or an act of arson, and the conspicuousness of such individuals in institutions encouraged theorizing about the connection between violence and mental illness. In 1932 Antoine Porot of the University of Algiers, who dominated Algerian psychiatry for over two decades, published a study of criminality in which he pointed to the Algerians' propensity for violence.[8] In this essay, Porot and his colleague

D. C. Arrii wrote at length about the impulsiveness of Algerian Muslims, contrasting their behaviour with that of members of an ethnic minority, the Kabyle. According to Porot and Arrii, Algerians were violent by heredity, congenital compulsives who could not channel their aggression to socially constructive ends. Their impulses were such that they frequently led to homicide. Contrary to the pattern found in Europeans, Algerian melancholics turned not to suicide but to murder. In explaining this phenomenon, Porot and Arrii argued that the Algerians' personality structure precluded introspection or reflection and led them to externalize violent feelings. They were convinced that the reason for such behaviour was to be found in the structure of the Algerian brain.[9]

In their 1936 study of the inmates of Zomba Asylum in Nyasaland, Shelley and Watson found over half of the inmates classified as criminal lunatics, most having committed arson or murder.[10] This pattern was in contrast with comparable institutions in England, where larceny was the most common crime, followed by arson and sexual offences.[11] While these researchers suggested that the darkness of night in rural Africa and the availability of weapons might encourage murder, they were convinced that such crimes also reflected certain features of the African personality. In many cases the victim was attacked with great ferocity and horribly mutilated. The criminal would very often make no attempt to escape and would be arrested at the scene of the crime. Over half of the crimes committed by African schizophrenics were violent; among European schizophrenics, in contrast, only 12 per cent of crimes involved attacks on other people. A similar pattern was found among affective psychotics, although here the number of patients involved was minuscule. From this evidence the researchers concluded that the 'nearer that one descends to the state of primitive man, the more keen is the desire to kill. The native whose threshold of control is injured by disease is frequently homicidal whereas the European defective is more inclined to commit theft, or to perpetrate a sexual assault'.[12] They argued that in the primitive it was a biological virtue to respond to perceived danger with the fight-or-flight mechanism, and it was this mechanism that explained the high incidence of homicide among native psychotics: 'It cannot be expected that the native can exercise complete control over such powerful instincts after such a comparatively short period of contact with civilising influences.'[13]

During his years at Mathari, as we have seen, Carothers had encountered many cases that could not readily be classified. Similar cases had meanwhile been documented in Southern and French West Africa. Laubscher, for example had commented upon the number of unclassified patients, many of them violent, at Queenstown, linking these cases with a pattern of high rates of homicide and low rates of suicide.[14] In West

Africa, Aubin, Gallais, Planques and Tooth had all noted a similar proportion of unclassifiable patients.[15] According to Carothers, many of these patients suffered from what he termed 'frenzied anxiety'. He argued that the African was prone to develop a twilight or confusional state which might last for days or even weeks, and usually ended in spontaneous recovery. The initial symptom was an overwhelming anxiety, which was often followed by a violent outburst, sometimes leading to murder. In explaining this syndrome, Carothers referred to his theory of the African mind, in which he identified a lack of personal responsibility. In the African, bewitchment often took the place occupied by conscience in the European psyche, resulting in a propensity to emotional outbursts. As he put it: 'Emotion easily dominates the entire mind: and when it does, the latter's tenuous grip on the world of things is loosened, and frank confusion takes the place of misrepresentation. All the neuroses seen in European individuals are here, as a rule, resolved on social lines, and the structure of psychosis is so altered by the lack of conscious integration that these are apt to take amorphous or abortive forms.'[16] In this sense 'frenzied anxiety' was a significant illness because it exposed the underlying structure of personality. Essentially it was a pathology that arose from the frontal lobe idleness which Carothers had identified in his first years at Mathari.[17]

The idea that schizophrenia was poorly defined in the African was based largely on the presence of these 'frenzied anxiety' states rather than upon the enhanced recovery rates for schizophrenic patients. 'Frenzied anxiety' was explained by reference to the supposed low incidence of suicide. Presumably, the psychotic African directed his hostility outwards and would commit murder or assault, where a European psychotic would turn the aggression upon himself.[18] When this theory about externalized aggression was being constructed, case-histories of African patients were rarely taken. Many patients had appeared initially before a district magistrate, where their evidence was heard through an interpreter, but there was seldom reliable information about the arson, assault or murder with which they had been charged. The same was true of their clinical records, and even Carothers made little attempt to distinguish between 'frenzied anxiety' and schizophrenia. The syndrome did suggest to him, however, that African psychotics were dangerous and that a proclivity for senseless violence was an integral part of the African personality. It therefore sounded a warning to settlers in their dealings with black workers. In Southern Rhodesia, Kenya and Algeria, settlers were concerned about the threat posed by African majorities and in some cases those fears were well founded. For example, in Southern Rhodesia the uprisings of 1895 and 1896 saw almost 10 per cent of the white population killed. However, the history of colonial societies suggests that whites had little reason to fear Africans, while Africans had good reason to fear their white employers.

The legal histories of Kenya and Southern Rhodesia are filled with stories in which, on the slightest provocation, white employers killed African workers. Those cases that came to trial led invariably to a charge of culpable homicide or assault rather than a more serious offence, and it was rare for a white man or woman to be gaoled for the killing of an African.[19] For example, in August 1916 a miner named Frederick West was charged with culpable homicide. The deceased was an African named Antonio who was working with the accused. When Antonio slipped and dropped and broke a windlass he was holding, the accused, in front of a number of witnesses, kicked him several times in the stomach. Antonio died from his injuries. West was found guilty of assault and was fined £25.[20] In May 1910 a storeman named MacLaren Forbes was charged with the shooting of an African named M'Tuna. The deceased was one of three Africans working at Forbes's store. On the night of the murder, Forbes demanded that the men play cards with him. When they refused, he became angry and shot M'Tuna in the head.[21] On 12 February 1915 at Hillside, a suburb of Salisbury, a Mrs Samuels became angry when one of her servants, a man named Tom, refused to follow orders. Mrs Samuels shot him in the head, killing him instantly. The case was heard before a district magistrate, but the attorney general of the day declined to pursue the matter and so Mrs Samuels was never charged.[22] These cases are representative; in any one year in Southern Rhodesia or Kenya an abundance of such killings took place.[23]

The relationship between employers and employees was often violent. Outbursts of uncontrollable rage were characteristic of the behaviour of white farmers and mine managers towards their black employees. That violence had its own sociology and cannot be understood outside the context in which labour was bought and sold. The legal framework for labour relations in British colonies was enshrined in various masters-and-servants ordinances. By diminishing the status of African workers and enhancing the powers of employers, those ordinances encouraged the kind of brutality which in the Battlefields case, in Southern Rhodesia, saw two African workers beaten to death by their white employers because one of them was suspected of theft.[24] These individual cases, like the broader histories of settler societies themselves, suggest that the theory of the violent African was, to a large extent, based upon a crude inversion.

The 'violent African' theory contained a number of enthusiasms favoured by ethnopsychiatrists. It suggested that the African had little self-control of the kind found in the European, and could easily lapse into irrational behaviour. That defect threatened all white employers in their dealings with individual blacks and made any indigenous mass movement potentially dangerous. Because Africans could not control themselves it fell to government to provide whatever constraints were necessary. The kind of political regime implicit in this theory was authoritarian: a democratic government would necessarily lead to social chaos. This, of course, was the conclusion reached by Carothers in his study of the Mau Mau and by Mannoni in his account of Malagasy nationalism.

One of the comforting myths of the Atlantic slave trade was the idea of the happy African whom providence had spared the sensitivities which so troubled white people. In the first half of this century, American medical journals played their part in perpetuating that myth.[25] The same idea was found in the ethnopsychiatric literature, and quickly became an article of faith.[26] Laubscher did find 10 cases of manic-depression among the 359 male inmates at Queenstown Asylum and 12 among the 195 women, but he pointed to its atypical profile and concluded that true manic-depressive psychosis, like depression itself, was rare among Africans and Cape Coloureds.[27] He believed that the incidence of suicide increased with civilization and that the African's psychology was antithetical to self-destruction, being 'built on the principle of blaming someone else or something else for his shortcomings'.[28] In studying the question of suicide, he canvassed magistrates in native reserves. During a two-year period, in a region containing over eight hundred thousand people, Laubscher discovered only fourteen suicides and four attempted suicides.[29] These results coincided with his experience at Queenstown Hospital, where over a fifteen-year period there were two attempted suicides among the 1,700 male and female patients.

In his 1950 survey of the Gold Coast, Tooth found no case of depressive psychosis and explained this pattern by reference to the African habit of sharing problems rather than fretting over them and the African mental patient's lack of self-reproach.[30] Carothers was less certain than Tooth or Laubscher about the absence of such illness but he concluded that since depression was linked with a high degree of personal integration and a sense of personal responsibility, it might be expected to be rare.[31] Writing in 1956 of Tanganyika, Smartt noted in contrast that depression was more striking in African men than women, and appeared in sharp contrast to the Africans' usual happy demeanour.[32] Upon arrival at hospital many patients were mute and painfully slow in their actions. Hypochondria was common, but the ideas of sexual guilt almost universal in European depressives were absent. The other major difference from the usual profile was the low risk of suicide and the rapidity with which such patients could shift into a mood of savage rage.

The orthodox view regarding depressive illness and suicide was imbibed by the first generation of black African-born psychiatrists. At the First Pan–African Psychiatric Conference, held in Abeokuta in 1961, T. Asuni presented a paper on suicide based upon research carried out at the Aro Hospital and coroners' reports from western Nigeria for the period 1957 to 1960. He found that the recorded rate of suicide was 1 per 100,000, which by world standards was extremely low.[33] He concluded that the rate of suicide was consistent with the low incidence of depressive illness, and his results tended to substantiate the opinions of Carothers, Laubscher and Tooth.[34]

Depression is the clinical name for intense personal suffering. In European cultures it is a disorder often associated with guilt, religious doubt and artistic originality, characteristics often identified as the very foundation of Western subjectivity. It is also of course the most common psychiatric illness and takes a huge toll in suffering and loss of life through suicide. The criteria for its diagnosis have changed little since the eighteenth century.[35] It is characterized by disturbed mood, self-debasing behaviour and self–castigation. The wish to die is also common. Its physical symptoms may include loss of appetite, sleeplessness, fatigue or exhaustion, inability to concentrate, and unexplained aches and pains. Up to twenty-nine symptoms are associated with it, covering a bewildering range of psychological and somatic disturbances.[36] Frequently, patients complain not of being depressed but of having a bad taste in the mouth or of a loss of energy. According to a standard British text, 'it may be impossible to get a clear statement of mood disorder from these patients; they may even deny that they are sad or depressed in any way'.[37]

For psychiatrists working in exotic locations, however, diagnosis requires a clear understanding of what constitutes a normal mood, and an ability to distinguish depression from grief, anger and sadness. Whatever the context, it is essential that the physician be familiar with the patient's culture in order to make a judgement about his or her sense of self-worth. Since most psychiatrists working in Africa lacked such familiarity, the identification of depression fell back upon the incidence of suicide or attempted suicide. In any setting suicide is a complex event, and the epidemiology on the subject is notoriously weak. In the colonies, where most births and deaths took place outside hospitals, the problems of identifying suicide were all the more serious. Carothers himself commented upon the lack of reliable data on suicide, while Laubscher's efforts in surveying suicide were at best rudimentary. During the colonial era such limitations did nothing, however, to discourage the idea that the African was immune to depressive illness. If African men and women were incapable of this kind of despair, then presumably they were also bereft of what, in European eyes, were treasured human qualities: the ability to feel guilt and the ability to doubt. This was certainly the opinion of Carothers who explained away the problem of depression by reference to the psychopathic nature of the African personality. In academic discourse this view was first seriously questioned only in 1955.

Margaret Field had begun working in the Gold Coast in the 1930s as an ethnologist. Having returned to Britain twenty years later to study psychiatry, she developed the idea that psychiatry could be useful in explaining the witchcraft that was so common in West Africa. It was her publications that helped to re-shape prevailing views about depressive illness.[38] Her work was also important for what it revealed of the limitations of psychiatry in dealing with cross-cultural contexts and the limitations of anthropology in the interpretation of psychiatric material.

In the period from 1920 until 1944 there had been a marked increase in witchcraft in rural areas of the Gold Coast, and many new shrines had been built, to which supplicants would come seeking relief from bewitchment. In a brief study published in 1955 Field noted that this increase coincided with widespread social problems resulting from the commercialization of agriculture and the introduction of industrial mining. Social change and Western education had caused considerable anxiety, and sterility, the result of gonorrhoea, was common.[39] According to Field, such a climate was conducive to witchcraft and to fears of bewitchment. She argued that witches were often mentally disturbed and that women who confessed to being witches, bemoaning the harm they had caused others, were severely depressed.[40] Among the supplicants who visited shrines, many of whom had suffered some personal loss, were also a number of mentally ill men and women. Elaborating upon this initial study in *Search for Security*, Field attacked the orthodoxy that mental illness was rare or relatively insignificant among primitives. She argued forcefully that in colonial Africa much mental illness went unrecognized because it wore the garments of traditional ideology.[41] In contrast to the ethnopsychiatrists, she did not draw her case material from asylum inmates, and, perhaps most important, her subjects were women rather than men.

Field provided a brief account of the social and economic climate of life in rural Ghana and outlined in some detail what she termed the 'ideological background' of witchcraft. She rejected the idea that mental illness was confined to Western-educated elites and that the stresses of transition forced Africans to assimilate mutually incompatible systems of belief. On the contrary, she argued that Africans were capable of assimilating Christian doctrine while retaining a commitment to paganism. She saw the power of witchcraft as derived from the same source as depressive illness, both of them relying upon the idea of the victim's being wicked. In the Gold Coast, the worst crime was to be a witch, and Field discovered that it was common for acutely depressed women to accuse themselves of witchcraft. The power of witches was kept alive by depression and by the fantastic delusions of sin and guilt which beset such individuals. As Field explained: 'Witchcraft meets, above all else, the depressive's need to steep herself in irrational self-reproach and denounce herself as unspeakably wicked. If depression were stamped out, I doubt if even the drunkards and other paranoid failures, with their urge to project blame on others, could keep witchcraft alive.'[42] Field referred to various forms of depression among women, including involutional depression, which she claimed was as recognizable in rural Ghana as it was in Europe. She also made reference to schizophrenia, paranoia and obsessional compulsive disorders, all of which she believed were common.

At one level, Field's argument was free of the kinds of problems that compromised ethnopsychiatry, but by employing European psychiatric concepts she ended up pathologizing Ghanaian culture. Whatever the limitations of her method, however, her work encouraged subsequent researchers to explore a problem long overlooked.

The Aro–Cornell project of the early 1960s, for example, estimated the prevalence and type of mental disorders in a number of villages and an urban centre among the Yoruba of western Nigeria, and compared the results with those from a study begun in 1948 in Stirling County in the rural north west of the United States.[43] While Leighton and his co-workers were not concerned specifically with depression, their research revealed important information about its incidence in Nigeria. Although the category was difficult to translate into Yoruba, it proved four times more common in the Nigerian sample than in the North American cohort.[44] During the 1960s there was a flood of publications on depressive illness in Africa, and Western-trained psychiatrists who for two generations had been unable to find any evidence of depression now found it in abundance. Researchers noted the importance of the psychosomatic symptoms through which Africans, as well as Europeans, experienced depression. While feelings of worthlessness and guilt were still considered rare, the profile of depression described in these articles was in most respects the same as that found in the clinical texts which had been used since the 1930s. The symptoms presented by patients had not changed, nor had the nosologies; what had changed was the capacity of clinicians to recognize them.

There has been no shortage of explanations for this failure, ranging from demographic influences on the size of urban populations to inadequate patient histories and a paucity of reliable data – all technical or procedural factors assumed to have hampered the practice of science.[45] No one has suggested that the correspondence between colonial ideology and ethnopsychiatric orthodoxy was anything other than coincidental. In writing of depression, however, the ethnopsychiatrists were describing a type of suffering that was linked to some of their most cherished values. That such suffering could not be found among Africans suggested a difference between the races as profound as those identified by Galton and de Gobineau in the previous century. That fact had implications for policy and for any assessment of nationalist claims for independence. Depression was closely associated with a sense of responsibility and the facility for self-reflection. The absence of these qualities in individuals seeking political power threatened chaos. Although ethnopsychiatry did not formally acknowledge these connections, their relevance to Carothers's study of the Mau Mau and Mannoni's comments on the massacres in Madagascar is obvious.

From the beginning of the colonial period, researchers were not perturbed if patterns of mental illness in Africans, including depressive illness, failed to conform to established categories. Because they accepted an evolutionist model which allowed for significant differences between the advanced European and the more primitive non-European peoples, variations from the expected patterns did not compromise the veracity of the classificatory systems being employed. It was only with the dawn of the independence decades that the absence of depression became problematic; a changed climate suggested that the science was flawed.

Yet another persistent theme in ethnopsychiatry was that African societies were bereft of creativity. In particular they were presumed to lack a capacity for invention or experiment. According to Carothers, Mannoni and Ritchie, the African adult merely followed rules laid down by his culture, without questioning their merit or the necessity for his compliance. Like his parents and grandparents, he lived in an unchanging world in which there was no innovation and no divergence from a rigid conformity. The body of knowledge in such societies was so limited that it could be mastered by a twelve-year-old child. Unfamiliar situations did not arise, and so initiative was unnecessary. There were no exceptional individuals; in fact, as Mannoni suggested, in a strict sense there were no individuals at all.[46]

The idea that primitive societies were static was not new, but few scientists clung to it with such tenacity as the ethnopsychiatrists. Among social anthropologists it faded with the development of intensive field-work during the 1920s. One of the key features of Malinowski's research, for example, was the distinction he drew between formal rules and what people actually did. In his work on the Trobriands, Malinowski often wrote of divergent behaviour in which an individual deliberately trans-

gressed social conventions, choosing instead to indulge personal preference. He found such behaviour to be not only common but habitual. He
concluded that in their response to conventions the Trobrianders resembled the peoples of Europe. The psychiatrists of the colonial period took
little interest in social anthropology, and it is not surprising that the work
of Malinowski had no influence upon them. In the social context in which
they worked, their views about compliant traditional behaviour were
unremarkable.

The men and women who were admitted to Blida and Mathari were
most often wage labourers living in mine compounds or urban locations.
They were a generation that had experienced radical change, and in many
cases they had shown extraordinary adaptability. Far from being
immersed in a static social order, they were the members of an emerging
urban class. The kinds of Africans who were depicted as members of
static societies never came to the attention of district commissioners, and
they were the people least likely to find their way through the gates of a
colonial asylum. In contrast to social anthropologists, who sought out the
pristine African, the ethnopsychiatrists worked instead with the men and
women whose lives had been most transformed by colonial rule. Consequently, their fiction about static social orders was created against the tide
of clinical work, and also confounded the practitioners' own social
experience: the households of both Carothers and Ritchie were maintained by African servants who in a single generation had left village life
behind.

Beside the issues of violence and social transgression, ethnopsychiatry
contained a range of self-contradictory propositions. Paramount among
these was the idea that primitive societies were pathological and that
African peoples enjoyed a spontaneous and free sexuality. Freud had
drawn an analogy between primitive religion and obsessional neurosis on
the one hand, and witchcraft and paranoia, on the other. The appeal for
him of this analogy was that it placed primitive societies into the kind of
evolutionist schema that underpinned much of psychoanalytic theory.
And yet in Freud's clinical and meta-psychologies a weak or undeveloped
superego and the spontaneous expression of sexuality were suggestive of a
type of mental health. In his later years Freud never tired of reminding his
readers that a developed superego and the loss of sexual pleasure were the
price Europeans paid for their culture. In Freudian terms at least, African
sexuality and, to a lesser extent the impulsive aggressiveness to which
Ritchie and Laubscher, Porot, Mannoni and Carothers pointed, were
evidence of mental health. The ethnopsychiatrists, however, including
those most sympathetic to psychoanalytic theory, reached the opposite
conclusion.

In general, the ethnopsychiatrists tended to view societies either as organisms which could become diseased or as analogous to individuals who were prone to breakdown and debility. The analogy was drawn from the medical models of illness with which they worked daily. It was simply a convenient means for interpreting social process. Significantly, the nationalist generation, and in particular Aimé Césaire and Frantz Fanon, often spoke of European culture as diseased. It was with self-conscious irony that in his *Discourse on Colonialism*, Césaire wrote of the 'European sickness', by which he meant alternately colonial racism, fascism or, on occasion, European culture as a whole. Fanon borrowed from ethnopsychiatry the idea that one party to the colonial encounter was sick and substituted the European for the African. He also adapted the theory of African violence to justify nationalist demands for independence.[47] It is ironic that Fanon's polemic on the subject of violence, which so outraged liberal sensibilities, was simply a restatement of a scientific orthodoxy.

In the clinical literature, the personality of the African was found deficient in various ways. Sometimes emphasis was placed upon an inability to delay gratification, sometimes upon poor planning or self-control, sometimes upon untruthfulness. In each instance, the various flaws were seen to constitute a particular character structure. The work of Carothers and Ritchie was based upon a series of assumptions about the subjectivity of an ideal individual – a male citizen whose behaviour was rational, predictable and self-interested; who was loyal and responsible and conformed readily to the expectations his society had of him. If he had any ruling passion it was disinterest or, at best, a passion for science, which was assumed to embody that virtue. The qualities absent in this ideal subject were passion, intuition, sexual precocity and nurturance, the very qualities which in Western cultures are often associated with females. This portrait of maturity presented a similar set of prescriptions to those found in the work of Erich Fromm, Erik Erikson and, to a lesser extent, Wilhelm Reich.[48] It is only in the past twenty years, with the advent of the women's and gay liberation movements, that these kinds of prescriptions about the ideal subject (and the ideal citizen) have been submitted to critical scrutiny. It no longer seems reasonable to suggest that a single model of subjectivity is sufficient to characterize a population.

Carothers and Ritchie wrote at length about the African's inability to feel or to express gratitude, and the same theme was taken up by Smartt and Gordon. In *Prospero and Caliban*, a whole section was devoted to this question, which Mannoni believed impaired relations between Europeans and colonial peoples. According to Mannoni, when the bonds of dependence which bound the native to the colonizer were broken, the native would immediately become hostile; no matter how much generosity was showered upon him, the native did not express gratitude because dependency precluded it. The inequality of which Mannoni wrote had nothing to do with political power or social advantage; it was an inequality of spirit.

The ingratitude of the native was of course a common complaint of white settlers. Such complaints were fuelled by a frustrated or aggrieved paternalism and were most often made of domestic servants.[49] The idea of the ungrateful native characterized the colonial vocation as a thankless task and served to highlight the selflessness of those who sought to build a civilization in the African wilderness. Gratitude is of course an important mark of civility and one of the first social graces in which middle-class European children are versed. Where it is absent, smooth social relations are difficult if not impossible. In fact, in *Prospero and Caliban* Mannoni characterized the colonial relationship in terms of the absence of gratitude and the prevalence of rancour.

The mature person was presumed to have a particular set of values and beliefs which was expressed in a passion for science and a commitment to what can best be termed 'the experimental spirit'. All of the ethnopsychiatrists were committed to science, and despite the influence of Freud all of them conceived of science and its method in strictly positivist terms. According to Mannoni, Ritchie and Carothers, Western man based his beliefs and oriented his behaviour according to technical or positive knowledge, while the primitive trusted blindly in tradition rather than experience.[50] As Mannoni put it: 'The characteristics of the scientific approach to reality are in fact the same as those of democratic society and of the highly-developed personality.'[51] The European worker served an apprenticeship in a material world in which the acquisition of technical skills, through conscious effort, fostered independence and a thirst for justice.[52] For the African, in contrast, techniques were simply sets of rules which had to be obeyed, not knowledge to be appropriated.

Like Karl Jaspers, Mannoni wrote of Descartes as a heroic figure embodying the best of the European spirit. He praised Descartes's career as typifying the difference between the infantile state in which the primitive lived and the desire for independence which was the chosen fate of Western man. According to Mannoni, the yearning for perfection at the heart of Western civilization was bought at the price of a particular European anguish. In light of this idealized portrait the deficiencies of the African were obvious: every quality identified as laudable in the European was also described as being conspicuously absent in the African. It would be a mistake, however, to see this portrait as an empty abstraction lifted from the margins of European philosophy. The ideal subjects in the ethnopsychiatric literature were the settlers who dominated colonial societies: white male entrepreneurs of the kind found in Max Weber's history of the Protestant ethic, and eulogized even today in the rhetoric of the National Party of South Africa. It was common for settler societies to portray themselves and in particular their forebears as heroic yet vulnerable through their women to degeneracy, caused by contamination by black men. That set of ideas formed a vital element in the white settler cultures of South Africa and Southern Rhodesia. The ethnopsychiatric fiction was simply a refashioning of that myth against the background of African inferiority. Among the ethnopsychiatrists Mannoni's was the only dissenting voice. While he adhered to the idea of heroic founders, Mannoni saw the later colonists as racist and uncreative.

Perhaps the most ambiguous idea in the ethnopsychiatric literature was the 'clash of cultures'. From the beginning of this century, European psychiatrists had remarked that contact with Western culture appeared to increase the incidence of mental illness in Africans. This idea appeared in the work of Gordon, Smartt, Shelley, Watson, Carothers, Field, Mannoni and E. B. Forster,[53] and it was appropriated for rather different ends by Frantz Fanon, who believed that colonialism and Western racism drove many Africans mad.[54] Shelley and Watson argued that contact with settler culture had brought many changes and in the susceptible African such change might be sufficient to cause breakdown.[55] They insisted that this problem was confined to 'mentally feeble stock', but their analysis would place the majority of the black population in that category.

One of the most notable applications of the 'clash of cultures' thesis was Raymond Prince's 1960 essay on 'brain fag' among Nigerian students.[56] His research was prompted by the seemingly high proportion of Nigerian psychiatric patients who were what he termed 'brain workers'. Such patients included young Nigerians in the United Kingdom, as well as patients seen at Aro and at the University College Hospital in Ibadan. The typical case was that of a young man complaining of a burning sensation in his head and an inability to read. On closer examination, these patients displayed intellectual and sensory impairment and persistent pain in the head and neck. Dizziness and loss of balance, and a general weakness throughout the body were also common symptoms. The majority were unmarried Yoruba men between the ages of fifteen and thirty years. Among the sample of ten cases cited by Prince, most suggested that too much study was the precipitating factor for their illness. Prince was far from convinced. In his search for a deeper understanding of these cases, however, he encountered certain obstacles due to the personality of his subjects. As he complained: 'There is one major difficulty in attempting to make speculative comments upon the psycho–dynamics of Nigerian's neurosis. This lies in the Nigerian's apparent lack of any need to engage in the elaborate introspections and soul searchings in the way the European does.'[57] Prince's patients were reluctant to provide information about their condition and unable to achieve significant insight into its causes.

In explaining 'brain fag', Prince turned to the character of Nigerian culture, in particular to the 'intense oral tradition' arising from prolonged breast-feeding. Among the Yoruba, education was viewed as the road to social advancement, and the students in Prince's cohort admitted that failure would have been a calamity. Prince concluded that the syndrome was due to a fusion of European learning techniques with the Nigerian personality. The Nigerian was reluctant to assume responsibility and disliked isolated endeavour. He was characterized by a blind acceptance of authority and a paralysis of will. Consequently, Nigerian students were unsuited to a type of education that demanded self-reliance. When faced with such a situation, they tended to develop psychosomatic disorders as a means of escaping responsibility both for studying and for their own plight. Prince made no recommendations for treatment; the conclusion implicit in his study was that young Nigerians should be discouraged from engaging in intellectual work.

Concern about the effects of Westernization was also a common theme in the literature from the independence decade. In 1962 the Ghanaian-born psychiatrist E. B. Forster published an article on the effects of social change upon the African personality.[58] He argued that the rate and extent of social change in Ghana had been very great and that the nationalist desire for Ghanaians to manage their own affairs had given rise to overconfidence. There had been little appreciation of what he termed 'true values', and of the distinction between fantasy and reality. In particular, social change had brought with it problems of identity: 'When the struggle for self-determination reached fever point and scored valuable concessions to the people, it brought with it certain emotional difficulties which were reflected in a heightened perception of one's own weaknesses and an anxiety over the overt manifestations of these deficiencies.'[59] As a result there had been an increase in the numbers of psychoneurotic cases seen at out-patient clinics and a change in the types of disorders presented.[60]

Forster referred to basic flaws in the African personality arising, he believed, from deficient child-rearing practices. He also noted the presence of an 'archaic weakness' in the African mind which in the case of illiterates diminished the ability to discriminate. As Africans were exposed to Western culture, he argued, it was essential that they develop internalized controls. Unfortunately, in many cases the influence of traditional mores was too strong to allow adjustment to the demands of a new society, and the result was an increase in mental illness.

Although Forster did not quote from Ritchie, Prince or Smartt, he shared with them the assumption that the African lacked the ability to change. Like a child he would be unable to enter into the world of adults without parental guidance. The African was unsuited to an urban existence and deficient in the resources needed to adapt easily to new situations. The thesis, however, contained a number of contradictions. The most obvious of these were the simultaneous claims that African societies were tradition bound and that Africans lived a carefree existence in which sublimation played little part. Africans were at one and the same time utterly abandoned in their behaviour, particularly their sexual behaviour, and slaves to custom, to patterns of sociability presumed to be identical in rural and urban settings. Individuals' ability to adapt to a colonial or post-colonial society was seen as dependent entirely upon their capacity to change cultural affiliation. Discussion of such change was restricted to psychology, and the concept of culture was abstracted from any social or economic context such as wage labour or urbanization.

The 'clash of cultures' thesis was evolutionist, and its politics had two strands. The first was a historical argument concerning African backwardness, its causes, and the rate of change that could be tolerated. The thesis suggested that the lack of material and cultural development on the continent was due to the absence of that impulse to innovation which had been a conspicuous part of European history. According to Prince and Forster, most aspects of African culture were unsuited to the construction of a modern society and would have to be abandoned. When change did come, it would have to be controlled, if an increase in the incidence of mental illness among the emerging middle class was to be avoided. On the grounds of social utility alone, demands for political independence had to be treated with caution. The second strand of the argument was more potent and presented a politics of the African intellectual. The men of whom Prince and Forster wrote belonged to the nationalist generation that came to power in the 1960s, and the judgement made of them was harsh. They were portrayed as having the worst possible qualities for political leadership, combining an inability to accept responsibility or to show initiative with a predisposition to mental illness. Their Western education merely destabilized them. As individuals they were unreliable; as a class they were dangerous. Within settler communities, by 1960 only the most vociferous opponents of majority rule publicly voiced such criticisms of those demanding independence.

9 From psychiatry to politics

With the coming of independence, ethnopsychiatry had to change. The first step in this direction was the professionalization of European psychiatry in Africa, marked by conferences held in Bakuva in 1958 and in Abeokuta in 1961. The Bakuva conference was the first time that psychiatrists from throughout the continent were brought together to discuss their professional concerns. At Abeokuta there were representatives from twenty-two countries, and funding came from a variety of sources including the omnipresent drug manufacturers Ciber–Geigy and Roche. The conferences were important in helping to establish the credentials of psychiatry among the other, better-known and better-funded medical disciplines. They also opened the way for a revaluation of orthodoxies and for research into hitherto-overlooked subjects such as indigenous modes of diagnosis and treatment. In the foreword to the report from Bakuva there is an overview of the challenges facing psychiatry on the continent, migratory labour being singled out as particularly important.[1] Professor Sir Aubrey Lewis's inaugural address at the Abeokuta conference pointed to a number of problems facing African societies and noted that social change, depriving many individuals of a sense of purpose, would lead to anxiety and insecurity.[2] In passing, he observed that there was no evidence suggesting that mental illness in the African differed markedly from that found in the European. This issue was, of course, not so easily resolved, and over the coming decades research continued into the epidemiology of mental disorders in the sub-Saharan region.[3]

The second step towards change took the form of a series of articles and books by the West Indian-born psychiatrist Frantz Fanon, aimed at exposing the political foundations upon which ethnopsychiatry rested. Fanon, born in Martinique in 1925, had fought for the Free French forces during World War II, and after the war had studied medicine, specializing in psychiatry, at Lyon. In 1953 he had accepted on a whim a post at Blida-Joinville, Algeria's largest psychiatric hospital, located some 20 kilometres outside Algiers. Fanon is the one psychiatrist from the colonial era whose name is familiar to a wide audience. For a time his book *The Wretched of the Earth* seemed uniquely relevant to understanding the relationship between the First and Third Worlds.

Fanon was the most eclectic of writers; a Marxist of sorts and an acquaintance of Jean-Paul Sartre, he was also much influenced by the body of literature known as Negritude. Poets of Negritude such as Césaire and Léopold Senghor sought to understand and to change colonial reality by explaining the colonial relationship in terms of a clash of fundamentally different cultures: European culture, concerned with material development, and black culture, with spiritual values. By treating alienation simultaneously as a purely personal experience and as the experience characteristic of a race, Negritude envisioned an abstract solidarity of the whole Negro race irrespective of the social or economic realities defining the lives of groups or individuals. Its supporters claimed that Negritude played a progressive role in the anti-colonialist movements by giving African peoples a sense of pride in the achievements of their race. It was, however, an avocation of Western-educated intellectuals, and its central idea of racial solidarity helped to obscure the deep class divisions within colonial societies. Because Fanon was a psychiatrist by training, his attitude towards the colonial experience was also shaped by ethnopsychiatry, which he first encountered as a medical student in Mannoni's *Prospero and Caliban*. His critique of ethnopsychiatry had two facets. In his political works he struggled with a cluster of problems posed by the theory of African inferiority, and directly attacked Mannoni and Carothers. In his clinical research he attempted to establish a new foundation for psychiatric practice. Because his clinical writings are little known, Fanon's readers have rarely seen his popular work in the context of the psychiatric theory that inspired it.

His first book, *Black Skin, White Masks*, written while he was a medical student, dealt mainly with colonial racism in the Antilles, which to this day remain under French rule. Its long and bitter critique of *Prospero and Caliban* is in some respects surprising. The purposes informing his and Mannoni's work were strikingly similar: both presented a psychology of colonialism dealing with both parties to the colonial experience, both explained how colonial rule was possible and necessary, and both set out to uncover the psychological and, by implication, the political preconditions for the development of an independent personality. Finally, both purported to be applicable to the situation of all colonized peoples.[4] Curiously, Fanon accepted Mannoni's account of the Prospero complex; he agreed that there was a connection between colonial racism and sexual guilt, and gave a similar account of the psychology of colonial violence. He opposed Mannoni, however, with regard to the concepts of inferiority and dependence, and the impact of colonialism upon indigenous culture. Fanon confused Mannoni's use of the Adlerian concept of 'inferiority' with his own term 'colonial inferiority'. For Mannoni the term 'inferiority' applied to a certain type of personality directed by self-will; it had nothing to do with any lack of political or moral courage (in fact, the opposite was the case). In Fanon's work, 'inferiority' was synonymous with racial denigration and the lack of civil liberties characteristic of colonialism. This confusion was compounded by Fanon's belief that the Malagasy was indeed a dependent type but that the dependence, rather than prefiguring colonial contact, was its most notable product.

According to Fanon, the arrival of the French did not, as Mannoni supposed, bring minor changes to the Malagasy personality. On the contrary, it obliterated that personality.[5] There were no common interests or values which could serve as a meeting-ground between the French and Malagasy worlds; the intrusion of the one necessitated the elimination of the other. The cultural and psychological shock attendant upon colonization 'inferiorized' the Malagasy, producing what he called the 'colonial personality' and what Mannoni termed the Caliban type. In his later writings Fanon referred to this process as the feature that distinguished colonialism from other forms of oppression.

Underlying Fanon's criticisms was the conviction that Mannoni's analysis was a justification for French imperialism. Fanon believed that by linking colonialism with certain qualities supposedly latent within the psyche of the Malagasy Mannoni had denied the role of social and political factors in the development of the 'colonial personality'. This was certainly true, but it was also true of *Black Skin, White Masks*, in which the concept of race (taken directly from Negritude) was dominant and there was as little reference to history, gender, nationality or class as there was in Mannoni. Consequently, Fanon's critique can be used effectively against his own work. Fanon carried his engagement with Mannoni to Algeria, and there were frequent references to *Prospero and Caliban* in each of his African works. To an extent that encounter set the boundaries of Fanon's intellectual career.

Fanon's first attempt at producing a counter to Mannoni's portrait of the colonial subject was an essay entitled 'The North African Syndrome', first published in 1952.[6] During the four years he spent in Lyon, Fanon had become familiar with the large number of North African men who flocked to that city in search of work. As expatriates, they often found their way to the out-patient departments of public hospitals, where they were treated with the same contempt that awaited them in the city's factories and hostels. As a medical student, Fanon soon encountered the disorder known colloquially as the 'North African Syndrome'. Expatriate workers would present themselves to physicians with a series of vague complaints. The physicians would be unable to identify the problem, and patients would leave armed with prescriptions or courses of treatment which they would then fail to follow. Within weeks they would return complaining of the same symptoms. From the hospital staff's experience of these 'malingering' North Africans grew an oral tradition which explained the disorder. It was seen to serve the patient's need to escape from work and enjoy the warmth and inactivity of the hospital environment: in short, to become a social parasite. Fanon, appalled by this tradition, argued that the Muslim's illness was a genuine response to the strains of expatriation and to the racism he encountered in metropolitan France. Treating these patients required recognizing the reality of their suffering and changing the social conditions which made their lives a misery. In short, the answer to these medical problems was political action.

Expatriation was a feature of labour patterns throughout Africa – for example, John Chavafambira was a migrant worker from Southern Rhodesia, although this fact was peripheral to Sachs's understanding of his life. Though expatriation was never mentioned in the clinical literature, it was such individuals who were most likely to find their way to Ingutsheni or Mathari. In this context 'The North African Syndrome' was a reminder of the unwillingness of physicians such as Carothers and Sachs to accord their patients suitable biographies. To Fanon it also suggested that they were complicit in the political and social oppression which caused such illness.

While employed at Blida, Fanon produced papers on confessional behaviour, the provision of day care for Muslim patients and Muslims' attitudes towards mental illness. He also wrote a brief review of the ethnopsychiatric literature from British and Francophone Africa.[7] Each of these articles was addressed to the problem of providing effective care for inmates of colonial asylums and replacing ethnopsychiatric theory with what he conceived to be an authentic scientific perspective. Although these articles presented the only contemporary critique of ethnopsychiatry, in subsequent reviews of the discipline they have been ignored.[8]

In 'The Attitude of the Maghrebian Muslim towards Madness', published in 1956 in collaboration with Dr Francois Sanchez, Fanon attacked in particular what he called the 'School of Algiers'.[9] Although Tooth and Carothers had noted the value of traditional systems in providing care for the insane, they had ignored the ways in which those systems functioned. Such an attitude was common; consequently physicians knew little about the fears or expectations of the men and women who filled the wards of colonial asylums. Fanon and Sanchez set out to correct that situation, at least in the case of the North African Muslim. They pointed out that Europeans believed that the mad were implicated in their own illness. For example, if a patient was aggressive, that aggression was seen as expressing, however imperfectly, the patient's will. The insane were perceived both as having lost control of themselves and as using their illness to their own advantage – such as expressing antagonism towards family members. To Western eyes the insane were not innocent. In contrast, for Maghrebian Muslims the mentally ill were merely the innocent victims of spirits which temporarily possessed their minds. It was not the patient's fault if he insulted his mother or tried to attack a stranger, and no one would dream of accusing him of disrespect or of harbouring murderous wishes. In principle the sick person was never excluded from the community, as his underlying personality was assumed to remain intact no matter how severe or prolonged the psychosis. Fanon and Sanchez explained that 'if a recovery comes about the patient is able from that time to take up again his place in society without fearing mistrust or ambivalence on the part of the group'.[10] Because no stigma was attached to mental illness, a man or woman might speak without embarrassment of a family history of insanity. It might even be mentioned in a marriage contract, with the husband agreeing to take his wife periodically to a shrine or a marabout (traditional healer).[11] Any person who was mentally ill was fed, cared for and maintained. While conceding that traditional means of treatment and care were, from a quantitative point of view, unsatisfactory, Fanon and Sanchez noted that on the human plane these methods were admirable.

The majority of the insane were seen by Muslims as attacked by malevolent spirits, and accepted as ill. A second, far smaller group, by European standards also ill, was believed to have divine insight and venerated. Pointing out the error of European observers who had taken this esoteric group as representative, Fanon and Sanchez commented: 'It is not the madness which arouses respect, patience, indulgence; it is the man attacked by madness.'[12] They cited no documentary evidence supporting the notion that Muslims venerated the insane, intimating that the idea, like the North African syndrome, arose largely from an oral tradition. In a practical sense, their paper demonstrated the importance of accommodating a knowledge of traditional beliefs within a modern psychiatric programme. It also highlighted the ethnocentrism of Western psychiatry. Neither at Mathari, Blida nor Ingutsheni was allowance made for the ways in which patients or their relatives understood the causes or the experience of psychosis. With the assistance of his colleagues, Fanon did make some attempt at Blida to improve the care for Muslim patients by altering the hospital's regime to suit their specific needs. Those attempts were not always successful, and Fanon was later to admit that his own cultural presuppositions were often entirely unsuited to the North African environment.

During the colonial period, one of the most popular beliefs among white communities was that Africans were habitual liars. This idea found its way into the work of Carothers, Porot and Ritchie, where it was enshrined as fact. In Algeria Fanon discovered that the European community considered the North African a liar by nature, incapable of admitting culpability for any wrongdoing. In an article published in 1955 with a Blida colleague, Dr R. Lacat, Fanon set out to analyse this problem in terms of the colonial situation itself.[13] Once again this article brought him closer to a politics of ethnopsychiatry. Fanon and Lacat argued that confession was a complex act which could only be understood by reference to the relationship between the individual and the community. For instance, when a medical or legal official was attempting to establish culpability for a crime, attention had to be paid to the meaning of the act and its justification for the criminal. In effect, the official had to understand the way in which the criminal resolved for himself the questions of guilt and responsibility.

A Muslim who made a confession would often later claim that he had done so under duress. Alternatively, he might maintain his innocence even when confronted by incontrovertible proof of his guilt. In explaining such behaviour Fanon and Lacat examined the nature of the confessional act. Confession served as a form of ransom which reintegrated the transgressor into the community from which he felt temporarily outcast. However, where there was no bond between the individual and the community by which he was being punished, confession served no purpose for him.[14] According to Fanon and Lacat, in Algeria the Muslim population felt no sense of accountability toward the colonial legal system. If the Algerian confessed he did so without guilt because he felt in no way obligated to the authority which demanded his contrition. The Algerian Muslim did lie, then, but only because of the nature of the society in which he was forced to live. His lying was a reflection of his alienation. Fanon and Lacat laid the blame for Algerian lying at the door of French colonialism. They did not suggest that a natural community of interests between the Muslim and the colonialist could be easily created. Their only solution was to call for greater sensitivity on the part of physicians and courts in dealing with Algerians.

In 'Sociotherapy in a Ward for Muslim Men', Fanon and J. Azoulay explored the difficulties that arose when methods of care and treatment invented in Europe were applied in a colonial context.[15] Fanon had established a successful programme of socio-therapy for European (French Algerian) women at Blida involving patients' meetings, the creation of a newspaper, regular social events and work therapy. A knitting workshop made embroidery, curtains and tablecloths, while a sewing group assembled robes from material bought from the patients' own savings. For the long-term inmates, many of whom had been at Blida for years, the opportunity to wear bright new clothes – the product of their own labour – was valuable in alleviating a hitherto monotonous existence. Of these changes Fanon and Azoulay observed 'not only has the asylum life become less laborious but the pattern of departures increased quite plainly'.[16] What had proved suitable in the treatment of French Algerian women, however, was a failure when applied to a ward of Muslim men.

Since Fanon spoke no Arabic (having abandoned an early attempt to master the language) he had to employ an interpreter when conversing with patients. As a result the subtleties of the language were often lost, making it impossible for patients to convey their meaning to the physician. In addition the use of interpreters provoked hostility by reproducing the relationship of subordination experienced before any colonial official. Quoting Merleau-Ponty, Fanon and Azoulay lamented the fact that speaking a language meant supporting the weight of a particular culture; unfortunately, the language barrier on the ward coincided with the social barriers of the colonial order itself.

Although the aims of the new regime were explained in some detail to the inmates at a general meeting, the programme met with indifference. The daily meetings failed to stimulate contact between patients and staff, and after only a brief period were suspended. The games, singing and discussion groups set up to create a sense of team spirit and co-operativeness failed to hold the patients' interest, and they soon returned to playing cards and dominoes, listening to the radio and sleeping. Attempts to organize theatrical evenings also failed. The newspaper attracted only one contribution from a patient, a paranoiac who protested that masculine roles in a hospital play were to be performed by women. None of the patients and only a few of the staff read the paper, which came to be written almost entirely by Fanon himself. Most patients avoided the new work schedules and resisted attempts on the part of the staff to develop a community spirit. Fanon and Azoulay commented: 'Thus, not only had we been unable after these months and after many efforts to interest the Muslim patients in a type of collective life which operated in the European quarters, but the atmosphere of the service remained unbearable.'[17] The conditions on the ward, with chronic overcrowding and the absorption of most of the staff's time in mundane tasks, precluded therapeutic success. Junior staff were occupied with changing linen, settling disputes between patients and segregating difficult or violent inmates. As Fanon and Azoulay admitted, the atmosphere was oppressive, with frequent resort to punishment by confinement in cells and withdrawal of privileges. The introduction of a socio-therapy programme merely succeeded in increasing the workload of the junior staff, and this in turn aroused their resentment of changes they believed futile.

Examining the reasons for the failure, Fanon and Azoulay emphasized the interaction between the biographical and the cultural aspects of the programme. Socio-therapy, derived from psychiatric practice in France, presupposed a set of circumstances very different from those found in North Africa. The onus was on the patient to adapt to methods, values and behaviours common to the metropole. To create a therapeutic environment, the hospital programme would have to be reorganized in accordance with a philosophy of cultural relativism. Fanon and Azoulay pointed to difficulties which arose because of a lack of reliable information about Muslim society. The bulk of the work produced by the Algiers School had dealt with motor and neuro-vegetative phenomena; there had been no research on the sociology of mental illness, and no effort had been made by French ethnologists to grasp the totality of the Muslims' emotional life. This set the psychiatrists the task of designing a programme in line with the particular needs of Algerian patients: 'There was a hurdle to get over, a transformation of values to be made. Let us say that it was necessary to pass from the biological to the institutional, from the material to the cultural.'[18] Physicians had to be armed with an understanding of the dominant values shaping Muslim aesthetics, morality and sociability.

In the absence of research, Fanon and Azoulay attempted to identify those dominant values. The bulk of their analysis was devoted to economic factors and the development of new classes under the impact of French colonialism. Although they did not argue the point openly, the article suggested the existence of important connections between the colonial system and the incidence of mental illness. Four spheres of Muslim life were distinguished, each with its own set of values and characteristics. First, Muslim society was theocratic in spirit, with Islamic belief dominating civil law, morals, science and philosophy. Second, Algeria was a patriarchal society in which the father ruled with absolute authority. The family itself was organized as an extended unit, with many individual families forming a single large conglomerate. The natural social unit was the clan, which was governed by a *djema* or council. In traditional society, the largest group in which the individual found his identity was the clan and not, as in Europe, the nation. Third, Algeria was ethnically complex and composed of various minority groups. The largest of these was the Kabyle, which, although sharing the majority's religion, had its own language and identity. Fourth, Algerian society included a landless, unskilled working class from which most of the patients at Blida were recruited.

Prior to the French conquest, land was held communally, and the major economic issue was the richness of particular plots of land or the acquisition of animals for farming. Upon their arrival the French forced a redistribution of resources, with the collective land being expropriated by large private owners. The resultant class system saw a division between a few major landholdings owned mostly by Europeans and a mass of small proprietors, or *fellahs*, eking out a painful existence on tiny parcels of the worst land. While in the past peasant farmers had often been poor, it was not until the expropriation of communal land that they had been subject to what Fanon and Azoulay called 'proletarianization'.[19] Many farmers were forced by this combination of circumstances to take up day labour, which further divided the peasantry into smallholders and landless labourers. With the introduction of new technologies on the large estates, the demand for labour decreased and this forced landless labourers to seek work in the cities, where, in the absence of industry, they found little opportunity for employment. Through the combined action of land alienation and the mechanization of agriculture, there developed a landless sub-proletariat, the victims of increasing social inequalities. The emergence of a permanent migrant labour force in metropolitan France was the final result of this complex process.

Nomadism, which for centuries had been an integral part of Algerian life, had always been accompanied by a sedentary attachment of some kind, and individual identity was guaranteed through tribal affiliation. In contrast, the new nomadism of those seeking work in metropolitan factories was quite different: it led to a degenerative detribalization in which normal ties between the individual and the community were eroded if not completely destroyed. The bulk of the Muslim patients at Blida were the victims of this process. Of 220 males at Blida, 78 were found to be landless peasants who had been forced to seek work in the cities. Of this group only 20 had specialized skills, the rest having had to accept menial work. Only 35 owned any land.[20]

According to Fanon and Azoulay, the implications of this study for a psychotherapeutic programme were obvious. The meetings between patients and staff had failed because the staff had no conception of suitable topics for conversation. Likewise, the proposed festivals and choral evenings were inappropriate because they ran counter to normal practice within Islamic culture. The Muslim indifference to theatre and team games was inevitable, since such activities had no place in the peasant's life experience. Although the films shown had been carefully chosen with emphasis upon action cinema set in the familiar North African landscape, their psychological orientation had been quite alien to the Muslim audience. Films such as *King Solomon's Mines*, *Rio Grande* and Jean Cocteau's *The Wedding of Sand* held little appeal to peasant farmers. The patient newspaper had attracted few readers because few of the patients could read. The set tasks of weaving or basket making were quite beyond the experience of these men, while the attempt to set up a raffia workshop was doubly fated to fail: the Muslims regarded this type of work as suitable only for women. Fanon and Azoulay concluded that work therapy could succeed only if it was redirected towards manual labour. When this was combined with the setting up of a Moorish cafe – the regular celebration of Muslim festivals and occasional visits by a story-teller – the first steps towards establishing a therapeutic environment had been achieved.

An immediate reaction upon reading 'Sociotherapy' is astonishment at the authors' naivety – not only their admitted ignorance of the lives of their Muslim patients but their enthusiasm for the traditions of Western psychiatry, which, as they recognized, provided little insight into their patients' lives. Contrary to the protestations made in *Black Skin, White Masks*, Fanon was not free of the vision of a universal psyche with its eternal patterns of need, growth and maturation, each separated by the same perennial crises. Race and racial identity dominated Fanon's first book; 'Sociotherapy' was his attempt to divest himself of such prejudices. Beyond this, what was significant about the article is its use of social factors to explain mental illness. In 'The North African Syndrome' a formal connection was assumed between expatriation and the psychosomatic disorders suffered by migrant workers, but Fanon offered no analysis of the causes of expatriation. His patients at Blida were drawn from the same population as those migrant workers, but only with a theory of imperialism or a concept of social class could he explain why they were oppressed. Fanon's Muslim patients were marginal men, the heroes of *The Wretched of the Earth*, trapped between a decaying culture and the fate of a modern poverty. A 'cure' for these men had to include the opportunity to find employment and thereby to lead a reasonable life. Yet about these issues Fanon and Azoulay said nothing. In writing of the hospital as a social milieu, they were confident about what was needed to create a dis–alienating or curative environment and of how disordered behaviour was generated by oppressive confinement. With regard to the wider social order, they remained hesitant. Fanon's enthusiasm for what he was later to term 'national culture' and the importance he attached to traditional mores in the maintenance of individual identity appeared in embryonic form in 'Sociotherapy'. Over time he came to see national culture as filling the gap in his analysis between the individual (psychiatry) and the race (Negritude).

By 1960 Fanon had come to believe that there was a causal connection between the colonial system and mental illness, thereby accepting the implications of his clinical studies. In *The Wretched of the Earth*, for example, he referred obliquely to 'Sociotherapy' when he commented: 'We have since 1954 in various scientific works drawn the attention of both French and international psychiatrists to the difficulties that arise when seeking to cure a native properly, that is to say, when seeking to make him thoroughly a part of the social background of the colonial type.'[21] It took some years for Fanon to arrive at the conclusion that in the colonial world psychiatry was political work.

Whereas in his first book Fanon had attacked ethnopsychiatry largely on methodological grounds, in *The Wretched of the Earth* he was chiefly concerned with its political implications. Yet a comparison of the two studies makes it apparent that he did not progress easily towards that political critique. He vacillated between accusing the ethnopsychiatrists of methodological naivety, of ignoring the social context of the subject, of political duplicity and of moral weakness in the face of social injustice; it was only in *A Dying Colonialism* and *The Wretched of the Earth* that he attacked them as agents of colonialism. For instance, in his first book Fanon conceded that although Mannoni was misguided, his 'analytic thought is honest'.[22] In 'Syndrome', 'The Attitude' and 'Confession' he sought to replace the existing orthodoxy based upon racist assumptions with a genuine psychology. In his final works he abandoned his commitment to science in favour of a commitment to political action. Even so, the shadow of ethnopsychiatry hung heavily over his theory of revolutionary nationalism, in which the figures of Carothers and Mannoni were far more important than those of Marx and Lenin, the theorists among whom Fanon sought to place himself.

The belief that race determined culture was far older than Negritude and has its origins as one of the shibboleths of imperialism. Ritchie and Mannoni, for example, referred to the role of culture in the development of personality. Both ethnopsychiatry and Negritude assumed culture to be a function of race, and this implied that disparities in power between Europeans and Africans were deserved and inviolate. It was for that reason that, in what is probably his most important essay, Fanon set out to analyse the relationship between race, culture and personality.[23] In 'Racism and Culture', he argued that colonialism was a dynamic system which, like its supporting ideology, changed with modifications in the prevailing means of production, and he suggested how this in turn was linked with the emergence of the colonial personality. *A Dying Colonialism* and the fourth chapter of *The Wretched of the Earth*, 'On National Culture', contained Fanon's views on the role of culture within the decolonization process.

Fanon distinguished two modes of colonial racism. The first was 'vulgar racism', in which the inferiority of the native was proved by reference to physiology. Claims that the African possessed a smaller brain than the European or that he was intellectually retarded were as common to ethnopsychiatry as they were familiar to readers of Victorian ethnography. Fanon made specific reference to the work of Carothers as an exponent of this science. The second, 'cultural racism', was a more sophisticated form in which the object was no longer the physiology of the individual but the cultural style of a people. References to the lazy cortex were replaced by studies of 'Occidental values'. Although he made no mention of Mannoni, there was no doubt that for Fanon *Prospero and Caliban* was the leading example of cultural racism. Vulgar racism was, he argued, becoming obsolete. The European experience of Nazism, with its apparition of a colonial system at the heart of Europe, had made the African colonies an embarrassment for liberal democratic regimes. Combined with the growing opposition to colonialism among the working classes in the metropoles, this had helped to undermine the less sophisticated justifications for colonialism. Finally, the evolution of techniques (by which Fanon meant changes to the prevailing means of production) had altered forever the relationship between Europe and the Third World.

Fanon's argument was that the form racism took was dependent upon the mode of the colonial relationship and that racism, rather than being a psychological flaw, had to be understood in terms of the political and economic function it served – systematic oppression. He hoped to convince his readers that the research of Carothers and Mannoni corresponded to the dominant ideologies accompanying distinct phases of colonial history and was nothing more than an adjunct to imperialism. Yet his argument was ambiguous. He misled his readers into believing that vulgar and cultural racism were neatly sequential; in fact there were, for example, elements of each in the work of Carothers and Ritchie. More important, his critique was compromised by his endorsement of the theory of African inferiority.

In *A Dying Colonialism* Fanon explored the indigenous response to European domination through what he termed 'the colonial personality' – an idealized portrait of men and women made deficient and fearful by the destruction of their natural means of sociability. He pointed in particular to a cultural withdrawal which he suggested accompanied colonialism and allowed the indigenous population to retain a semblance of its originality. Under colonial conditions the Algerian's response to even genuine offers of help became undiscriminating, as he perceived 'the doctor, the engineer, the school teacher, the policeman, the rural constable, through the haze of an almost organic confusion'.[24] In the case of medical care, the Muslim would approach the hospital and the physician with fear rather than hope, his attitude being comparable to that of the phobic. Within Fanon's theory this process is framed exclusively in terms of culture, and there is little reference to capital or to the creation of new classes or to the influence of urbanization.

In *The Wretched of the Earth* Fanon claimed that colonial occupation called a halt to the development of indigenous culture in almost every field of activity.[25] He also suggested that the destruction of local culture was part of colonialist policy. Under such conditions, local culture 'becomes a set of automatic habits, some traditions of dress and a few broken-down institutions'.[26] Paradoxically, in *The Wretched of the Earth* Fanon's choice of the peasantry as the revolutionary class arose out of his belief in the revolutionary significance of cultural withdrawal. He considered the peasantry 'a coherent people who go on living, as it were, statically, but who keep their moral values and their devotion to the nation intact'.[27] Such an attachment was vital to the maintenance of an independent identity and, ultimately, to the development of a revolutionary consciousness. This argument was of course borrowed from Negritude, Fanon substituting the particularities of culture for a myth about racial identity. It associated traditionalism with the nation and the urban setting with cultural degeneration.

In 'Colonial Wars and Mental Disorders', the fifth chapter of *The Wretched of the Earth* and a chronicle of Fanon's experience in Tunisian hospitals treating the victims of the Algerian revolution, Fanon contended that colonialism was the cause of mental illness. He now suggested that the African inferiority to which the ethnopsychiatrists had pointed was, like those disorders arising directly from the Algerian revolution, a reactional phenomenon. According to Fanon, colonialism produced a colonial personality characterized by, among other features, a profound sensitivity. The daily confrontations, typically violent, between the colonized and the colonial system inflicted successive psychic injuries leading to the erosion of self-respect. These continuous assaults upon personality were at their zenith during the period between the wars: 'There is thus during this calm period of successful colonisation a regular and important mental pathology which is the direct product of oppression.'[28] This pathology involved self-doubt, hypersensitivity and a propensity for violence. Fanon saw in this subjective aspect of colonialism the 'tinctures of decay' that might well plague the newly independent African nations.[29] Of the three terms in this syndrome, only violence was taken directly from the ethnopsychiatrists.

In Fanon's writings there is no single model describing colonial alienation but rather a number of partly conflicting, partly complementary accounts of the impact of colonialism upon personality. This is because his concern with psychology had three distinct aspects: his clinical involvement at Blida and later at Charles Nicolle in Tunis with the victims of colonialism, his personal or autobiographical interest, best seen in his study of Martinique, and his concern with the politics of social structure and mental illness. The colonial peoples who appeared as the subjects in each of these aspects differed in class origins, cultural affiliations and colonial situations. Yet in his political works Fanon did not make these distinctions. He had begun his anatomy of colonialism with the idea, drawn directly from ethnopsychiatry, that all colonial peoples were the same. That idea, reinforced by his encounter with Negritude, which subordinated class and nationality to race, was an idea he never managed to transcend. In pursuing this line of argument, Fanon ignored the most important lessons to be learnt from his own research on Martinique and North Africa.

According to Fanon, settler colonialism created a mythology which both justified and perpetuated European rule. It was that set of myths about the native's laziness and brutality which was acquiesced in by the colonized themselves and codified in the science known as ethnopsychiatry. In *The Wretched of the Earth* Fanon conceded that the colonized were lazy and that the Algerian was violent. He explained that where colonial rule was stable this propensity to violence was channelled into self-hatred and muscular tension, these attributes defining the colonial personality. His theory owed far too much to a science whose politics was very different to his own.

In his attacks upon the ethnopsychiatrists Fanon always sought to maintain a contrast between their work and his. He achieved this by a prejudiced rendering of the texts which in the case of Mannoni resulted in serious distortions. This is understandable in that in so many respects his portrait of the colonial subject was a recapitulation of Mannoni's and Carothers's theory of African inferiority. His clinical writings suggest that during his years at Blida and Charles Nicolle he treated the usual variety of illnesses found in any colonial asylum. Those disorders must have included organic diseases such as dementia and syphilis, the very disorders which filled the wards of Mathari and Ingutsheni. Because he made no mention of such illnesses either in his clinical or in his popular works, he created the impression that all his patients were the victims of colonial alienation. This confusion was not helped by the fact that the insights found in the clinical papers about the relationship between mental illness and proletarianization were not incorporated into *The Wretched of the Earth*. In his clinical practice Fanon acknowledged that his patients were ill and in need of treatment, which, as a physician, he provided. He would not have presumed, however, that the withdrawal of the French from Algeria would have cured the schizophrenic or syphilitic inmates of Blida. In *The Wretched of the Earth* he came perilously close to just such a conclusion.

Despite its flaws, Fanon's critique of ethnopsychiatry has much to tell us about that science. In 'The North African Syndrome' Fanon drew attention to the pathologies of migrant labour, explaining the costs of expatriation, which were borne also by the patients at Blida. In 'Confession' and 'The Attitude' he exposed the ethnocentrism of colonial psychiatry. In his popular works, such as *The Wretched of the Earth* and *A Dying Colonialism*, he laid bare the connection between psychiatry and colonialism; in his hands the psychopathology of the African became a weapon for attacking French and British imperialism.

In *The Wretched of the Earth* Fanon used the theory of African inferiority invented by Carothers and Ritchie to fashion a critique of colonialism. His own writings were in a Marxist sense practical, and they were always intended to bring about political change. Through them he managed to defeat ethnopsychiatry as polemic, but in the process he ignored its importance as a science and its influence upon his own imagination. For example, in *The Wretched of the Earth* Fanon presented his concept of the colonial personality without any reference to a systematic theory of class (such as is contained in the clinical papers) or even ethnicity. As a result, the colonized remained an amorphous mass identified solely by their relationship to a dominant European culture. He failed to distinguish formally between the indigenous middle class or *évolués* like himself and the landless peasants who formed the bulk of his patients at Blida. Consequently, at times he wrote of the African peasantry as if its relationship to European culture were identical to that of Western-educated intellectuals. In the end, *The Wretched of the Earth* became a battleground on which the metaphysicians of Negritude struggled for supremacy with the science of Carothers, Mannoni and Ritchie. The outcome was a theory of the colonial personality just as disembodied as the doctrine Fanon was attempting to crush. In one sense, Fanon's failure to complete his critique of ethnopsychiatry was unimportant: the winds of change were sufficiently strong to destroy the foundations upon which the science of ethnopsychiatry rested. It was important, however, in another sense. During the 1960s and 1970s the analysis of colonialism presented in *The Wretched of the Earth* helped to shape theorizing about social class, nationalism and political transformation. Unfortunately, that theory carried within it a set of prescriptions about personality and human nature which the ethnopsychiatrists themselves had helped to create.

10   Conclusion

Theorizing about the primitive mind began in earnest in the nineteenth century. It was not until the 1920s, however, when asylums appeared in the colonies of Britain and France, that first-hand research into mental illness among African peoples was begun. The psychiatry of the colonial period was distinctive in various ways: the environment, the patients and the social location of physicians all differed from those encountered in the metropoles. In colonial Africa as in Europe, however, the profession was dominated by men. Arguably their masculinity influenced the way practitioners defined the ideal citizen, and the emphasis they placed upon violence. Margaret Field, the only woman among their ranks, produced unconventional work.

In terms of philosophy, the ethnopsychiatrists were a disparate group. Their intellectual affiliations ranged from British eclecticism to psychoanalysis. They worked independently of each other, most often in intellectual isolation. They had no professional association, no journals, and we know from Carothers that they did not have access to each other's research. It seems likely that Fanon was the first psychiatrist to have read the work of both Francophone and Anglophone specialists.[1] Despite their differences, the work produced by European psychiatrists conformed so well to a coherent set of ideas about race, class and gender that the ethnopsychiatrists can be classified as a school.

The ethnopsychiatrists shared a number of professional and intellectual interests. They were all senior state employees and, as male members of ruling minorities, shared a common social position. As intellectuals, the ethnopsychiatrists were members of the most exclusive white minorities in Africa. In Southern Rhodesia and Kenya this intellectual elite consisted of a small number of lawyers, missionaries, civil servants and farmers who were distinguished either by their education or their interest in the arts or the sciences. As can be seen from the writings of Karen Blixen, Doris Lessing and Llewellyn Powys, however, intellectual sophistication was not greatly valued.

Among the ethnopsychiatrists only Mannoni and Fanon acknowledged

137

the existence of colonialism or commented upon its relevance to the study of personality and the treatment of mental illness. The term colonialism appears so rarely in the literature that it is almost possible to survey the science without being aware of the context in which it was written. The ethnopsychiatrists supposed that their work had nothing to do with politics or wider social processes. They had no formal interest in relations between black and white communities and they ignored the ways in which colonial contact had reshaped African societies. Racism was a question that concerned neither Laubscher nor Ritchie, while, at the end of his career, Carothers was deeply hurt by the suggestion that his research was racist. Their science was about the individual or the race; it was not about ethnic or national groups, subsistence farmers or migrant labourers. Mannoni and Fanon were the only specialists who wrote about colonialism and the ideology of white superiority.

Mannoni believed that colonial racism was the work of petty officials, the kind of mediocre men who were driven to seek in the colonies the success that had eluded them at home. It was a vice fed by frustration, and could be explained by reference to the psychology of the individual. Fanon, in contrast, believed that racism served particular social and economic interests. Far from being the work of disaffected colons it was an expression of the ethos of the European bourgeoisie. The liberal view of racism, held by Mannoni, supposed that racism was an aberration of the human spirit which could be overcome by appeals to reason. The liberal view also assumed that racism and science were antithetical. Both of these ideas were wrong.

Ethnopsychiatry carried within it two key assumptions: that the colonial vocation was noble, and that the disabilities suffered by Africans were considerable. From these ideas came an explanation of the plight of white settlers throughout Africa and a warning that sudden political change would lead to violence and social disintegration. The clinical literature explained what many settlers firmly believed: that it was the African personality which forced otherwise democratic governments and men to adopt anti-democratic policies of the kind pursued by the French in Madagascar and the British in Kenya. The more the ethnopsychiatrists examined the African, the more keenly they felt the necessity for the existing colonial relations, and the more they felt the superiority of white society. Significantly, they were writing at a time when that superiority had come under serious attack from African nationalism and anti-colonial sentiment in Europe.

The ethnopsychiatrists did not write about mental illness among settlers, and white society was rarely discussed. It was always present, however, in their language: it appeared as order, reason, standards, discipline, sexual continence, self-control, altruism and prestige. Its antithesis was savagery, violence, laziness and sexual promiscuity. Like the concept of race in earlier literatures, the emphasis on the virtues (belonging to whites) and vices (belonging to blacks) was so strong that it erased all gradations from both societies. In the place of social complexity it produced a smooth, mythical homogeneity. And yet settler societies were anything but uniform, and their composition varied over time and place. In Kenya, for example, a significant number of settlers came from upper-middle-class and landed gentry backgrounds, while in Southern Rhodesia, Algeria, and South Africa there were large working class-minorities. Furthermore, in each of those latter colonies there were significant numbers of impoverished whites, the very people who were either excluded or forcibly expelled from Kenya.[2]

The period from 1920 to 1960 was one of extraordinary change within both Europe and Europe's African empires. It was also a period of sharp decline in the status of Britain and France as world powers. Many contemporary intellectual and artistic movements such as Nihilism, Dada and Surrealism supposed human nature to be fundamentally irrational, and social disintegration inevitable. Such ideas were also prominent in the works of Nietzsche and Freud, both of whom believed that savage impulses were a powerful presence within even the most civilized men and women. To many, these beliefs were given credence by the events of 1914–18, and were reinforced by the rise of fascism. Such ideas, however, found little resonance among the bourgeoisie of the day in part because they were antithetical to the imperial project. The idea of European superiority was also challenged in a rather different way by social anthropology. The doctrine of cultural relativism suggested that primitive societies were complex and operated according to rules just as elaborate as those which governed Europeans. Through colonial contact, some Europeans found their assumptions about themselves and their culture challenged. In social anthropology, unlike ethnopsychiatry, that confrontation encouraged various forms of self-examination and self-criticism.[3]

Most ethnopsychiatry was produced in the period when the demise of colonialism had become obvious. That can be seen in Mannoni's work on Madagascar and Carothers's monograph of the Mau Mau both of which were, to an extent, studies of the inevitability of change. A more subtle but no less telling source of change was suggested in Sachs's biography of John Chavafambira, which described the impact of urbanization and wage labour upon the life of one man. The same period also saw radical critiques of colonialism written by a new class of European-educated blacks. Césaire and Fanon drew an analogy between colonialism and

Nazism, and the irrationality which the ethnopsychiatrists had perceived within African culture was in their hands attributed to Europeans themselves. In Francophone Africa the cultural renaissance movement known as Negritude was influential in shaping the nationalist discourse, and eventually in defining the boundaries of the independence project. In British colonies the less influential doctrine of the African Personality served much the same purpose. The men and women who led the fight for independence were intellectuals who had been exposed to Western education at mission schools. As members of an indigenous intelligentsia they had been subjected to the slights of colonial racism about which Patrice Lumumba, for one, wrote with such poignancy.[4]

Mannoni believed that white settlers were an effete class because they lacked the vitality and ethos of a genuine bourgeoisie. Whatever the merits of his argument, the power of settlers was fragile. For a time whites held a monopoly over the legitimate means of violence and had some control over the management of colonial economies. They also owned the dominant culture. But their power was provisional. With the exception of South Africa, settler power lasted little more than the span of a single lifetime. By 1945, in most colonies settlers had already lost considerable prestige. That loss was reflected in the ethnopsychiatric literature which, in various ways, mirrored the tensions, anxieties and preoccupations of settler societies and the surviving texts convey something of the nostalgia, resentment and fear which were their dominant characteristics.[5] Settlers were anxious about the potential violence of Africans (Carothers/Porot), they were alarmed by 'Black Peril' (Laubscher) and they feared sharing political power (Mannoni). The ethnopsychiatrists idealized European society and refused to acknowledge the instability of the world in which they lived. Expatriates tend to view their former home society as static; however, in the work of Carothers and his contemporaries the image created of Europe was more than static, it was immutable. Consequently, far from encouraging self-inquiry or self-doubt ethnopsychiatry fostered an unreasonable confidence in the colonial project and an exaggerated fear of Africans. The doctrine of African inferiority not only described the limits to change, it contained the wish that change be impossible.

Administrators had little interest in theories about personality or race. For district commissioners and magistrates the question of race or difference was unproblematic. Their work was to settle disputes over marriage, divorce or land ownership, and did not require the making of wider judgements. Beside its narrow focus, official rhetoric was also open to scrutiny by imperial governments, and legislation along with colonial administration had frequently to be justified in terms of democratic principles. As a consequence, the discussion of Africans in official rhetoric was often ambiguous and lacked the purity of the psychiatric vision. Like all theories of temperament or human nature, ethnopsychiatry constructed ideal boundaries for the power of both dominant and subordinate groups.[6] In every colony such boundaries existed at law and were enforced in the structure of colonial economies. Those boundaries were also reinforced by a variety of symbolic devices which are embodied in the theories of African inferiority and hypersexuality.

Within ethnopsychiatry the term 'primitive' was used to characterize Africans, and no distinctions were acknowledged between town and countryside. Even so, the texts were structured around distinct classes of urban wage labourers and peasants. That distinction was evident in discussions of intellectual work and mental illness. Carothers often wrote of the intellectual failings of Africans as wage labourers, and in the work of Mannoni, Biesheuvel, Laubscher and Ritchie there were references to the ill-effects of Western education on the African mind. The intellectuals about whom the ethnopsychiatrists wrote were the Africans contesting with settlers for political power, and included the leaders of the nationalist generation. They were perceived as deficient in those qualities the ethnopsychiatrists regarded as essential to citizenship: self-governance, sublimation and discipline.

Like any science, ethnopsychiatry changed and developed over time. African inferiority, which was initially explained in terms of physical endowment and brain structure, became in the hands of later practitioners a function of cultural patterns and child-rearing conventions. The shift between somatic and psychological models was suggestive of the varied genealogies upon which the science was based and illustrates the instability of the social environment in which psychiatrists worked. However, in creating a theory of African inferiority the ethnopsychiatrists tried to ignore those changed circumstances and to produce an image of relations between blacks and whites which by 1945 had become untenable.

On the surface it appeared that social anthropology and ethnopsychiatry had much in common. That, however, was not the case. Ethnopsychiatrists were not interested in indigenous culture and they ignored the anthropological literature about their African patients. The sciences also differed in terms of their clienteles. The majority of the patients examined by ethnopsychiatrists were wage labourers, or at least lived in urban locations. For their part, anthropologists worked in villages and with few exceptions showed little interest in the social and demographic changes wrought by colonialism. Because the ethnopsychiatrists stood at the point of urbanization, they were better placed than were anthropologists to document and to understand the changes which would lead eventually to the disintegration of colonialism. While they gave no acknowledgement of that fact, their strategic location did force the ethnopsychiatrists to confront, in an oblique fashion, the major political questions of the day.

White settlers were much given to self-justification. The more violent they were, the more they tended to speak about their own civility and the violence of blacks. The same was true of sexuality. Although miscegenation was the preserve of white men, it was African men who were accused of wanting to rape white women. Civility was problematic for whites in Africa for two main reasons; settlers were in general recruited from among the less successful members of the European middle and artisan classes and tended to be sensitive about their class status. They also, on occasions, felt discomfort about their abuse of African labour. They were frequently criticized from home about their labour practices, and they put some effort into defending themselves against charges of brutality. The disquiet of Europeans over their own civility can also be seen in their evaluation of Africans. Settlers judged African behaviour against the kinds of internal self-controls or restraints regarding sexual conduct, citizenship, self-respect, the value of work, and the roles of men and women that cultured Europeans were expected to possess. Yet they also wanted blacks to be docile and undiscriminating labourers, a mass of humanity which was both conformist and capable of constant toil. It was because Africans lacked such habits that they had to be disciplined by the means of forced labour. Each of these concerns was refracted through the ideal of internal governance and it produced a particular theory about the subjectivity of Africans. In contemporary European history doctrines of individuality, based upon particularities of class, gender and ethnicity have been important in defining the boundary between the public and private domains. They have also been influential in designating the rights and obligations of citizens.

Most psychiatric texts are fabricated from the case-histories of individual patients. In schools as dissimilar as British eclecticism and psychoanalysis, the case-study both explicates and justifies the theory. By contrast, within ethnopsychiatry there were few case-studies and little reference to the kinds of particularities found in texts about Europeans. With the exception of Sach's *Black Anger*, there were no biographies; in general, ethnopsychiatry produced a literature without anecdotes. It was also a literature without individuals. Fanon's patients in Algeria and Tunisia were simply Muslims, Ritchie's Malozi were transposed into Africans, and Mannoni's Malagasy were colonial subjects. Those transpositions were important, and in order to understand their significance it is best to begin with the puzzle of depressive illness.

The idea that African peoples were immune to physical and emotional suffering goes back to the days of the trans-Atlantic slave trade. That idea also formed a durable element in the ethnopsychiatric canon. For almost fifty years, European psychiatrists could find no evidence of depressive illness among their African patients. They also found that sexuality was less problematic in African men and women, and that a lack of sublimation, in both sexual conduct and in the expression of anger, distinguished the African psyche. The problem of depression was connected to two major themes in the literature: to the clash of cultures thesis and to the causes of violence. In both the colonial and metropolitan literatures it was also allied to the concept of the individual.

As many scholars have argued, the concept of the individual in modern Western cultures is both highly institutionalized and historically specific. The obvious tensions between societies which demand conformity from their citizens and the doctrine of the sovereignty of the individual has been a theme in intellectual debate at least since Max Weber.[7] In evaluating their African patients, the ethnopsychiatrists employed a particular category of the person which carried within it a set of prescriptions drawn from that same milieu. In their hands, however, personhood had less to do with the possession of life-plans or consciousness than with self-control, especially in regard to sexual continence, and the sublimation of aggression. Laubscher, Mannoni, Smartt and Ritchie, for example, all deplored the sexual conduct of Africans, their lack of individuality and the rigid conformity to rule they believed typified African societies. Carothers found the Kikuyu were fear ridden, but their fears were the property of the group, not the person. He felt they should develop instead the kinds of internal governance characteristic of the British working class. According to Mannoni, among primitives there was no disharmony between the social being and the inner personality. The oriental face was firmly wedded to the whole being and the individual was held together by the collective shell. That shell provided a persona, which was more inclusive than the 'moral skeleton' found in Europeans. Mannoni believed the Malagasy were not individuals.[8]

Within European history there is a connection between the patterns of internal governance and the pacification of populations, a process which has been theorized most notably in the work of Weber, Elias and Foucault.[9] (Weber wrote about the bourgeoisie, Elias about the nobility and Foucault, in an oblique fashion, about the working class). The central thesis in Norbert Elias's study of European manners was the connection between the growth and extension of state monopolies over the means of violence and the tightening self-control over the passions of the ruling classes. 'The peculiar stability of the apparatus of mental self-restraint which emerges as a decisive trait built into the habits of every civilised human being, stands in the closest relationship to the monopolisation of physical force and the growing stability of the central organs of society.'[10] According to Elias, where a strong central power emerged, it was accompanied by a change in personality type among the nobility; the growing complexity, differentiation and interdependence of societies led to increased levels of the self-control expected of individuals. Where the process was most advanced, self-restraint became habitual.

According to Elias, in Western Europe this took place first among the nobility and then spread to the lower strata. In the early modern period masters were expected to exercise internal governance over their own passions and external governance over the behaviour of their wives, children and servants. As new capitalist and trade relations spread, masters from both the nobility and the 'industrious classes' began to condemn idleness, to stress discipline and exalt work. Instead of working hard to satisfy immediate needs and then stopping, what was demanded of labour was ceaseless toil. Writing in the 1940s Elias traced this development through the spread of 'manners', while Foucault has written of the same process in terms of surveillance and internalized authority. The modern Western notion of internal governance, be it in the form of civility (Elias), or work (Weber), or surveillance (Foucault), depended upon the existence of centralized states, the Christian churches, production for exchange, wage labour and incorporated populations, none of which existed in colonial Africa.

The form of obedience with which each of these theorists dealt revolved around the establishment of modern forms of subjectivity and the idea of freely rendered rather than forced compliance. As Foucault has suggested, those who failed to conform, such as the mad, ethnic minorities, women, or subordinate classes, were pathologized and subject to ostracism and systematic incarceration. While such a process may have been characteristic of Western Europe, it was foreign to colonial Africa if only because the power of the state was never so extensive. Despite these major differences in social context, the ethnopsychiatrists never tired of lamenting the absence of internal governance among Africans.

The science of ethnopsychiatry was invented on behalf of a declining colonial class to which the ethnopsychiatrists themselves belonged. Its subject matter was that of a rising class, the urban African. Black wage labourers and urban dwellers formed the majority of the inmates at Blida, Mathari and Ingutsheni, and it was they who inspired the theorizing of Carothers and his generation. This was seen, for example, in Carothers's study of African employees. It was also evident in Fanon and Azoulay's essay on socio-therapy in a ward for Muslim men, as well as in Fanon's final book, *The Wretched of the Earth*. The ethnopsychiatrists were the only social scientists to study urbanized Africans exclusively, and they did so from a vantage point which was unusual. In the lives of their patients, they saw vividly the impact that new economic relations were having upon indigenous cultures. Their position was one from which practitioners could easily look backwards to the pre-eminence of their own class and forwards to the rise of the class that would replace them. The sciences' nostalgia comes from the backward glance and the desire to restore what had already passed irrevocably. With the exception of Fanon, the ethnopsychiatrists refused to look towards the future, even though their own research contained ample evidence of the changes overwhelming colonial societies.

White settlers did not have to be told that their African workers were dangerous, lazy and unreliable, and their domestic servants stupid. Judging from the fiction or daily newspapers produced in the period between the World Wars, it seems that settlers complained of little else. Ethnopsychiatry was therefore irrelevant in the sense that it did not tell settlers anything they did not already know. Its importance lay in elevating that knowledge from the realm of anecdote to the realm of science. The voices of Carothers and Ritchie gained an international audience and to anyone who would listen, be it staff at the Rhodes–Livingstone Institute or the British parliamentarians who read Carothers's study of the Mau Mau, they represented admirably the interests of white settlers besieged by black majorities. The science validated a fundamental element within settler culture and justified the idea that their politics were forced upon them by the behaviour of Africans. The liberalism of their critics at home was a luxury which, so the science showed, they could not afford. It justified settlers' conduct towards African employees, and established the virtue of the societies they had built under the most trying of circumstances. The work of Carothers and his contemporaries provided a theory about the African as a flawed man or woman; it also explained the failings of Africans as citizens. Ethnopsychiatry was the settlers' most eloquent response to the challenge of African nationalism.

In the work of Carothers and Ritchie, Mannoni, and Smartt, the ideal subject was based on a vision of a bourgeois man who was already, at the opening of World War I, obsolete. He was the small, independent producer, who worked in the capitalist vocation identified by Max Weber; the father of a family who lived in a world he could both understand and, within his own domain, control. That man was the measure against whom the African was found wanting. Because he belonged to a history that had already passed, this figure suggests why ethnopsychiatry was imbued with such a mood of nostalgia. Over a thirty-year period the ethnopsy-chiatrists managed to create another symbol which politically was far more potent: the figure of the colonial subject. It was in the creation of that shadowy presence that the legacy of this modest science was most enduring.

Notes

1 INTRODUCTION

1. For example in 1940 the European population of Angola was 44,000, of Mozambique 27,000, and in Tanganyika 10,000. See Lewis Gann and Peter Duigan, *White Settlers in Tropical Africa* (Westport: Greenwood Press, 1977).

2. For an account emphasizing the diversity of the settler community see Alistair Horne, *A Savage War of Peace: Algeria 1954–1962* (London: Macmillan, 1977). For a study of settler society in the city of Bône, see also David Prochaska, *Making Algeria French* (Cambridge: Cambridge University Press, 1990).

3. Dane Kennedy, *Islands of White: Settler Society and Culture in Kenya and Southern Rhodesia 1890–1939* (Durham, NC: Duke University Press, 1987), p. 4.

4. Colin Leys, *European Politics in Southern Rhodesia* (London: Oxford University Press, 1959), pp. 14, 17.

5. Adam Kuper in his history of the British school takes this date as being crucial in the development of the discipline. It was in that year that W. H. R. Rivers died, and Malinowski and Radcliffe-Brown each published major works. See Adam Kuper, *Anthropologists and Anthropology: The British School 1922–1972* (Harmondsworth: Penguin Books, 1973).

6. A. C. Haddon, *Reports of the Cambridge Anthropological Expedition to Torres Straits* Vol. II: *Physiology and Psychology* (Cambridge: Cambridge University Press, 1901), p. 42.

7. For example see R. Littlewood and M. Lipsedge, *Aliens and Alienists* (London: Penguin Books, 1982), Ari Kiev, *Transcultural Psychiatry* (New York: Free Press, 1972) and Suman Fernando, *Race and Culture in Psychiatry* (London: Croom Helm, 1988). In general, monographs on the subject are addressed to specialist issues and to a specialist audience; e.g., Georges Devereux, *Basic Problems of Ethnopsychiatry* (Chicago: University of Chicago Press, 1980). Among the few works that examine the history and politics of the discipline are John Cox (ed.), *Transcultural Psychiatry* (London: Croom Helm, 1986), and Megan Vaughan 'The Madman and the Medicine Man: Colonial Society and the Theory of Deculturation' in her *Curing Their Ills: Colonial Power and African Illness* (London: Polity Press, 1991). For an anthropology of mental illness in a colonial society, see Lawrence Fisher, *Colonial Madness: Mental Health in the Barbadian Social Order* (New

Brunswick: Rutgers University Press, 1985). For a guide to the literatures of both the colonial and contemporary periods, see David Westley, *Mental Health and Psychiatry in Africa: An Annotated Bibliography* (London: Hans Zell Publishers, 1993).

2 PSYCHIATRY AND COLONIAL PRACTICE

1. Elliot Valenstein, *Great and Desperate Cures: The Rise and Decline of Psychosurgery and Other Radical Treatments for Mental Illness* (New York: Basic Books, 1986). It is difficult to underestimate the importance of technologies in the modern history of Western psychiatry. In fact, it is tempting to write that history by recounting the introduction of new techniques. For an example of such historiography, see M. H. Beaubrun et al., 'The West Indies', in John Howells (ed.), *World History of Psychiatry* (London: Bailliere/Tindall, 1975), pp. 507–27.
2. John Howells and P. Osborn, 'Great Britain', in Howells, *World History of Psychiatry*, p. 200.
3. John K. Wing, *Reasoning about Madness* (Oxford: Oxford University Press, 1978), p. 49.
4. Sigmund Freud, *Totem and Taboo: Resemblances between the Psychic Lives of Savages and Neurotics*, trans. A. A. Brill (New York: Vintage Books, 1946), p. 3.
5. *Ibid.*, p. 14.
6. *Ibid.*, p. 49.
7. *Ibid.*, p. 85.
8. *Ibid.*, p. 116–17.
9. *Ibid.*, p. 117.
10. E. B. Forster, 'The Theory and Practice of Psychiatry in Ghana', *American Journal of Psychotherapy* 16 (1962), p. 30.
11. *Ibid.*
12. E. B. Forster, 'A Short Psychiatric Review of Ghana', in *Mental Health Disorders and Mental Health in Africa South of the Sahara* CCTA/CSA–WFMH–WHO meeting of specialists on mental health, Bukava. CCTA Publication No. 35 (1958), p. 37.
13. See *Mental Health Disorders*, pp. 20, 28, 31.
14. See F. B. Hylander, 'Summary Information on Mental Diseases in Ethiopia', in *Mental Health Disorders*, pp. 35–36.
15. See 'Mental Hygiene and Mental Health in Mozambique' (anon.), in *Mental Health Disorders*, pp. 45–9.
16. Megan Vaughan, 'Idioms of Madness: Zomba Lunatic Asylum, Nyasaland, in the Colonial Era', *Journal of Southern African Studies* 9: 2 (1983), p. 220.
17. *Ibid.*, p. 219.
18. For an account of the patients' diet and a description of the physical conditions see Vaughan, 'Idioms of Madness', pp. 222–4. For a less critical view of Zomba see H. Shelley and W. H. Watson, 'An Investigation Concerning Mental Disorder in the Nyasaland Natives', *Journal of Mental Science* 341 (1936): 702–25.
19. See Shelley and Watson, 'An Investigation', pp. 715–17.

20. *Ibid.*, p. 704.
21. *Ibid.*, p. 710.
22. Under Watson's direction a small number of patients was being cared for at an 'approved institution', at the Utale Mission of the Monfort Marist Fathers. The five patients involved were visited on a regular basis by a physician from Zomba. This was the first attempt at an 'out-patient' programme and it signalled a change from a custodial to a curative philosophy. *Annual Report of the Public Health Department,* The Federation of Rhodesia and Nyasaland, Salisbury: Government Printer (1955), p. 33.
23. *Annual Report of the Public Health Department,* The Federation of Rhodesia and Nyasaland, Salisbury: Government Printer (1959), p. 43.
24. ZNA, *Public Health Estimates Chief Accountants Office: British South Africa Company,* T 5/3/1 1899 to 1900.
25. ZNA, *Estimates,* year ending 31 March 1903, T/5/3/4.
26. ZNA, *Annual Report of Southern Rhodesia Department of Public Health,* year ending 31 March 1905, p. 6.
27. ZNA, *Annual Report, Department of Public Health,* year ending 31 December 1907.
28. In that year the cost of Ingutsheni was £1,739 while the cost of housing twenty-seven nationals in South African institutions was £1,609. ZNA, *Annual Report, Department of Public Health,* year ending 31 December 1910.
29. ZNA, *Annual Report, Department of Public Health,* year ending 31 December 1911.
30. ZNA, 'Inspection of Ingutsheni': Inspector of Chests for the Auditor General, 10 June 1914.
31. In 1916 the cost per capita per diem was 1s 4d at Ingutsheni, 4s 6d at Salisbury Hospital and 5s 1d at Umtali Hospital. ZNA, *Annual Report, Department of Public Health,* year ending 31 December 1916.
32. ZNA, *Annual Report, Department of Public Health,* year ending 31 December 1916.
33. In December 1917 Ingutsheni housed 42 European male, 132 African male and 22 African female patients. The European staff was increased with the appointment of two extra attendants. ZNA, *Annual Report, Department of Public Health,* year ending 31 December 1917.
34. ZNA, *Annual Report, Department of Public Health,* year ending 31 December 1919.
35. A review of the budget estimates for the hospital for the six-month period ending 30 June 1924 shows a mere £50 allowance for drugs, disinfectants and surgical appliances for an institution of some 204 patients. The total allowance for that period was a little over £3,000. See ZNA correspondence, Ingutsheni Mental Hospital, Feb. 1924–Dec. 1928, Department of Public Health, S 1173/1439.
36. ZNA, Correspondence staff: salaries and conditions, medical director to the secretary of the dept of the colonial secretary 22/4/1924. Subject: submission made by the European staff at Ingutsheni. Ingutsheni correspondence Feb. 1924–Dec. 1925, *Department of Public Health,* S1173/143.
37. ZNA, Return for quarter on the use of mechanical restraint and seclusion, 30 September 1925. Lunacy Form No. 6, the auditor general S1173/143,

Ingutsheni Hospital.

38. ZNA, *Annual Report, Department of Public Health*, year ending 31 December 1932.

39. 'The Lunacy Ordinance of 1908' reprinted in *State Law of Southern Rhodesia 1908 to 1910*, XI (Salisbury: Government Printer, 1909), pp. 1244–63.

40. Prior to the enactment of the 1936 law Rodger was asked by the minister of health to write a review of the legislation as it would affect the day-to-day running of the mental hospital. Rodger provided a critique of the existing Ordinance and also expressed his support for the new legislation. He stressed the importance of early treatment for curable illnesses and the need to rid mental illness of the stigma attached to it. See ZNA, Memo: Dr Rodger to the minister of health 'Mental Disorders Bill', Dept of Internal Affairs S246/477, Ingut MH 20/1/1936 ZNA. See also comments made on the Bill by R. J. Morton, the solicitor general: 20/9/1935. Morton pointed to distinctions to be made between idiots, imbeciles and the insane, and the determination to treat criminal lunatics in the same way as any other sick person.

41. See ZNA, *Annual Report, Department of Public Health*, year ending 31 December 1936.

42. ZNA, *Annual Report, Department of Public Health*, year ending 31 December 1938, p. 42.

43. ZNA, *Annual Report, Department of Public Health*, year ending 31 December 1938, p. 44.

44. See D. Henderson and R. D. Gillespie, *A Text-book of Psychiatry* (London: Oxford University Press, 1956), pp. 421–22.

45. Two such cases are representative. Mrs F. D. Wright was admitted to Ingutsheni in June 1938. She was the wife of a farmer who, after protracted negotiations between her husband, the hospital and the Department of Internal Affairs was treated for a further ten months without payment. Mr Wright was also allowed extra time to pay the outstanding account for treatment already received. Department of Internal Affairs 18 June 1938: letter from Blackwell, secretary of Department to the auditor general and the medical director.

The second case is that of Stanley Albert Probart who was admitted initially to Ingutsheni and then transferred in March 1938 to Grahamstown Mental Hospital in South Africa. Probart had lived alone on a farm at Wankie when he became ill. He owed money to the Lands Department and his estate boasted more debts than assets. His transfer to Ingutsheni and his subsequent removal to Grahamstown generated correspondence between the auditor general, the chief native commissioner, the Department of Public Health and the hospitals involved over who would pay Probart's bill. See ZNA, *Department of Public Health* file No. 494/37 1938.

46. ZNA, district commissioners' files: letters on lunatics, Chipinga District S1057/3, 1942–1950.

47. ZNA, Department of Internal Affairs 3/2/1941. Nervous Diseases Hospital Correspondence S 2014/4/4.

48. ZNA, *Annual Report, Department of Public Health*, year ending 31 December 1943.

49. *Ibid.*

50. ZNA, *Annual Report, Department of Public Health*, year ending 31 December 1946, p. 10.

51. ZNA, *Annual Report, Department of Public Health* year ending 31 December 1947.

52. In June 1962 a psychiatric facility named the Chainana Hills Hospital was opened at Lusaka. It was staffed by brothers from the Order of St John of God and female nurses from the Franciscan Order of the Divine Brotherhood. Initially it catered for African patients, and Europeans continued to be sent to Bulawayo. The facility appointed a psychiatrist in 1962. By the middle of the following year it had a daily average of 250 patients. See ZNA, *Annual reports, Department of Public Health*, 1962, 1963.

53. ZNA, *Annual Report, Department of Public Health*, year ending 31 December 1957.

54. John. A. Carman, *A Medical History of Kenya: A Personal Memoir* (London: Rex Collings, 1976), p. 12.

55. KNA, Medical Department: Report 2/122, file no. 47/225: 'Admission of European Lunatics to South Africa'.

56. The South African authorities never welcomed this arrangement, as it only added to their own problems in providing adequate mental health care. From April 1931 the South African government restricted the numbers of lunatics and feeble-minded patients it would take from neighbouring colonies such as Kenya. KNA file no. PM 49/44: memo from under secretary of External Affairs, South Africa, to the colonial secretary, Kenya, 20 April 1931, 'Admission of patients to mental hospitals in the Union'.

57. See KNA, *Annual Report*, 1921, pp. 95–8.

58. *Ibid.*, p. 97.

59. KNA, *Annual Report*, 1929, p. 34.

60. Of the thirty-two deaths for 1927 the causes are listed as follows: epilepsy, four; heart failure, six; general debility, seven; malaria, two; and amoebic dysentery, two. The same pattern is found throughout the 1920s. See KNA, *Annual Report*, 1927, p. 42.

61. KNA, Medical Department, 1930: file no. 16/719 Deposit 2/9.

62. KNA format for 'Medical report on a prisoner remanded on a capital charge': Medical Department, 1930: file no. 3/292 TC829 62.

63. KNA, *Annual Report*, 1931, p. 43.

64. KNA, *Annual Report*, 1931 p. 35a.

65. According to Gordon's estimates the native female wards were overcrowded to the extent of 50 per cent above their intended capacity and the native male wards to 33 per cent. See KNA, *Annual Report*, 1932 pp. 53, 56.

66. KNA, letter Portuguese consul general, Nairobi to the medical superintendent, Mathari, 25 January 1933; subject: suitable diet for Portuguese citizens while in custody. Mathari correspondence file 24/1180/189, letter no. 5/33.

67. Letter from the medical superintendent of Mathari to the director of medical and sanitary services, 21 February 1938: KNA file no. Af. M286.

68. See letter from T. H. Maney, senior medical officer to the director of medical and sanitary services, 22 March 1932: KNA letter no. 3/7/145/32.

69. Letter from the director of medical and sanitary services to the senior medical officer, European Hospital Nairobi, 4 April 1932: KNA no. 26, 182/133 Vol 111.

70. Letter from the medical superintendent, Mathari to the director of medical and sanitary services 16 January 1940: KNA ref no. 31. See also letter from the acting crown counsel to the Attorney General's Office, 31 January 1940, in which counsel points out that patients suffering from delirium tremens cannot legally be admitted to Mathari unless they are also lunatics. KNA ref no. 122/3/111/59.

71. KNA, *Annual Report*, 1937, p. 71.

72. For an account of Cobb's career see Carman, *A Medical History*, pp. 74–6.

73. Interview with Dr J. C. Carothers at Havant, England, November 1986.

74. Maintenance of charges at Mathari Mental Hospital: KNA Medical Department file no. 2/380, 1944.

75. Letter from commissioner of prisons, Fort Hall to the director of medical services, Nairobi, 25 June 1946: KNA ref. no. Pris. 20/3/1.

76. Letter from the district commissioner, Fort Hall, to the medical officer, Fort Hall, 8 September 1947: KNA ref. no. 20/3/1.

77. Letter from the district officer, Machakos, to the medical officer in charge, native civil hospital, Machakos, 7 December 1950: KNA ref. no. L&O 17/6/2/207.

78. Letter from the senior medical officer, Nyanza Province to the director of medical and sanitary services, Nairobi, 14 March 1950: KNA ref. no. NP 6/50/245.

79. For a synopsis of this circular of 13 July 1939 see Dispatch from the Colonial Office, London to the officer administering the government of Kenya: 'Detention of lunatics in prisons', 13 September 1952: KNA ref. no. SSD 130/320/01.

80. See correspondence for the Medical Department's *Annual Reports* for the years 1947, 1948 and 1949: KNA file no. TC 787 3/40, pp. 29–31.

81. Correspondence for *Annual Reports*, 1949, p. 39.

82. Correspondence for *Annual Reports*, 1948, p. 41.

83. *Ibid.*

84. This problem did not end with the changing of the Act, and irregularities in the committal procedure remained common. One such case is that of the patient Phuita Maguru, who was committed to Mathari in 1950. Maguru's papers had been signed by a third-class magistrate, and therefore his detention at the asylum was illegal. According to correspondence his was the third such case from Fort Hall in a single month, and it appears common for patients to have arrived at the hospital with their papers 'hopelessly out of order'. See KNA letter from the medical superintendent of Mathari to the district commissioner, Fort Hall daily correspondence, Central Province 1932–1956: ref. no. AF.M 24/50.

85. Estimates, Mathari Mental Hospital for 1951: *Medical Department*, 18 April 1950: KNA ref. no. 3/564 TC 867.

86. E. L. Margetts, 'Psychiatric facilities in Kenya', in *Mental Health Disorders*, p. 43.

87. *Ibid.*

88. Crawford, B. K. A. 'The Developing Psychiatric Services in Kenya' in Lambo, T. A. (ed.) *First Pan-African Psychiatric Conference Report* (Ibadan: Government Printer, 1962), pp. 185–186.

3 SOME CONTEMPORARY REVIEWS OF COLONIAL MENTAL HEALTH SYSTEMS

1. He noted that there was a wide disparity between the official numbers of mentally ill, that is the numbers held in asylums, and the actual numbers of lunatics. See R. Cunynham Brown, *Report 111 on the Care and Treatment of Lunatics in the British West African Colonies, Nigeria* (London: Crown Agents, 1938), p. 12.
2. J. C. Carothers, 'A Report on the Psychiatric Services on Nigeria, 1955'. A draft copy was supplied by Carothers in Portsmouth in November 1986.
3. Carothers found that in the south that epileptics were shunned by their communities and fared far worse than the insane. See his Report, pp. 3–4.
4. Carothers estimates that 21 per cent of the criminally insane were held on such charges which did little more than confuse the distinction between lunatic and ordinary prisoners.
5. Carothers, Report, p. 15.
6. His recommendations covered all aspects of administration and servicing. Carothers provided a survey of the needs of each region and also of the needs of different categories of patients. He pointed to the importance of staff recruitment and training and the need for legislative change to bring Nigerian practice into line with contemporary English law. In an appendix he presented plans for the ideal principal mental hospital.
7. Carothers, Report, p. 34.
8. Tooth divided the country into three sectors: north, forest and coastal. In the north magic and witchcraft were seen as the cause of insanity. The insane were usually treated in the home; seldom mistreated or shackled, they were well fed and allowed to enjoy the company of children. In the forest region the mad were feared as a source of evil, and mental illness was a disaster. Madness was usually attributed to poisoning or magic. In the coastal region lunacy was a disgrace and as a consequence a girl with a mad relative might not be able to find a husband. Geoffrey Tooth, *Studies in Mental Illness in the Gold Coast* (London: Colonial Office, 1950).
9. Cunynham Brown had found that mental defectives constituted an average of 15.5 per cent of asylum populations, while Tooth's figure for the Gold Coast was only 3.5 per cent. Tooth commented, however, that his sample size was small and therefore could well be unrepresentative. Tooth, *Studies*, p. 51.
10. F. Fanon, J. Dequeker, R. Lacat, M. Micucci and F. Ramée, 'Aspects actuels de l'assistance mentale en Algérie', *L'Information psychiatrique*, 4th series, 1 (1955), pp. 11–18.
11. Fanon et al., 'Aspects', p. 13.
12. See F. Fanon and J. Azoulay, 'La socialthérapie dans un service d'hommes musulmans: difficultés méthodologiques', in *L'Information psychiatrique*, 4th series 9 (1954), pp. 349–61.
13. KNA, *Committee of Inquiry Report: Mathari Mental Hospital, 1933*: Medical Department, file no. 47/354, pp. 1–17.
14. *Ibid.*, p. 8.
15. *Ibid.*, p. 9.
16. *Ibid.*, p. 11.

17. Transcripts of evidence by Dr MacKenzie before the committee.
18. Evidence by Dr MacKenzie, transcripts of *Committee of Inquiry Report*, p. 74.
19. Evidence of Henry Telford Low, transcripts of *Committee of Inquiry Report*, p. 114. Low's evidence concerning the conditions for European patients was verified by Mr Arthur Warren. For fifteen years Warren's wife had been an inmate of Ingutsheni and he described the conditions in which she lived as 'awful'. Her room was small and dirty and she was given no medical treatment.
20. 'Memo submitted by the Toc H Committee in report of the commission', submissions and letters March to August 1942.
21. Letter from Coloured Community Service League to the medical director, Salisbury, 9 January 1945: ZNA correspondence, Department of Public Health, S 2410/15/1 file no. 6, 1945 to 1950.
22. Letter from the medical director to the secretary of internal affairs, 16 January 1946: ZNA correspondence, Department of Public Health, S 2410/15/1.
23. See, for example, David Rothman, *The Discovery of the Asylum* (Boston: Little, Brown, 1970); Andrew Scull, *Museums of Madness* (London: Allen Lane, 1979); Michel Foucault, *Discipline and Punish* (New York: Random House, 1979).
24. Scull, *Museums*, p. 222.
25. Foucault, *Discipline*, p. 193.

4   TOWARDS A THEORY OF THE AFRICAN MIND

1. See for example, E. M. Green, 'Psychosis among Negroes: A Comparative Study', *Journal of Mental and Nervous Disease* 41 (1914), pp. 697–708 and John. E. Lind, 'The Dream as a Simple Wish-Fulfilment in the Negro', *Psychoanalytic Review* 1 (1913/14); pp. 295–300.
2. H. L. Gordon, 'Psychiatry in Kenya Colony', *Journal of Mental Science* 80 (1934): pp. 167–71.
3. 'An Inquiry into the Correlation of Civilisation and Mental Disorder in the Kenyan Native', presented to a meeting of the Kenya Branch of the BMA, Nairobi, 18 December 1935, subsequently published in *East African Medical Journal* 12 (1935–36), pp. 327–35.
4. Gordon, 'An Inquiry', p. 333.
5. H. L. Gordon, 'Sexual Perversions', *Kenya and East African Medical Journal* 6 (1929–30): 122–30.
6. H. L. Gordon, 'Is War Eugenic or Dysgenic?: That Is Does War Improve or Impair the Physical or Mental Qualities of Future Generations?', *East African Medical Journal* 19 (1942), p. 94.
7. An abstract of Gordon's findings was published by a colleague, James Sequeria who concluded: 'If it is proven that the physical basis of mind in the East African differs from that of the European, it seems quite possible that efforts to educate these backward races on European lines will prove ineffective and possibly disastrous. It has long been recognised among highly civilised races that the educational methods applied to the normal child cannot be applied to the backward defective.' Sequeria hoped that further research into this subject could be funded by either the League of Nations or

the Carnegie or Rockefeller Trusts. See James. H. Sequeria, 'The Brain of the East. African', *British Medical Journal* 7 (1932), p. 581.

8. See F. W. Vint, 'A Preliminary Note on the Cell Content of the Prefrontal Cortex of the East African Native', *East African Medical Journal* 9 (1932–3), pp. 30–1.

9. Cited in Vint, 'A Preliminary Note', pp. 52, 54.

10. F. W. Vint, 'The Brain of the Kenyan Native', *Journal of Anatomy* 68 (1934), pp. 216–23.

11. *Ibid.*, p. 217.

12. *Ibid.*

13. H. L. Gordon, 'Editorial', *East African Medical Journal* 2 (1934), pp. 39–42.

14. Attempts at aptitude testing were also few. One exception was the work of R. A. C. Oliver. Oliver carried out a series of tests on the intelligence of Kikuyu and white adolescents using white boys from the Prince of Wales School, Kabete and Kikuyu boys from the Alliance School, an academically selective Protestant college. The test used by Oliver was prepared by Oliver and presented in English. The Europeans had an advantage in terms of language by attending a superior school, while the Africans were older. The average score for the Europeans was 312.34 while that for the Africans was 266.40. Oliver argues that the reason for this variation is race, tests on American Negro adolescents, also of Bantu stock, having produced similar results. See R. A. C. Oliver, 'The Comparison of the Abilities of Races: With Special Reference to East Africa', *East African Medical Journal* 9 (1932), pp. 160–78.

15. This account of the life of Carothers was provided to me during a series of interviews at his home in Havant, England in November 1986.

16. Carothers used as his text Henderson and Gillespie's *Text-book of Psychiatry*, a manual which went through eight editions between its original date of publication and 1956. Even in the editions published after World War II it contains a long section expounding upon the merits of both positive and negative eugenics programmes. See D. Henderson and R. D. Gillespie, *A Text-book of Psychiatry*, 8th edn (London: Oxford University Press, 1956), pp. 45–59.

17. Carothers retired at the age of forty-seven in order to be eligible for employment in the British health service. At that time employment was restricted to physicians under the age of fifty.

18. J. C. Carothers, 'Some Speculations on Insanity in Africans in General', *East African Medical Journal* 17 (1940), pp. 90–105.

19. A similar pattern was found in the asylum in Southern Rhodesia, for it was among African women at Ingutsheni that the first lobotomies were performed. Presumably as at Mathari these women were perceived as the most difficult patients to manage. See Carothers, 'Some Speculations', p. 92.

20. Of 107 admissions at Mathari reviewed by Carothers, only 2 were cases of manic-depressive psychosis. Carothers, 'Some Speculations', p. 102.

21. See Henderson and Gillespie, *A Text-book*, pp. 300–42.

22. Carothers, 'Some Speculations', p. 99.

23. *Ibid.*, p. 100.

24. *Ibid.*, p. 99.

25. J. C. Carothers, 'A Study of Mental Derangement in Africans and an Attempt

to Explain its Peculiarities, More Especially in Relation to the African Attitude to Life', *Journal of Mental Science* 93 (July 1947), pp. 548–97.

26. He excluded military personnel treated at the military hospital during the war and patients of Arab descent. Carothers, 'A Study', p. 47.

27. The rate of certification on the reserves was 2.3 per 100,000 while the rate for Africans living away from home was 13.3 per 100,000. Carothers, 'A Study', p. 58.

28. *Ibid.*, p. 73.

29. At Mathari Carothers noted the absence of obsessional forms of behaviour among the inmates and concluded that obsessive–compulsive neurosis was probably absent from the African psyche. In an African setting such individuals would appear entirely normal rather than pathological as they do in a European culture with its emphasis upon individual choice. 'Primitive culture is essentially obsessive-compulsive': Carothers, 'A Study', p. 83.

30. During my interviews with Carothers in Portsmouth in October 1986 he also referred to the typical cases of depressive illness he encountered at Mathari. However, in his published work his position on the absence of such illness among the African is consistent with that of his contemporaries.

31. Carothers supplied case-notes on the following patients who were admitted to Mathari with frenzied anxiety. The first case was that of a Mkamba man aged about thirty who had been living on a reserve with his wife and three children. On 10 January 1941 he was tried for the murder of his wife and youngest son. Before committing the murders he had told his sister-in-law that he was going to die and that he was worried about his wife. A medical examination found no evidence of mental or physical disorder. At his trial the accused explained to the court that his troubles had been caused by an old man in his village and that two days before the crime he had found charms at the entrance to his home. When Carothers first interviewed the man he was in good mental health but suffered amnesia about the crime. He told Carothers: 'If I had not killed my wife I would have died.' Carothers commented that the man was compelled to commit a murder and that any death would do to appease the gods. He was found guilty of murder but was deemed insane at the time of the crime (case file no. M:1005).

The second case was that of a Mkamba man aged about forty. He was certified insane by a local magistrate on 18 February 1939. He had been singing constantly at night and had killed a number of cattle belonging to other villagers. His speech was incoherent, and the magistrate had no hesitation in certifying him. By the time he arrived at Mathari, at the beginning of April, he was completely sane and in good physical health. An interview revealed a rather slow and selfish man who explained his temporary insanity as being due to his first wife whom he had wanted to abandon. He remained well and was discharged from Mathari at the end of April (case file no. M:398).

32. Carothers, 'A Study', p. 71.

33. J. C. Carothers, 'Frontal Lobe Function and the African', *Journal of Mental Science* 97 (1951), pp. 12–48.

34. *Ibid.*, p. 27.

35. 'If one asks any African a question, he is very apt to give the answer that he

thinks you want.' Another way to interpret such behaviour is to locate it within the context of relations between master and servant. See Carothers, 'Frontal Lobe Function', p. 31.

36. See Elliot. S. Valenstein, *Great and Desperate Cures: The Rise and Decline of Psychosurgery and Other Radical Treatments for Mental Illness* (New York: Basic Books, 1986), pp. 84ff.

37. Carothers, 'Frontal Lobe Function', p. 38.

38. *Ibid.*, p. 46.

39. C. G. F. Smartt, 'Mental Maladjustment in the East African', *Journal of Mental Science* 102 (1956), p. 444.

40. During the colonial era the standard medical text on illness among the African was Michael Gelfand's *The Sick African*. This monograph, over eight hundred pages in length, went through three editions between 1943 and 1957. Gelfand worked at Salisbury Native Hospital in Southern Rhodesia and he was eventually awarded the OBE. From its second edition *The Sick African* contained a chapter on mental illness, and Gelfand relied almost entirely upon Carothers. See Michael Gelfand, *The Sick African: A Clinical Study*, 3rd edn (Cape Town: Juta, 1957).

41. See J. C. Carothers, *The African Mind in Health and Disease*, (Geneva: World Health Organization, 1953), chapters 2 and 3.

42. Carothers was so impressed by the veracity of Vint's research that he went so far as to comment that the literature on the brain of the African stands or falls according to the quality of Vint's publications. See Carothers, *The African Mind*, p. 77.

43. See P. Gallais, G. Miletto, J. Corriol, and J. Bert. 'Introduction a l'etude de l'Eeg physiologique du noir d'Afrique' *Medecine Tropicale* 11 (1951), pp. 128–46. See also P. Gallais, J. Corriol, and J. Bert, 'Etude preliminaire des rythmes electro-encephalographiques chez le noir: analyse de 50 sujets'. *Medecine Tropical* 9 (1949), pp. 687–95.

44. A South African study carried out in 1953 failed to reproduce the French results. A. C. Mundy-Castle compared EEGs from a group of sixty-six normal Bantu men and women, all of whom worked as domestics or gardeners in Johannesburg, with a control group of seventy-two normal Europeans. The majority of the Europeans were younger and better educated than the African subjects. Using the same procedures as Gallais et al., Mundy-Castle could find no major difference between the two groups. He concluded that the French studies were of interest but had not been validated. See A. C. Mundy-Castle, B. L. McKiever and T. Prinsloo, 'A Comparative Study of the Electroencephalograms of Normal Africans and Europeans of Southern Africa', *Electroencephalography and Clinical Neurophysiology Journal* 5 (1953), pp. 533–43.

45. Carothers, *The African Mind* , pp. 42–54.

46. Carothers commented that infantile experience 'is no doubt of fundamental importance, but it seems that, though this experience sounds a very poor keynote for the time that follows, all later African education cripples the hands which might play a melody of sorts, in other cultures'. Carothers, *The African Mind*, p. 97.

47. The most important element in the process of intellectual development is the

achievement of what Piaget terms 'subjective relativism'. For an account of this process see Jean Piaget, *Judgment and Reasoning in the Child* (London: Routledge & Kegan Paul, 1969), esp. pp. 130–4.

48. Carothers, *The African Mind*, p. 100.
49. *Ibid.*, p. 102.
50. *Ibid.*, pp. 106–7.
51. *Ibid.*, p. 87.
52. Margaret Mead, review of Carothers, *The African Mind*, in *Psychiatry* 17 (1954), p. 304.
53. In passing Carothers noted the importance in African culture of the spoken word and suggested that this might well explain some of the key features of the mentality of primitive peoples. Mead believed this insight was important and perhaps it was for that reason that Carothers later developed the idea. See J. C. Carothers, 'Culture, Psychiatry and the Written Word', *Psychiatry* 22 (1959), 307–20, and 'Hysteria, Psychopathy and the Magic Word' *Mankind Quarterly* 16:2 (1975), pp. 93–102. The first article found an enthusiastic audience and in his book *The Guttenberg Galaxy* Marshall McLuhan acknowledges the inspiration he had found in Carothers's essay. See *The Guttenberg Galaxy* (London: Routledge & Kegan Paul, 1962), pp. 18–20, 22, 26–8, 32–4.
54. Mead, review, p. 306.
55. See for example Melville Herskovits, review of *The African Mind*, in *Man* 25–26 (February 1954), p. 30.
56. Jules Henry, 'A Reply to Mead's Review of Carothers' Book', *Psychiatry* 17 (1954), p. 402.
57. *Ibid.*
58. See J. C. Carothers, 'The Nature–Nurture Controversy', *Psychiatry* 18 (1955), pp. 301–4. Carothers was deeply affected by the criticism aroused by *The African Mind* and six years after its publication he wrote a second defence, arguing that individual statements from the monograph had been taken out of context. See 'Further Thoughts on the African Mind', *East African Medical Journal* 6 (1960), pp. 457–63.
59. Carothers's work did attract some criticism from his contemporaries although none of it was comprehensive. In 1958 H. J. Simons, from the University of Cape Town, produced a critique of what he termed 'the East African School of Medical Psychology'. Quite correctly Simons pointed out our inability to distinguish between environmental and inherited characteristics, a distinction central to Carothers's work. He also pointed out that at the time Carothers was working at Mathari, Kenya was in a state of social and political turmoil and questioned why Carothers never commented upon that fact. See H. J. Simons, 'Mental Disease in Africans: Racial Determinism', *Journal of Mental Science* 104 (1958), pp. 377–88.
60. Almost twenty years after the release of his first monograph Carothers published a second full-length work on the African. *The Mind of Man in Africa*, released by a British commercial press in 1972, was very much a recapitulation of the earlier study. See J. C. Carothers, *The Mind of Man in Africa* (London: Tom Stacey, 1972).

5 THEORY INTO PRACTICE: CAROTHERS AND THE
   POLITICS OF MAU MAU

1. See O. W. Furley, 'The Historiography of Mau Mau', in B. A. Ogot (ed.),
   Hadith 4: Politics and Nationalism in Colonial Kenya (Nairobi: East African
   Publishing House, 1972), p. 121. For the most impressive recent study of
   British violence during the rebellion see Robert. B. Edgerton, *Mau Mau: An
   African Crucible* (New York: Free Press, 1989).
2. See John Wilkinson, 'The Mau Mau Movement: Some General and Medical
   Aspects', *East African Medical Journal* 7 (1954), pp. 294–314.
3. Michael Kirby, 'The Unhappiness of the Kikuyu: Or the Seeds of Mau Mau',
   East African Medical Journal 10 (1957), pp. 529–32.
4. *Ibid.*, p. 529.
5. Of the Kikuyu Kirby wrote: 'The witchdoctors are all powerful and highly
   respected and can set their victims' nervous systems vibrating to produce
   frenzied and murderous actions. No wonder, therefore, that the usually
   cowardly race of Kikuyu have caused such trouble to the military and police
   forces.' See 'The Kikuyu', p. 531.
6. L. S. B. Leakey, *Mau Mau and the Kikuyu* (London: Methuen, 1952), p. 27.
7. See L. S. B. Leakey, *Defeating Mau Mau* (London: Methuen, 1955), esp. pp.
   127–41.
8. Frank Furedi, 'The Social Composition of the Mau Mau Movements in the
   White Highlands', *Journal of Peasant Studies* 1 (1974), p. 488.
9. *Ibid.*, pp. 491–3, see also David. W. Throup, *Economic and Social Origins of
   Mau Mau* (London: James Currey, 1986), pp. 4–8.
10. According to Throup in the period from 1941 to 1948 the population of
    Nairobi grew at an annual rate of 17 per cent. See Throup, *Social Origins*, p. 8.
11. See Throup, *Social Origins*, p. 248.
12. Letter from S. R. Mortimer, Member for Health, Lands and Local Govern-
    ment, Nairobi, to J. C. Carothers, Havant, 20 November 1953, ref no. OFF/
    13A. Carothers's personal files.
13. In the letter the terms of the appointment were specified. Carothers was to be
    paid on the same salary scale he was then receiving in the United Kingdom.
    He was also to be paid an honorarium of £100 for the period of his visit or else
    a daily allowance of £3. A return air fare was included.
14. J. C. Carothers, *The Psychology of Mau Mau* (Nairobi: Government Printer,
    1954).
15. *Ibid.*, p. 2.
16. F. D. Corfield, in his official history of the Mau Mau, provides a detailed
    account of the oaths and their content. He claims that many of the oaths were
    taken in daylight to heighten the initiates' fear and as they developed the oaths
    came more and more to violate customary law and Christian belief. The most
    extreme oaths featured menstrual blood and public sexual intercourse with
    sheep and adolescent girls. Some involved the violation of tribal taboos which
    terrified the initiates. See F. D. Corfield, *Historical Survey of the Origins and
    Growth of Mau Mau* (London: Her Majesty's Stationery Office, 1960), esp.
    pp. 163–9.
17. Carothers, *Mau Mau* p.21.

18. For a study of the movement's career in Southern Rhodesia, see D. G. H. Flood, *The Concept of Self-help in African Education as Exemplified by the Role and Function of the Jeanes Teacher in Southern Rhodesia Between the Wars* (Dip. of Education thesis, Institute of Education, University of Birmingham, May 1966).

19. According to Carothers, 'Morality in Africans lacks general application'. Carothers, *Mau Mau*, pp. 25–6. See also pp. 26–8.

20. Gordon also made the wry comment that being a bit queer did not prevent anyone from getting a job in East Africa. See H. L. Gordon, 'Mental Instability among Europeans in Kenya', *Kenya and East Africa Medical Journal* 4 (1927–8), pp. 316–24.

21. During the years of the emergency this idea was common as if the rebellion could be explained by the Kikuyu's failure to absorb the teachings of the Christian missions. In an editorial reviewing *The Psychology of Mau Mau* one physician noted the importance of Christianity in Carothers's report, commenting that he had shown the views of the missionary and the psychologist to be in accord. See 'Editorial', *East African Medical Journal* 31 (1954): 337.

22. Corfield, *Historical Survey*, p. 5.

23. He wrote of Carothers's report: 'It is a penetrating document, and I have consulted it freely to supplement my own knowledge of the African.' See *Historical Survey*, p. 8.

24. Corfield argued that the problem lay not in the presence of white settlers so much as in the African's poor use of the land, which increased the demand for larger and larger plots. See *Historical Survey*, pp. 20–1.

25. Jaspers chose these three individuals as embodiments of the European spirit, and while he acknowledged their limitations he treated them as heroic figures. See Karl Jaspers, *Leonardo, Descartes, and Weber*, trans. Ralph Manheim (London: Routledge & Kegan Paul, 1965), esp. pp. 44–46. See also Karl Jaspers, *The European Spirit*, trans. Ronald Smith (London: SCM Press, 1948).

26. See D. Henderson and R. D. Gillespie, 'Psychopathic States', in *A Textbook*, pp. 389–402.

6   AFRICAN INTELLIGENCE, SEXUALITY AND PSYCHE

1. See Francis Galton, *Hereditary Genius: An Inquiry into its Laws and Consequences* (1892; 2nd edn Gloucester: Peter Smith, 1972), p. 36.

2. The Australian-born psychologist Stanley Porteus is best remembered for his invention of the Maze Test, which purportedly provided a culture-free assessment of intelligence. This test, which was used widely as an adjunct to other more sophisticated models, required the subject to construct an exit from a maze drawn on a sheet of paper. His research was notable for the minuscule size of the test samples and for the intellectual shallowness of its central concepts. See Stanley Porteus, *Primitive Intelligence and Environment* (New York: Macmillan, 1937) and *The Psychology of a Primitive People* (New York: Books for Libraries Press, 1931). For a whimsical and unreliable account of his career, which spanned more than fifty years, see Stanley Porteus, *A Psychologist of Sorts* (Palo Alto: Pacific Books, 1969).

3. For a brief account of Biesheuvel's career see H. A. Bulhan, 'Psychological Research in Africa: Genesis and Function', in *Race and Class* 1 (1981), pp. 25–41.

4. Cited in S. Biesheuvel, *African Intelligence* (Johannesburg: South African Institute of Race Relations, 1943). See pp. 21, 220.

5. *Ibid.*, p. 31.

6. *Ibid.*, pp. 50–1.

7. *Ibid.*, p. 83.

8. *Ibid.*, p. 99.

9. *Ibid.*, p. 103.

10. Biesheuvel commented that the performance of African children in the standard tests of the kind used by Flick is probably from ten to thirty points below the level they would have reached under better circumstances. He noted the lack of facilities in schools for Africans, the size of classes and the dearth of qualified teachers. See *African Intelligence*, p. 114.

11. See Stanley Porteus and Marjorie Babcock, *Temperament and Race* (Boston: Richard. G. Badger, 1926), in which the authors denounce what they call 'race levellers' such as Franz Boas, who discounted the importance of inherited racial characteristics.

12. This approach brought Biesheuvel close to the work of later 'progressive' English writers on class and education such as Bernstein. See Basil Bernstein, *Class, Codes and Control*, vol. I (London: Routledge & Kegan Paul, 1971).

13. Biesheuvel, *African Intelligence*, p. 183.

14. *Ibid.*, p. 187.

15. In Southern Rhodesia and South Africa sexual anxiety was such that whites feared contracting syphilis from servants handling cutlery and crockery. See annual reports of the Bulawayo district commissioner, 1936 to 1942: ZNA S235/514–7; S1563. For an account of the ways in which sexual relations between blacks and whites were managed in Southern Rhodesia for the benefit of white men and to the disadvantage of the African community and white women see John Pape, 'Black and White: The "Perils of Sex" in Colonial Zimbabwe', *Journal of Southern African Studies* 4 (1990), pp. 699–720.

16. B. J. F. Laubscher, *Sex, Custom and Psychopathology: A Study of South African Pagan Natives* (London: George Routledge, 1937).

17. *Ibid.*, p. 28.

18. Laubscher, sensitive to suggestions that his interest in sexuality was prurient, offered several justifications for the scientific status of his research. (p. xv).

19. *Ibid.*, p. 49.

20. 'My scientific training and culture has given me one form of reality and his [the African's] mythology and culture pattern has given him another'. Laubscher, *Sex*, p. 221.

21. See Sigmund Freud, *The Future of an Illusion*, trans. W. D. Robson-Scott, (London: Hogarth Press, 1962), chapter 9.

22. One of the examples cited by Laubscher in proof of this veneer of culture was the African's facility to lie to a white man if he believed in so doing he would gain the approval of his family or his tribe. See Laubscher, *Sex*, p. 59.

23. *Ibid.*, pp. 236–7.

24. The ordinance states: 'Any person convicted of the crime of assault with intent to commit rape may be sentenced to be hanged or by the Judge's discretion to be sentenced to any lesser punishment [not specified] as the Judge considers sufficient.' See *The Ordinance No. 3 of 1903: Criminal Law Amendment Ordinance*. Although in the ordinance no reference is made to race, the death penalty was never imposed on a white man for any crime of rape or attempted rape. See also ZNA, 'Black Peril': S144/4.

25. Laubscher refers to eighteen cases of whom he claims only a small minority were circumcised. *Sex*, p. 270.

26. Archival records from Southern Rhodesia for the same period suggest that the rape of African women by African men was a common crime, especially in urban locations. These records are confined to cases that reached a district magistrates' court.

27. 'The active partners are usually the paranoids and the feeble-minded and the passive partners are the epileptics and dull schizophrenics and imbeciles.' Laubscher, *Sex*, p. 283.

28. Wulf Sachs, 'The Insane Native: An Introduction to a Psychological Study', *The South African Journal of Science* 30 (1933), pp. 706–13.

29. *Ibid.*, p. 713.

30. Wulf Sachs, *Black Anger* (New York: Grove Press, 1947). This was first released in the same year as Laubscher's *Sex*, under the title *Black Hamlet* (London: Geoffrey Bles, 1937).

31. Sachs, *Black Anger*, pp. 6–7.

32. *Ibid.*, p. 52.

33. *Ibid.*, p. 120.

34. *Ibid.*, p. 168.

35. Compare for example the statements made by Sachs on p. 168, where he described Chavafambira's flawed character, and p. 275; 'I had never regarded him as a patient: within the limits of his grim reality John was a relatively well–adjusted individual'.

7   THE AFRICAN FAMILY AND THE COLONIAL PERSONALITY

1. For an account of the pathologizing of the mother see David Spiegel, 'Mothering, Fathering and Mental Illness', in Barrie Thorne and Marilyn Yalom (eds.), *Rethinking the Family: Some Feminist Questions* (New York: Longman, 1982), pp. 95–110.

2. For a pioneering work see Eli Zaretsky, *Capitalism, the Family and Personal Life* (London: Pluto Press, 1976). For a more recent example of the literature on the emergence of the contemporary Western family form see Diana Gittins, *The Family in Question* (London: Macmillan Education, 1985).

3. Zaretsky argues that it is only under capitalism that the political economy of the family becomes obscured, making the family appear independent from the surrounding economy. As a consequence in the twentieth century the Western family has until recently been studied almost exclusively by psychologists and psychiatrists. See Zaretsky, *Capitalism*.

4. It was in Seacliff that many years later the novelist Janey Frame was incarcerated.

5. See Erik Olssen, 'Truby King and the Plunket Society: An Analysis of a Prescriptive Ideology', *New Zealand Journal of History* 1 (1981), pp. 3–23, and Kereen Reiger, *The Disenchantment of the Home: Modernizing the Australian Family, 1880–1940* (Melbourne: Oxford University Press, 1985), esp. pp. 142–7.

6. This account of the history of the Rhodes–Livingstone Institute is taken from Richard Brown, 'Anthropology and Colonial Rule: The Case of Godfrey Wilson and the Rhodes–Livingstone Institute, Northern Rhodesia', in Talad Asad (ed.), *Anthropology and the Colonial Encounter* (Ithaca: Humanities Press, 1975), pp. 173–97. For a history of British anthropology see Henrika Kuklick, *The Savage Within* (Cambrige: Cambridge University Press, 1993).

7. J. F. Ritchie, *The African as Suckling and as Adult: A Psychological Study* (Rhodes–Livingstone Institute Papers 9, 1943). The monograph was subsequently republished in 1968 under the same title by Manchester University Press.

8. Klein is best remembered for her work on the pre-Oedipal period of development and in particular for her pioneering work on envy. Her *Envy and Gratitude* contains almost nothing on gratitude.

9. Ritchie, *The African*, p. 12.

10. *Ibid.*, p. 13.

11. *Ibid.*

12. *Ibid.*, p. 33.

13. Ritchie commented that because of experiences in infancy 'the African could not create an orderly mythology, philosophy or religion. That is, he could not make a projection of order from a disordered mind'. *The African*, p. 37.

14. Ritchie did concede, however, that there were exceptions to this rule: 'Whenever I find an African who is distinctive in uprightness and stability of character and in his intelligence and commonsense view of life, I always try to learn something of his antecedents. Without exception so far, I have found that he has been for some time under the influence of a European of vigorous personality, yet kindly and never unjust.' *The African*, p. 49.

15. For the most popular expositions on the concept of narcissism see the work of Christopher Lasch, especially *The Culture of Narcissism* (New York: Norton, 1978) and *The Minimal Self* (London: Picador, 1984).

16. Ritchie, *The African*, p. 16.

17. T. A. Lambo, 'Growth of African Children: Psychological Aspects', in Lambo (ed), *First Pan-African Psychiatric Conference*, pp. 60–4.

18. *Ibid.*, p. 61.

19. After returning to Paris Mannoni trained as a psychoanalyst under Jacques Lacan at the Ecole Freudienne de Paris and he subsequently published a full-length study of Freud entitled simply *Freud* (Paris: Editions du Seuil, 1968).

20. Quoted in Elisabeth Roudinesco, *Jacques Lacan and Company: A History of Psychoanalysis in France, 1925–1985*, trans. Jeffrey Mehlam (Chicago: University of Chicago Press, 1986), p. 234.

21. Octave Mannoni, *Prospero and Caliban: The Psychology of Colonization*, trans. Pamela Powesland (New York: Frederick A. Praeger, 1964), p. 128.

22. *Ibid.*, p. 75.

23. *Ibid.*, p. 79.

24. *Ibid.*, p. 85.

25. The number of Malagasy killed is a matter for dispute. The official figure was eleven thousand, while the high commissioner at that time, Pierre de Chevigne, and one of the French generals involved, General Garbay, put the figure at between sixty thousand and eighty thousand. See Nigel Heseltine, *Madagascar* (New York: Praeger, 1971), pp. 180–1, and Bonar. A. Gow, 'Madagascar' in Michael Crowder (ed.), *The Cambridge History of Africa*, vol. VIII (Cambridge: Cambridge University Press, 1984), pp. 674–97.
26. Mannoni, *Prospero*, p. 105.
27. For an account of the ways in which sexual relations between blacks and whites were managed in Southern Rhodesia for the benefit of white men and to the disadvantage of the African community and white women see John Pape, 'Black and White: The "Perils of Sex" in Colonial Zimbabwe', *Journal of Southern African Studies* 4 (1990), pp. 699–720.
28. A good illustration is found in a short story by Llewelyn Powys, a long term resident of Kenya. 'How It Happens' is the story of a young Englishman named Gerald Littlemore who goes to Africa to make his fortune. He is soon dragged down by the heat and by the behaviour of his fellow whites who cohabit with black women. Driven by loneliness, Littlemore has sexual relations with a Nandy girl, contracts syphilis, and in despair commits suicide. The moral of the story is that the colonies are no fit place for decent young Englishmen. See Llewelyn Powys, *Ebony and Ivory* (London: Grant Ritchards, 1923), pp. 89–106.
29. Mannoni, *Prospero*, p. 108.
30. *Ibid.*, p. 110.
31. *Ibid.*, p. 24.
32. *Ibid.*, p. 7.

8   THE ELEMENTS OF ORTHODOXY

1. In the preface to *The African Mind* Carothers acknowledged the kindness and hospitality of P. Gallais and H. Aubin. However, Carothers had met these specialists for the first time in 1953, while researching his WHO monograph. See Carothers, *The African Mind*, p. 9.
2. *Ibid.*, p. 134.
3. *Ibid.*, p. 137.
4. See Henderson and Gillespie, *A Text-book*, pp. 305–8.
5. C. G. Seligman believed that schizophrenia was practically unknown in truly primitive societies, an observation that was later endorsed by the Hungarian-born psychiatrist Georges Devereux, who was convinced that schizophrenia was truly the psychosis of civilization. None of the ethnopsychiatrists working in colonial Africa would claim, however, that their charges were 'untouched primitives'. See C. G. Seligman, 'Anthropological Perspective and Psychological Theory', *Journal of the Royal Anthropological Institute* 62 (1932), pp. 193–228.
6. This is borne out by a later study by Nancy Waxler, who compared a group of schizophrenic patients from Mauritius with a comparable group of patients from asylums in Great Britain. See E. Nancy Waxler, 'Culture and Mental Illness: A Social Labelling Perspective', in *Journal of Nervous and Mental Disease* 6 (1974), p. 386.

7. A much earlier study by a South African psychiatrist on the effectiveness of ECT with 'Bantu' patients supports Waxler's argument. Dr J. S. Du T. De Wet studied a group of schizophrenic Bantu women who were admitted to the Tower Hospital in the Eastern Cape province in the period 1952 to 1954 and compared their responses with those of a comparable group of European patients. The study is marred by the absence of proper case-histories for any of the women and also by the smallness of the sample. De Wet found no evidence that the use of ECT enhanced the rate of discharge from Tower Hospital and concluded that in the case of Bantu patients 'with courses of 30 fits given at the rate of 2 per week, ECT may actually delay the discharge of patients who recover spontaneously during the course' (p. 748). See J. S. Du T. De Wet, 'Evaluation of a Common Method of Convulsive Therapy in Bantu Schizophrenics', *British Journal of Psychiatry* 103 (1957), pp. 739–57.

8. A. Porot and D. C. Arrii, 'L'impulsivite criminelle chez l'indigene algerien: ses facteurs', *Annales Medico-psychologiques* 90 (1932), pp. 588–611.

9. See, for example, A. Porot and C. Sutter, 'Le primitivisme des indigenes nord-africains: Ses incidences en pathologie mentale', *Sud Medical et Chirur-gical* (April 1939), pp. 226–41.

10. Shelley and W. H. Watson, 'An Investigation', pp. 702–29.

11. *Ibid.*, p. 711.

12. *Ibid.*, pp. 711–12.

13. *Ibid.*, p. 729.

14. Carothers, *The African Mind*, p. 153.

15. *Ibid.*, pp. 157–8.

16. *Ibid.*, p. 161.

17. Carothers's views on 'frenzied anxiety' were not supported by any clinical data. He did, however, keep case-notes on homicides both for the inmates at Mathari and for the murderers held at HM Prison, Nairobi. One such note, dated 25 April 1949, presents a list of psychiatric homicides held at Mathari. The list is divided between men and women and includes forty-nine patients, six of whom were women. Almost two-thirds of this group are classified as schizophrenic (fifteen) or as feeble-minded (twelve), while nine are diagnosed as suffering from an organic psychosis. A second file, also dated 25 April 1949, covers 100 murderers held at Nairobi Gaol. One of Carothers's duties as senior medical officer at Mathari was to review each homicide case before trial and, if the person was found guilty, to again examine the prisoner before execution. During the period of World War II Carothers kept records of the 100 homicide cases he was called to review. He later classified these according to the cause of the crime. The most common causes cited are alcohol (twenty-three), quarrels about possessions (sixteen), witchcraft (eleven), sex (ten), and feeble-mindedness (eight); psychosis is cited only four times. These two files suggest that 'frenzied anxiety' cases were classified as schizophrenic and that 'frenzied anxiety' did not play a prominent role as the cause of murder, at least during the six years covered by the study.

18. This idea was sometimes applied to all non-Western peoples. See Paul. K. Benedict and Irving Jacks, 'Mental Illness in Primitive Societies', *Psychiatry* 17 (1954), pp. 377–89.

19. One murder that did result in the gaoling of a white woman occurred in Kenya in 1934. Mrs Helen Selwyn, a farmer's wife from Kitale in the Rift Valley

Province, was charged with the murder of a Suk named Keyen Luyamoinon. Mrs Selwyn had Keyen and three other Suk, whom she suspected of stealing cowbells, beaten with strips of rubber tyre. Three days later Keyen died. Mrs Selwyn was charged with murder, found guilty of manslaughter, and gaoled for twelve months. What was so unusual about the case was not the murder itself but the consequences. See Transcripts of Supreme Court Criminal Case No. 110 of 1934: 'The Selwyn Case', *Colonial Office* correspondence CO 533/450/8.

20. *Rhodesian Herald*, 4 August 1916.
21. *Rhodesian Herald*, 6 May 1910.
22. *Rhodesian Herald*, 26 February 1915.
23. A review of the records from the High Courts of Bulawayo and Salisbury in the period 1905 to 1930 shows just how common these cases were. In Southern Rhodesia the refusal of white juries to convict white men for the murder of Africans even in the face of the most damning evidence led to two major crises. The so-called Battlefields and Laidlaw cases of 1908, in which white employers were charged with beating Africans to death, and the Lewis case of 1911 resulted in changes to the jury system in the colony following severe criticism from the high commissioner. See Criminal Cases: High Court of Southern Rhodesia S628 no.150–2000. See also Shirley Weleba, 'Trial by Jury in Southern Rhodesia 1900–1912', (Ph.D. dissertation, University of Southern California, 1969).
24. This case, in which four white men were charged with culpable homicide, was heard in the Salisbury High Court in November 1908. The men were charged with having beaten to death two African workers who were employed at the Battlefields mine compound in the Hartley district. The deceased, who were suspected of petty theft, had in fact been tortured over a period of days. Despite overwhelming evidence of their guilt of at least culpable homicide, the accused were acquitted of all charges. The case caused a scandal and precipitated a crisis in the Southern Rhodesian legal system. See 'The Battlefields Case', ZNA S 628 No. 416 (1908).
25. For example, see Siegfried Fischer, 'The Influence of Indian and Negro Blood on the Manic-Depressive Psychosis', *Journal of Nervous and Mental Disease* 97 (1943), pp. 409–20.
26. One dissenting voice was that of the French psychiatrist H. Aubin working in West Africa, who found that depressive illness was common and that it showed up starkly in contrast to the African's usual mood. He also believed that self-mutilation leading to suicide was common. See H. Aubin, 'Introduction a l'etude de la psychiatrie chez les noirs', *Annales Medico-psychologiques* 97, (February 1939), pp. 1–29; and 'Notes de psychologie pathologique chez le noir', *Hospital* 28 (May 1940), pp. 185–7. See also Carothers, *The African Mind*, p. 145.
27. Laubscher, *Sex*, p. 275.
28. *Ibid.*, p. 295.
29. *Ibid.*, p. 298.
30. See Tooth, *Studies in Mental Illness*, pp. 38–40.
31. Carothers wrote: 'The inability of the African depressive to recognise his depression as a mental rather than as a physical state seems to be simply a part

of his general lack of introspective ability and developed self–consciousness, which again are probably by-products of the habit of synthesis.' Carothers, 'Frontal Lobe Function', p. 42.

32. See Smartt, 'Mental Maladjustment'.

33. T. Asuni, 'Suicide in Western Nigeria', in Lambo (ed.), *First Pan-African Psychiatric Conference Report*, p. 166.

34. The orthodoxy about depressive illness in primitives was not confined to Africa but appeared in much later studies in sites as far removed as Melanesia. B. G. Burton-Bradley, for many years was the only psychiatrist in Papua New Guinea, found that schizophrenia was the most common psychosis and depressive delusions of the kind found in the European uncommon, even among those in transition between a traditional and modern lifestyle. See B. G. Burton-Bradley, *Stone Age Crisis: A Psychiatric Appraisal* (Nashville: Vanderbilt University Press, 1975), pp. 109–10; and also *Long-Long: Transcultural Psychiatry in Papua and New Guinea* (Port Moresby: Public Health Department, 1973).

35. This is apparent if one compares the standard psychiatric textbooks from the 1930s with the contemporary literature. See Henderson and Gillespie, 'Depression', in *A Text-book*, pp. 249–63; W. Mayer-Gross and Martin Roth, *Clinical Psychiatry* (London: Cassell, 1954) and Aaron Beck, *Depression: Causes and Treatment* (Philadelphia: University of Pennsylvania Press, 1967).

36. See Beck, *Depression*, pp. 21–39.

37. Henderson and Gillespie, *A Text-book*, p. 252.

38. M. J. Field, *Search for Security: An Ethno-Psychiatric Study of Rural Ghana* (New York: Norton, first published 1960, repr. 1970).

39. M. J. Field, 'Witchcraft as a Primitive Interpretation of Mental Disorder', *Journal of Mental Science* 101 (1955), p. 826.

40. *Ibid.*, p. 827.

41. Field, *Search for Security*, p. 13.

42. *Ibid.*, p. 38.

43. See H. Alexander et al., *Psychiatric Disorder among the Yoruba: A Report from the Cornell–Aro Mental Health Research Project in the Western Region, Nigeria* (Ithaca: Cornell University Press, 1963).

44. Subsequent research by Orley and Wing duplicated these findings among a group of Ugandan women who were found to suffer more frequently and more severely from depression than did a comparable group of women from south-east London. See John Orley and John Wing, 'Psychiatric Disorders in Two African Villages', *Archives of General Psychiatry* 36 (1979), pp. 513–20.

45. A good example of this kind of reasoning is found in Roland Littlewood and M. Lipsedge, *Aliens and Alienists*, pp. 68–86. For a contrary view see Arthur Kleinman, 'Culture and Depression' and Paul Bebbington, 'The Epidemiology of Depressive Disorders', both in *Culture, Medicine and Psychiatry* 2 (1978): pp. 295–6, and 297–341.

46. In another regard Mannoni was correct: the men and women of Madagascar were not the same kind of individuals as the people depicted in clinical psychiatry. The concept of the individual and of the person are both historically specific inventions, and the interior lives of men and women and

their personas are just as variable over time and place as are their material circumstances. Mannoni's interpretation of that difference placed the Malagasy (and the colonized) into an evolutionist model of personality and culture. Within the terms of that model the subordination of the Malagasy was affirmed. See Michael Carrithers, Steven Collins and Steven Lukes (eds.), *The Category of the Person: Anthropology, Philosophy, History* (Cambridge: Cambridge University Press, 1985).

47. See Frantz Fanon, 'Concerning Violence', in *The Wretched of the Earth*, trans. Constance Farrington (London: Penguin Books, 1967), pp. 27–84.

48. According to Dilman there is general agreement within the psychoanalytic tradition about what constitutes a mature personality. That person is loyal, steadfast, responsible and free from infantile or destructive emotions. He is free from greed and envy, can tolerate his own anger without fear, and is capable of forgiveness. See Ilham Dilman, *Freud and Human Nature* (Oxford: Basil Blackwell, 1983), esp. pp. 188–90.

49. For a history of such relations see Karen Hansen, *Distant Companions: Servants and Employers in Zambia, 1900–1985* (Ithaca: Cornell University Press, 1989).

50. This passion for inquiry is also presumed to provide the foundation for European culture. See Mannoni, *Prospero*, p. 188.

51. *Ibid.*, p. 194.

52. *Ibid.*, p. 195.

53. There were some dissenting voices, and in his study of the Gold Coast Tooth commented that there was no clear evidence of an association between Europeanization and psychosis. He was, however, in the minority. See his *Studies in Mental Illness*, p. 61.

54. See Fanon, 'Colonial Wars and Mental Disorders', in *The Wretched of the Earth*, pp. 200–50.

55. Shelley and Watson, 'An Investigation'.

56. See Raymond Prince, 'The Brain Fag Syndrome in Nigerian Students', *Journal of Mental Science* 106 (1960), pp. 559–70.

57. *Ibid.*, p. 566.

58. E. B. Forster, 'The Theory and Practice of Psychiatry in Ghana', *American Journal of Psychotherapy* 16 (1962), p. 7.

59. *Ibid.*, p. 12.

60. Forster claimed that in the period from 1952 until the end of 1956 he had treated a total of 138 patients suffering from an anxiety neurosis of a type not seen previously. See 'Psychiatry in Ghana', p. 12.

9   FROM PSYCHIATRY TO POLITICS

1. Foreword: 'Report: The Present Position in Different African Countries', in *Mental Health Disorders and Mental Health in Africa South of the Sahara* (Bukava, 1958), p. 89.

2. Aubrey Lewis, 'Inaugural Speech', *First Pan-African Psychiatric Conference* (1962), pp. 19–26.

3. Lewis's speech was entirely orthodox; see for example, *Africa: Social Change and Mental Health* (New York: World Federation of Mental Health, 1959).

4. Fanon vacillated somewhat on the relevance of his conclusions to other

colonial sites: see *Black Skin, White Masks*, trans. Charles L. Markhamm (London: MacGibbon & Kee, 1967), pp. 16, 172–3), while Mannoni was quite definite about the status of his conclusions: 'My direct knowledge of the colonial peoples leads me to believe that some of my conclusions are of general applicability.' Mannoni, *Prospero*, pp. 30–1. See also p. 44.

5. Fanon, *Black Skin*, p. 95.
6. Frantz Fanon, 'The North African Syndrome', first published in *L'esprit* (February 1952), and later in *Toward the African Revolution*, trans. Haakon Chevalier (London: Pelican Books, 1967), pp. 13–26.
7. Frantz Fanon, 'Réflexions sur l'ethnopsychiatrie', *Conscience maghrébine* 3 (1955), pp. 1–2.
8. Neither was there reference to Fanon's clinical publications in Edward. L. Margetts's comprehensive bibliography at the end of the *First Pan-African Psychiatric Conference*. That bibliography contained numerous citations from allied disciplines such as social anthropology as well as works from the nineteenth century. See Lambo, *First Pan-African Psychiatric Conference Report*, pp. 303–20.
9. Frantz Fanon and Francois Sanchez, 'L'attitude du musulman maghrébian devant la folie', *Revue pratique de psychologie de la vie sociale et d'hygiene mentale* 1 (1956), pp. 24–7.
10. *Ibid.*, p. 26.
11. *Ibid.*, p. 26.
12. *Ibid.*, p. 26.
13. Frantz Fanon and R. Lacat, 'Conduites d'aveux en Afrique du Nord'. *La Tunisie medicale*, 53rd session, Nice (5–11 September 1955), pp. 657–60.
14. *Ibid.*, p. 659.
15. Fanon and Azoulay, 'Socialtherapy', pp. 349–61.
16. *Ibid.*, p. 351.
17. *Ibid.*, p. 354.
18. *Ibid.*, p. 246.
19. *Ibid.*, p. 357.
20. *Ibid.*, p. 358.
21. Fanon, *The Wretched*, p. 200.
22. Fanon, *Black Skin*, p. 83.
23. Frantz Fanon, 'Racism and Culture', in *Toward the African Revolution*, pp. 39–54.
24. Frantz Fanon, *A Dying Colonialism*, trans. Haakon Chevalier (London: Pelican Books, 1965), p. 102.
25. Fanon, *The Wretched*, p. 191.
26. *Ibid.*, p. 191.
27. *Ibid.*, p. 101.
28. *Ibid.*, p. 201.
29. *Ibid.*, p. 200.

10 CONCLUSION

1. In 'Ethnopsychiatric Considerations' and in *The Wretched* Fanon provided reviews of the discipline and its ruling orthodoxies. However, those reviews were not read widely by practitioners. Carothers, who was the best travelled

of the ethnopsychiatrists, was unaware of the existence of Fanon's work when interviewed in 1986.

2. Albert Camus, for example, was born into a poor French family in Algiers which, as he later failed to persuade his Parisian friends, hardly made him or his mother beneficiaries of French colonialism.

3. For a history of the way British social anthropology adapted to the twin environments of metropolitan Britain and colonial Africa see Kuklick, *The Savage Within*.

4. See Patrice Lumumba, *La Pensée politique de Patrice Lumumba*. Selected and ed. by Jean van Lierde. (Paris: Presence Africaine, 1963).

5. The same kinds of sentiments are prominent in Paul Scott's portrait of the disintegration of the British Raj. See Paul Scott, *The Raj Quartet*.

6. For an account of the uses of science in defining social value see for example Stephan L. Chorover, *From Genesis to Genocide* (Cambridge: The MIT Press, 1980).

7. For a discussion of these and allied debates see T. Heller et al. (eds.), *Reconstructing Individualism: Autonomy, Individuality, and the Self in Western Thought* (Stanford: Stanford University Press, 1986) and V. Beechey and J. Donald, (eds.), *Subjectivity and Social Relations* (Milton Keynes: Open University Press, 1985).

8. Mannoni, *Prospero*, p. 41.

9. See Pavla Miller, *Assembling the School*, forthcoming.

10. Norbert Elias, *The Civilising Process: State Formation and Civilisation* (Oxford: Basil Blackwell, 1978), p. 235.

Bibliography

The material cited in chapters 2 and 3 is drawn largely from the National Archives of Zimbabwe and Kenya. The abbreviations used in footnotes for these sources are: Zimbabwe National Archive, ZNA, and Kenya National Archive, KNA.

BOOKS

Africa: Social Change and Mental Health. New York: World Federation of Mental Health, 1959.

Alexander, F. and Selesnick, S. *The History of Psychiatry.* New York: Harper & Row, 1966.

Alexander, H. et al. *Psychiatric Disorders among the Yoruba: A Report from the Cornell–Aro Mental Health Research Project in the Western Region, Nigeria.* Ithaca: Cornell University Press, 1963.

Asad, Talad (ed.) *Anthropology and the Colonial Encounter.* Ithaca: Humanities Press, 1975.

Beck, Aaron *Depression: Causes and Treatment.* Philadelphia: University of Pennsylvania Press, 1967.

Beechey, Veronica and Donald, James (eds.) *Subjectivity and Social Relations.* Milton Keynes: Open University Press, 1985.

Benedict, Ruth *Patterns of Culture.* Boston: Houghton Mifflin, 1959.

Biesheuvel, S. *African Intelligence.* Johannesburg: The South African Institute of Race Relations, 1943.

Bloch, Maurice *Marxism and Anthropology: The History of a Relationship.* Oxford: Oxford University Press, 1985.

Boas, Franz *The Mind of Primitive Man.* New York: Free Press, 1963.

Bohannan, Paul (ed.) *African Homicide and Suicide.* Princeton: Princeton University Press, 1960.

Bourguignon, Erika *Psychological Anthropology: An Introduction to Human Nature and Cultural Difference.* New York: Holt, Rinehart & Winston, 1976.

Burrow, J. W. *Evolution and Society: A Study in Victorian Social Theory.* London: Cambridge University Press, 1966.

Burton-Bradley, B. G. *Long-Long: Transcultural Psychiatry in Papua and New Guinea.* Port Moresby: Public Health Department, 1973.

Burton-Bradley, B. G. *Stone Age Crisis: A Psychiatric Appraisal.* Nashville: Vanderbilt University Press, 1975.

Carman, John A. *A Medical History of Kenya: A Personal Memoir.* London: Rex Collings, 1976.

Carothers, J. C. *The African Mind in Health and Disease: A Study in Ethnopsy-chiatry*. Geneva: World Health Organization, 1953.

Carothers, J. C. A report on the psychiatric services of Nigeria, 1955.

Personal papers of J. C. Carothers.

Carothers, J. C. *The Psychology of Mau Mau*. Nairobi: Government Printer, 1954.

Carothers, J. C. *The Mind of Man in Africa*. London: Tom Stacey, 1972.

Césaire, Aimé *Discourse sur le colonialisme*. Paris: Presence Africaine, 1950.

Césaire, Aimé *Cahier d'un retour au pays natal*. Paris: Presence Africaine, 1956.

Chorover, Stephan L. *From Genesis to Genocide: The Meaning of Human Nature and the Power of Behavior Control*. Cambridge: MIT Press, 1980.

Cohen, Stanley and Scull, Andrew (eds.) *Social Control and the State: Historical and Comparative Essays*. Oxford: Basil Blackwell, 1985.

Corfield, F. D. *Historical Survey of the Origins and Growth of Mau Mau*. London: Her Majesty's Stationery Office, 1960.

Cox, John, L. (ed.) *Transcultural Psychiatry*. London: Croom Helm, 1986.

Cunynham Brown, R. *Report 111 On the Care and Treatment of Lunatics in the British West African Colonies, Nigeria*. London: Crown Agents, 1938.

Curtin, Phillip (ed.) *Africa and the West: Intellectual Responses to European Culture*. Madison: University of Wisconsin Press, 1972.

Devereux, Georges *Basic Problems of Ethnopsychiatry*. Chicago: University of Chicago Press, 1980.

Dilman, Ilham *Freud and Human Nature*. Oxford: Basil Blackwell, 1983.

Driberg, J. H. *At Home with the Savage*. London: George Routledge, 1932.

Edgerton, Robert B. *Mau Mau: An African Crucible*. New York: Free Press, 1989.

Elias, Norbert *The Civilising Process: State Formation and Civilisation*. Oxford: Basil Blackwell, 1978.

Elkin, A. P. *The Australian Aborigines*. Melbourne: Angus & Robertson, 1974.

Erikson, Erik *Childhood and Society*. First published 1950. London: Pelican Books, 1970.

Evans-Pritchard, E. E. *The Nuer*. New York: Oxford University Press, 1940.

Evans-Pritchard, E. E. et al. (eds.) *Essays Presented to C. G. Seligman*. London: Kegan Paul, Trench, Trubner, 1934.

Fanon, Frantz *Peau noire, masques blancs*. Paris: Francois Maspero, 1952; translated by Charles L. Markhamm as *Black Skin, White Masks*. London: MacGibbon & Kee, 1967.

Fanon, Frantz *Les Damnés de la terre*. Paris: Francois Maspero, 1961; translated by Constance Farrington as *The Wretched of the Earth*. London: Penguin Books, 1967.

Fanon, Frantz *Pour la révolution africaine*. Paris: Francois Maspero, 1964; translated by Haakon Chevalier as *Toward the African Revolution*. London: Pelican Books, 1967.

Fanon, Frantz *A Dying Colonialism*; translated by Haakon Chevalier. London: Pelican Books, 1965.

Fernando, Suman *Race and Culture in Psychiatry*. London: Croom Helm, 1988.

Field, M. J. *Search for Security: An Ethno-Psychiatric Study of Rural Ghana*. New York: Norton, 1960; repr. 1970.

Fisher, Lawrence *Colonial Madness: Mental Health in the Barbadian Social Order*. New Brunswick: Rutgers University Press, 1985.

Foucault, Michel *The Birth of the Clinic*, translated by A. M. Sheridan Smith. New York: Random House, 1975.

Foucault, Michel *The History of Sexuality*. Vol. I; translated by Robert Hurley. London: Penguin Books, 1978.

Foucault, Michel *Discipline and Punish*. New York: Random House, 1979.

Freeman, Derek *Margaret Mead and Samoa: The Making and the Unmaking of an Anthropological Myth*. Canberra: Australian National University Press, 1983.

Freud, Sigmund *Totem and Taboo: Resemblances between the Psychic Lives of Savages and Neurotics*. First published 1913; translated by A. A. Brill. New York: Vintage Books, 1946.

Freud, Sigmund *Three Essays on the Theory of Sexuality*. First published 1905; translated and edited by James Strachey. New York: Avon Books, 1971.

Galton, Francis *Narrative of an Explorer in Tropical South Africa*. London: Ward, Lock, 1889.

Galton, Francis *Inquiries into Human Faculty and its Development*. London: J. M. Dent, 1908.

Galton, Francis *Hereditary Genius: An Inquiry into its Laws and Consequences*. (2nd ed. 1892) Gloucester: Peter Smith, 1972.

Gann, Lewis and Duigan, Peter *White Settlers in Tropical Africa*. Westport: Greenwood Press, 1977.

Gelfand, Michael *The Sick African: A Clinical Study*. Third edn. Cape Town: Juta, 1957.

Gelfand, Michael *A Service to the Sick: A History of the Health Services for Africans in Southern Rhodesia 1890 to 1953*. Salisbury: Mambo Press, 1976.

Gittins, Diana *The Family in Question*. London: Macmillan Education, 1985.

Gobineau, A. de *The Inequality of the Human Races*. New York: Howard Fertig, 1967.

Haddon, A. C. *Reports of the Cambridge Anthropological Expedition to Torres Straits*. Vol. II: *Physiology and Psychology*. Cambridge: Cambridge University Press, 1901.

Hansen, Karen *Distant Companions: Servants and Employers in Zambia, 1900–1985*. Ithaca: Cornell University Press, 1989.

Heller, Thomas et al. (eds.) *Reconstructing Individualism: Autonomy, Individuality, and the Self in Western Thought*. Stanford: Stanford University Press, 1986.

Henderson, David and Gillespie, R. D. *A Text-book of Psychiatry*. Eighth edn. London: Oxford University Press, 1956.

Henriques, Julian et al. *Changing the Subject: Psychology and Social Regulation*. London: Methuen, 1984.

Historical Survey of the Origins and Growth of Mau Mau. London: Her Majesty's Stationery Office, 1960.

Horne, Alistair *A Savage War of Peace: Algeria 1954–1962* London: Macmillan, 1977.

Howells, John (ed.) *World History of Psychiatry*. London: Bailliere/Tindall, 1975.

Jaspers, Karl *The European Spirit*; translated by Ronald Smith. London: SCM Press, 1948.

Jaspers, Karl *Leonardo, Descartes, and Weber*; translated by Ralph Manheim. London: Routledge & Kegan Paul, 1965.

Kardiner, Abram et al. *The Psychological Frontiers of Society*. New York: Columbia University Press, 1946.

Kennedy, Dane *Islands of White: Settler Society and Culture in Kenya and Southern Rhodesia 1890–1939*. Durham, NC: Duke University Press, 1987.

Kevlis, Daniel J. *In the Name of Eugenics: Genetics and the Uses of Human Heredity*. New York: Alfred A. Knopf, 1985.

Kiev, Ari *Transcultural Psychiatry*. New York: Free Press, 1972.

Kleinman, Arthur *Rethinking Psychiatry: From Cultural Category to Personal Experience*. New York: The Free Press, 1988.

Kraeplin, E. *One Hundred Years of Psychiatry*. London: Peter Owen, 1962.

Kuklick, Henrika *The Savage Within: The Social History of British Anthropology, 1885–1945*. Cambridge: Cambridge University Press, 1993.

Kuper, Adam *Anthropologists and Anthropology: The British School 1922–1972*. London: Penguin Books, 1978.

Lambo, T. Adeoye (ed.) *First Pan-African Psychiatric Conference Report*. Abeokuta: 1962.

Langham, I. *The Building of British Social Anthropology*. London: Reidel, 1981.

Laubscher, B. J. F. *Sex, Custom and Psychopathology: A Study of South African Pagan Natives*. London: George Routledge, 1937.

Leakey, L. S. B. *Mau Mau and the Kikuyu*. London: Methuen, 1952.

Leakey, L. S. B. *Defeating Mau Mau*. London: Methuen, 1955.

Lebra, W. (ed.) *Culture-bound Syndromes: Ethnopsychiatry and Alternate Therapies*. Honolulu: East–West Center, 1976.

Levy-Bruhl, L. *Primitive Mentality*. New York: Macmillan, 1923.

Levy-Bruhl, L. *The Notebooks on Primitive Mentality*; translated by Peter Riviere. London: Harper & Row, 1978.

Leys, Colin *European Politics in Southern Rhodesia*. London: Oxford University Press, 1959.

Littlewood, Roland and Lipsedge, Maurice *Aliens and Alienists*. London: Penguin Books, 1982.

Lumumba, Patrice *La Pensée politique de Patrice Lumumba*. Selected and edited by Jean van Lierde. Paris: Presence Africaine, 1963.

McCulloch, Jock *Black Soul, White Artifact: Fanon's Clinical Psychology and Social Theory*. New York: Cambridge University Press, 1983.

McCulloch, Jock *In the Twilight of Revolution: The Political Theory of Amilcar Cabral*. London: Routledge & Kegan Paul, 1983.

Malinowski, B. *The Sexual Life of Savages in North Western Melanesia*. London: Routledge & Kegan Paul, 1929.

Malinowski, B. *Sex and Repression in Savage Society*. New York: New American Library, 1955.

Mannoni, Octave *Prospero and Caliban: The Psychology of Colonization*; translated by Pamela Powesland. New York: Frederick A. Praeger, 1964.

Mayer-Gross, W. and Roth, Martin *Clinical Psychiatry*. London: Cassell, 1954.

Mead, Margaret *Coming of Age in Samoa*. London: Penguin Books, 1966.

Memmi, Albert *The Colonizer and the Colonized*; translated by H. Greenfield. Boston: Beacon Press, 1965.

Mental Health Disorders and Mental Health in Africa South of the Sahara. CCTA/ CSA–WFHM–WHO Meeting of Specialists on Mental Health, Bukava, 1958. CCTA Publication No. 35.

Orley, John *Culture and Mental Illness*. Makerere: East African Publishing House, 1970.

Piaget, Jean *Judgment and Reasoning in the Child*. London: Routledge & Kegan Paul, 1969.

Porteus, Stanley *The Psychology of a Primitive People*. New York: Books for Libraries Press, 1931.

Porteus, Stanley *Primitive Intelligence and Environment*. New York: Macmillan, 1937.

Porteus, Stanley *The Maze Test and Clinical Psychology*. Palo Alto: Pacific Books, 1959.

Porteus, Stanley. *A Psychologist of Sorts*. Palo Alto: Pacific Books, 1969.

Porteus, Stanley and Babcock, Marjorie *Temperament and Race*. Boston: Richard G. Badger, 1926.

Powys, Llewellyn *Ebony and Ivory*. London: Grant Ritchards, 1923.

Prochaska, David *Making Algeria French*. Cambridge: Cambridge University Press, 1990.

Reiger, Kereen *The Disenchantment of the Home: Modernizing the Australian Family, 1880–1940* Melbourne: Oxford University Press, 1985.

Ritchie, John. F. *The African as Suckling and as Adult: A Psychological Study*. First published 1943. Manchester: Rhodes-Livingstone Institute, 1968.

Rivers, W. H. R. *Psychology and Politics and Other Essays*. London: International Library of Psychology, 1923.

Rivers, W. H. R. *Psychology and Ethnopsychology*. London: International Library of Psychology, 1926.

Róheim, Géza. *Australian Totemism: A Psycho-analytic Study in Anthropology*. London: George Allen & Unwin, 1925.

Róheim, Géza. *Psychoanalysis and Anthropology*. New York: International University Press, 1950.

Rose, Nicholas *The Psychological Complex: Psychology, Politics and Society in England 1869–1939*. London: Routledge & Kegan Paul, 1985.

Rothman, David *The Discovery of the Asylum*. Boston: Little, Brown, 1970.

Sachs, Wulf. *Black Anger*. First published 1947. New York: Grove Press, 1969. Published in the UK as *Black Hamlet* (London: Geoffrey Bles, 1937).

Sapir, Edward *Culture, Language and Personality: Selected Essays*. Los Angeles: University of California Press, 1961.

Schram, Ralph *A History of the Nigerian Health Services*. Ibadan: Ibadan University Press, 1971.

Scull, Andrew *Museums of Madness*. London: Allen Lane, 1979.

Smith, Edwin *Knowing the African*. London: Lutterworth Press, 1946.

Slobodin, Richard. *W. H. R. Rivers*. New York: Columbia University Press, 1978.

Sow, I. *Anthropological Structures of Madness in Black Africa*. New York: International University Press, 1980.

Spiro, Melford E. *Oedipus in the Trobriands*. Chicago: University of Chicago Press, 1982.

Styron, William *Darkness Visible*. London: Jonathan Cape, 1991.

Thomas, A. and Sillens, S. *Racism and Psychiatry*. New Jersey: Citadel Press, 1974.

Thorne, Barrie and Yalom, Marilyn (eds.) *Rethinking the Family: Some Feminist Questions*. New York: Longman, 1982.

Throup, David, W. *Economic and Social Origins of Mau Mau*. London: James Currey, 1986.

Tooth, Geoffrey *Studies in Mental Illness in the Gold Coast*. Colonial Office, 1950. London: Colonial Research Publication No. 6.

Valenstein, Elliot S. *Great and Desperate Cures: The Rise and Decline of Psychosurgery and Other Radical Treatments for Mental Illness*. New York: Basic Books, 1986.

Wallace, Edwin R. *Freud and Anthropology*. New York: International University Press, 1983.

Westley, David *Mental Health and Psychiatry in Africa: An Annotated Bibliography* (London: Hans Zell Publishers, 1993).

Wing, John K. *Reasoning About Madness*. London: Oxford University Press, 1978.

Zaretsky, Eli *Capitalism, the Family and Personal Life*. London: Pluto Press, 1976.

ARTICLES

Abdi, Yusuf 'Problems and Prospects of Psychology in Africa'. *International Journal of Psychology*, Vol. 10, No. 3, 1975, pp. 227–34.

Aubin, H. 'Introduction a l'etude de la psychiatrie chez les noirs'. *Annales Medico-psychologiques*, No. 97, February 1939, pp. 1–29.

Aubin, H. 'Notes de psychologie pathologique chez le noir'. *Hospital*, No. 28, May 1940.

Bebbington, Paul 'The Epidemiology of Depressive Disorders'. *Culture, Medicine and Psychiatry*, No. 2, 1978, pp. 297–341.

Benedict, Paul K. and Jacks, Irving 'Mental Illness in Primitive Societies'. *Psychiatry*, No. 17, 1954, pp. 377–89.

Buchan, T. 'Depression in African Patients'. *South African Medical Journal*, No. 23, August 1969, pp. 1055–8.

Carothers, J. C. 'Some Speculations on Insanity in Africans and in General'. *East African Medical Journal*, No. 17, 1940, pp. 90–105.

Carothers, J. C. 'A Study of Mental Derangement in Africans, and an Attempt to Explain its Peculiarities, More Especially in Relation to the African Attitude to Life'. *Journal of Mental Science*, Vol. 93, July 1947, pp. 548–97.

Carothers, J. C. 'Frontal Lobe Function and the African'. *Journal of Mental Science*, Vol. 97, 1951, pp. 122–48.

Carothers, J. C. 'The Nature–Nurture Controversy'. *Psychiatry*, No. 18, 1955, pp. 301–4.

Carothers, J. C. 'Culture, Psychiatry and the Written Word'. *Psychiatry*, No. 22, 1959, pp. 307–20.

Carothers, J. C. 'Further Thoughts on the African Mind'. *East African Medical Journal*, No. 6, June 1960, pp. 457–63.

Carothers, J. C. 'Hysteria, Psychopathy and the Magic Word'. *Mankind Quarterly*, Vol. 16, No. 2, October/December 1975, pp. 93–102.

Césaire, Aimé. 'L'Homme de culture et ses responsabilités'. *Présence Africaine*, No. 24/25, 1959, pp. 116–22.

Cheetham, R. W. and Griffiths, J. A. 'Changing Patterns in Psychiatry in Africa'. *South African Medical Journal*, No. 26, July 1980, pp. 166–8.

Cooper, John. M. 'The Cree Witiko Psychosis'. *Primitive Man*, No. 6, 1933, pp. 20–4.

Demerath, N. J. 'Schizophrenia among Primitives: The Present Status of Sociological Research'. *American Journal of Psychiatry*, Vol. 98, 1941–2, pp. 703–7.

Devereux, Georges 'Cultural Thought Models in Primitive and Modern Psychiatric Theories'. *Psychiatry*, No. 21, 1958, pp. 359–74.

De Wet, J. S. Du T. 'Evaluation of a Common Method of Convulsive Therapy in Bantu Schizophrenics'. *British Journal of Psychiatry*, Vol. 103, 1957, pp. 739–57.

Doob, L. 'On the Future of Uncivilized and Civilized People'. *Journal of Nervous and Mental Disease*, No. 126, 1958, pp. 513–22.

Edgerton, Robert B. 'Conceptions of Psychosis in Four African Societies'. *American Anthropologist*, Vol. 68, 1966, pp. 408–25.

Fanon, Frantz 'La Socialthérapie dans un service d'hommes musulmans: Difficultés méthodologiques'. With Dr J. Azoulay. *L'Information psychiatrique*, 4th series, No. 9, 1954, pp. 349–61.

Fanon, Frantz 'Conduites d'aveux en Afrique du Nord'. With Dr. R. Lacat. *La Tunisie médicale*, 53rd session, Nice, 5–11 September 1955, pp. 657–60.

Fanon, Frantz 'Réflexions sur l'ethnopsychiatrie'. *Conscience maghrébine*, No. 3, 1955, pp. 1–2.

Fanon, Frantz 'Aspects actuels de l'assistance mentale en Algérie'. With Drs Dequeker, Lacat, Micucci and Ramée. *L'Information psychiatrique*, 4th series, No. 1, 1955, pp. 11–18.

Fanon, Frantz, 'L'Attitude du musulman maghbrébian devant la folie'. With Dr Francois Sanchez. *Revue pratique de psychologie de la vie sociale et d'hygène mentale*, No. 1, 1956, pp. 24–7.

Field, M. J. 'Witchcraft as a Primitive Interpretation of Mental Disorder'. *Journal of Mental Science*, Vol. 101, 1955, pp. 826–33.

Field, M. J. 'Chronic Psychosis in Rural Ghana'. *British Journal of Psychiatry*, Vol. 114, No. 506, 1968, pp. 31–3.

Fischer, Siegfried 'The Influence of Indian and Negro Blood on the Manic-Depressive Psychosis'. *Journal of Nervous and Mental Disease*, No. 97, 1943, pp. 409–20.

Forster, E. B. 'The Theory and Practice of Psychiatry in Ghana'. *American Journal of Psychotherapy*, No. 16, 1962, pp. 17–51.

Furedi, Frank 'The Social Composition of the Mau Mau Movements in the White Highlands'. *Journal of Peasant Studies*, No. 1, 1974.

Furley, O. W. 'The Historiography of Mau Mau', in Ogot, B. A. (ed.) *Hadith 4: Politics and Nationalism in Colonial Kenya*. Nairobi: East African Publishing House, 1972.

Gallais, P., Miletto, G. Corriol, J. and Bert, J. 'Introduction a l'etude de l'Eeg physiologique du noir d'Afrique'. *Medecine Tropicale*, No. 11, 1951, pp. 128–46.

Gallais, P., Corriol, J. and Bert, J. 'Etude preliminaire des rythmes electro-encephalographiques chez le noir: analyse de 50 sujets'. *Medecine Tropicale* No. 9, 1949, pp. 687–95.

Gordon, H. L. 'Mental Instability among Europeans in Kenya'. *Kenya and East Africa Medical Journal*, No. 4, 1927-8, pp. 316–24.

Gordon, H. L. 'Sexual Perversions'. *Kenya and East African Medical Journal*, No. 6, 1929-30, pp. 122–30.

Gordon, H. L. 'Psychiatry in Kenya Colony'. *Journal of Mental Science*, Vol. 80, 1934, pp. 167–71.

Gordon, H. L. 'An Enquiry into the Correlation of Civilization and Mental Disorder in the Kenyan Native'. *East African Medical Journal*, No. 12, February 1936, pp. 327–35.

Gordon, H. L. 'Is War Eugenic or Dysgenic? That Is Does War Improve the Physical or Mental Qualities of Future Generations?' *East African Medical Journal*, No. 19, 1942, pp. 86–96.

Green, E. M. 'Psychosis among Negroes: A Comparative Study'. *Journal of Mental and Nervous Disease*, No. 41, 1914, pp. 697–708.

Greenless, Duncan 'Insanity among the Natives of South Africa'. *Journal of Mental Science*, Vol. 41, 1895, pp. 71–8.

Harris, Grace 'Possession Hysteria in a Kenya Tribe'. *American Anthropologist*, Vol. 59, 1957, pp. 1046–66.

Kirby, Michael 'The Unhappiness of the Kikuyu, or the Seeds of Mau Mau'. *East African Medical Journal*, No. 10, 1957, pp. 529–32.

Kleinman, Arthur. M. 'Depression, Somatization, and the New Cross-Cultural Psychiatry'. *Social Sciences and Medicine*, Vol. 11, 1977, pp. 3–10.

Kleinman, Arthur M. 'Culture and Depression' *Culture, Medicine and Psychiatry*, No. 2, 1978, pp. 295–6.

Kleinman, Arthur M. 'Culture, Illness and Care'. *Annals of Internal Medicine*, Vol. 88, No. 2, February 1978, pp. 251–58.

Kleinman, Arthur M. 'The Cultural Meanings and Social Uses of Illness'. *Journal of Family Practice*, Vol. 16, No. 3, 1983, pp. 539–45.

Lambo, T. A. 'The Role of Cultural Factors in Paranoid Psychosis among the Yoruba Tribe'. *Journal of Mental Science*, Vol. 101, 1955, pp. 239–66.

Lambo, T. A. 'Neuropsychiatric Observations in the Western Region of Nigeria'. *British Medical Journal*, 15 December 1956, pp. 1388–94.

Lambo, T. A. 'Psychiatric Syndromes Associated with Cerebrovascular Disorders in the African'. *Journal of Mental Science*, Vol. 104, 1958, pp. 113–43.

Lambo, T. A. 'Malignant Anxiety: A Syndrome Associated with Criminal Conduct in Africans'. *Journal of Mental Science*, Vol. 108, 1962, pp. 256–64.

Lind, John E. 'The Dream as a Simple Wish-fulfilment in the Negro'. *Psychoanalytic Review*, No. 1, 1913/14, pp. 295–300.

Littlewood, Roland 'Anthropology and Psychiatry: An Alternative Approach'. *British Journal of Medical Psychology*, No. 53, 1980, pp. 213–25.

Mead, Margaret 'The Implications of Culture Change for Personality Development'. *American Journal of Psychiatry*, Vol. 17, 1947, pp. 633–46.

Minde, M. 'Mental Health: Past, Present and Future'. *South African Medical Journal*, November 1955, pp. 1124–7.

Minde, M. 'Early Psychiatry in Natal'. *South African Medical Journal*, March 1956, pp. 287–91.

Mundy-Castle, A. C., McKiever, B. L. and Prinsloo, T. 'A Comparative Study of the Electroencephalographs of Normal Africans and Europeans of Southern Africa'. *Electroencephalography and Clinical Neurophysiology Journal*, No. 5, 1953, pp. 533–43.

Muwazi, E. M. K. and Trowell, H. C. 'Neurological Diseases Among African Natives of Uganda'. *East African Medical Journal*, January 1944, pp. 2–19.

Nichols, L. A. 'Neurosis in Native African Troops'. *Journal of Mental Science*, Vol. 90, 1944, pp. 863–8.

Oliver, R. A. C. 'The Comparison of the Abilities of Races: With Special Reference to East Africa'. *East African Medical Journal*, No. 9, September 1932, pp. 160–78.

Olssen, Erik 'Truby King and the Plunket Society: An Analysis of a Prescriptive Ideology'. *New Zealand Journal of History*, No. 1, 1981, pp. 3–23.

Orley, John and Wing, John 'Psychiatric Disorders in Two African Villages'. *Archives of General Psychiatry*, Vol. 36, May 1979, pp. 513–20.

Pape, John 'Black and White: The "Perils of Sex" in Colonial Zimbabwe'. *Journal of Southern African Studies*, No. 4, 1990, pp. 699–720.

Porot, Antoine and Arrii, D. C. 'L'impulsivite criminelle chez l'indigene algerien: ses facteurs' *Annales medico-psychologiques*, Vol. 90, 1932, pp. 588–611.

Porot, Antoine and Sutter, C. 'Le primitivisme des indegines nord-africains: Ses incidences en pathologie mentale'. *Sud medical et chirurgical*, April 1939, pp. 226–41.

Porteus, Stanley 'Mental Tests with Delinquents and Australian Aboriginal Children'. *Psychological Review*, Vol. 24, No. 6, November 1917, pp. 32–42.

Price, Basil G. 'Discussion of the Causes of Invaliding from the Tropics'. *British Medical Journal*, November 1913, pp. 1290–6.

Prince, Raymond 'The Brain Fag Syndrome in Nigerian Students'. *Journal of Mental Science*, Vol. 106, 1960, pp. 559–70.

Rivers, W. H. R. 'Sociology and Psychology'. *Sociological Review*, No. 9, 1916, pp. 1–13.

Rosenstiel, A. 'An Anthropological Approach to the Mau Mau Problem'. *Political Science Quarterly*, Vol. 68, 1953, pp. 419–32.

Sabshin, M. et al. 'Dimensions of Institutional Racism in Psychiatry'. *American Journal of Psychiatry*, Vol. 127, December 1970, pp. 87–93.

Sachs, Wulf 'The Insane Native: An Introduction to a Psychological Study'. *The South African Journal of Science*, No. 30, 1933, pp. 706–13.

Seligman, C. G. 'Psychology and Racial Differences', in Hadfield, J. A. (ed.) *Psychology and Modern Problems*. London: University of London Press, 1935, pp. 51–106.

Sequeria, James H. 'The Brain of the East African'. *British Medical Journal*, No. 7, 1932, p. 581.

Shelley, H. and Watson, W. 'An Investigation Concerning Mental Disorder in the Nyasaland Natives'. *Journal of Mental Science*, Vol. 82, November 1936, pp. 701–30.

Simons, H. J. 'Mental Disease in Africans: Racial Determinism'. *Journal of Mental Science*, Vol. 104, 1958, pp. 377–88.

Smartt, C. G. F. 'Mental Maladjustment in the East African'. *British Journal of Mental Science*, Vol. 102, 1956, pp. 441–66.

Sutter, Jean 'L'epilepsie mentale chez l'Indigene nord-africain: etude clinique'. Thesis, University of Algiers, 1937.

Vaughan, Megan 'Idioms of Madness: Zomba Lunatic Asylum, Nyasaland, in the Colonial Era'. *Journal of Southern African Studies*, No. 9, 1983, pp. 218–38.

Vaughan, Megan 'The Madman and the Medicine Man: Colonial Society and the Theory of Deculturation', in Vaughan, Megan (ed.) *Curing Their Ills: Colonial Power and African Illness*. London: Polity Press, 1991.

Vint, F. W. 'A Preliminary Note on the Cell Content of the Prefrontal Cortex of the East African Native'. *East African Medical Journal*, No. 9, 1932–33, pp. 30–1.

Vint, F. W. 'The Brain of the Kenyan Native'. *Journal of Anatomy*, Vol. 68, January 1934, pp. 216–23.

Waxler, Nancy 'Culture and Mental Illness: A Social Labelling Perspective'. *Journal of Nervous and Mental Disease* No. 6, 1974, pp. 374–95.

Weleba, Shirley 'Trial by Jury in Southern Rhodesia 1900–1912'. Ph.D. dissertation, University of Southern California, 1969.

Wilkinson, John 'The Mau Mau Movement: Some General and Medical Aspects'. *The East African Medical Journal*, No. 7, 1954, pp. 294–314.

Index